Language
and the World

Essays New and Old

Richard L. Epstein

ARF

Advanced Reasoning Forum

With many thanks to Julia Gracie for copyediting.
Mistakes in the text are now due to me.

For more information contact:
    Advanced Reasoning Forum
    P. O. Box 635
    Socorro, NM 87801   USA
    www.AdvancedReasoningForum.org

paperback ISBN 978-1-938421-56-3
e-book ISBN 978-1-938421-57-0

Language and the World
Essays New and Old

Preface

History of the Essays

BENJAMIN LEE WHORF

Preface

Language and the world. A big subject. The structure of languages, metaphysics, knowing and wondering, things and mass and process, how to reason well, thought, ethics. All these and more are involved in understanding how we encounter the world with our languages.

The first three essays, "The World as the Flow of All", "Language and the World", and "Language-Thought-Meaning", set out the overall perspective. The other essays extend, or contradict, or support the ideas in these first three, leading to a large view of how we talk and understand, and how that affects how we live.

In part, this work is an exploration of the idea that language shapes how we encounter the world. I do not attempt to trace the history of "Whorf's Thesis", the use and misuse of that term, and the many ideas of what it's thought to be, for that is ably done by John Leavitt in *Linguistic Relativities* (Cambridge, 2011) and Penny Lee in *The Whorf Theory Complex* (John Benjamins Publishing Company, 1996).

This book is an exploration in essays by me and others as we try to understand, and to understand how we understand, an exploration leading, I hope, to less certainty and more wonder.

DEDICATED TO

Juan Francisco "Pancho" Rizzo
Eduardo S. "Eddie" Ribeiro

with gratitude for their criticism,
encouragement, and friendship
that helped shape this book.

A man too old to fend for himself prays:

> . . . I cannot go up to the mountains in the west to you,
> deer; I cannot kill you and bring you home . . .
> You, water, I can never dip you up and fetch you home
> again . . .
> You who are wood, you wood, I cannot carry you home
> on my shoulder.

This is not the speech of one who has plucked the fruits of nature
by brute force; it is the speech of a friend.

> Dorothy Lee, "Linguistic Reflection of Wintu Thought"

Even a great magician cannot pull a rabbit out of a hat if
there is not already a rabbit in the hat.

> from the film *The Red Shoes*, 1948

History of the Essays

ESSAYS NEW

Richard L. Epstein (1947–)
"The World as the Flow of All"
An earlier version of this essay appeared in *ETC.: A Review of General Semantics*, vol. 73, no. 3, pp. 213–232, 2016 (published in 2018).

Note on the composition of this essay
This essay grew out of my trying to explain to friends the ideas from a preprint *The Internal Structure of Predicates and Names with an Analysis of Reasoning about Process* (2010). The many discussions I had with Don Brown, Fred Kroon, Melissa Axelrod, Arnold Mazotti, and Esperanza Buitrago helped shape what I have said, and I am grateful to them.

I'm grateful also to João Marcos, who at the Universidade do Natal, Brazil, in February 2011 gave me my first opportunity to give a talk, in Portuguese, about this work, and to Petrucio Viana and Renata de Freitas who invited me to give a talk in English about this work at the XVI Encontro Brasileiro de Logica in Petropolis, Rio de Janeiro, Brazil, in May 2011, and to Ivan da Costa Marques who arranged for me to give the "same" talk in Portuguese there. Since then I presented this material in talks at the Philosophy Department of the Universidade Federal de Minas Gerais and at the Department of Linguistics at the University of New Mexico, and I am grateful to the participants whose comments led me to revise this.

For the conception of the world as flow I was much influenced by translating the stories in *The BARK of DOG*.

"Language and the World"
Written in 2020 for this volume. Some of this is derived from the previously published version of "The World as the Flow of All". The template analogy comes from my book *Propositional Logics*. I am grateful to Chris Sinha for his suggestions for improving this essay and his encouragement for my work in this book.

"Language-Thought-Meaning"
Written November 2013–October 2014 and revised slightly since.

"Why Event-Talk Is a Problem"
This was written in May–July 2019 to explain to colleagues the issues

I previously discussed only in relation to formal logic ("Events in the Metaphysics of Predicate Logic" in *Reasoning and Formal Logic*, Advanced Reasoning Forum, 2015) and in relation to issues of cause and effect ("Reasoning about Cause and Effect" in *Cause and Effect, Conditionals, Explanations*, Advanced Reasoning Forum, 2011).

"On the Genesis of the Concept of Object in Children"
Written in 2010 and revised slightly since.

"A New Turing Test"
This first appeared in the ARF Blog in July 2019.

"The Thing-Basis of Western Philosophy"
Written in 2020 for this volume, based in part on an earlier version of "The World as the Flow of All".

"The Metaphysical Basis of Logic: Masses and Things"
First written in 2014 and revised since.

"Languages and Logics"
Written in 2020 for this volume.

ESSAYS OLD

I have reproduced the use of single and double quotation marks and placement of punctuation relative to those as they appear in the original papers. I have kept the formatting of the text and the references as in the originals. Figures are placed as closely as possible to their placement in the originals.

Dorothy Demetracopoulou Lee

"Conceptual Implications of an Indian Language"
Philosophy of Science, vol. 5, no. 1, 1938, pp. 89–102.

"Categories of the Generic and the Particular in Wintu˙‘ "
American Anthropologist, vol. 46, no. 3, 1944, pp. 362–369.

"Linguistic Reflection of Wintu Thought"
International Journal of American Linguistics, vol. 10, 1944, pp. 181– 187. The version here is from *Freedom and Culture*, a collection of essays by Lee, edited by C. Moustakas and D. Smillie with the approval of Lee, Prentice-Hall, 1959, reprinted Waveland Press, 1987, pp. 105–112.

"Symbolization and Value"
Originally published in *Symbols and Values, an Initial Study*,
Thirteenth Symposium of the Conference on Science, Philosophy,
and Religion, 1954. The version reprinted here is from *Freedom
and Culture*, Prentice-Hall, Inc., 1959, pp. 78–88.

Benjamin LeeWhorf

"Grammatical Categories"
Published posthumously in *Language*, vol. 21, no. 1, 1945,
pp. 1–11, with the following editorial note:

> This paper was written late in 1937 at the request of Franz Boas,
> then editor of the International Journal of American Linguistics.
> The manuscript was found in the Boas collection by C. F. Voegelin
> and Z. S. Harris. The author died on July 26, 1941. BB

I guess that "BB" refers to Bernard Bloch, editor of *Language* at
that time. No indication is given of who edited it for publication.
The original is listed in "Index to the Franz Boas Collection of
Materials for American Linguistics" by Voegelin and Harris
(*Language*, vol. 21, no. 3), but neither the curators of that
collection at the American Philosophical Society nor the
curators of the Whorf collection at Yale can find it.

I have replaced words and phrases in all capitals with italics
in conformity with the works Whorf published in his lifetime.

"Science and Linguistics"
Technology Review (Massachusetts Institute of Technology), vol.
42, pp. 229–231 and pp. 247–248, no. 6 (April 1940).

"The Relation of Habitual Thought and Behavior to Language"
In *Language, Culture, and Personality: Essays in Memory of
Edward Sapir*, Sapir Memorial Publication Fund, 1941, pp. 75–93.
Reprinted in *ETC.*, 1944, from which this reprint is done.

"Languages and Logic"
Technology Review (Massachusetts Institute of Technology),
vol. 43 (April, 1941), pp. 250–252, 266, 268, 270, 272.

These four papers were reprinted in *Language, Thought, and
Reality: Selected Writings of Benjamin Lee Whorf,* edited by John
B. Carroll, The MIT Press, 1956. Carroll made the following
changes in his versions: he introduced single quotation marks

where the original used only double ones, adding them in a seemingly random pattern; he used all capital letters for what in the original appeared as lower case italics; he added and deleted connectives and words; he changed punctuation; he changed the text describing some of the figures; and he re-arranged the first figure in "Science and Linguistics" to make it unintelligible.

M. Dale Kinkade
"Salish Evidence against the Universality of 'Noun' and 'Verb' "
Lingua, vol. 60 (1983), pp. 25–40. Reprinted by permission of the publishers of *Lingua*.

Friedrich Nietzsche
" 'Reason' in Philosophy"
Originally published as "Die 'Vernunft' in der Philosophie" in Nietzsche, *Götzen-Dämmerung*, 1888. This version appeared as a chapter in *Twilight of the Idols*, translated by Walter Kaufman in *The Portable Nietzsche*, Viking Press, 1954, pp. 479–484.

Benson Mates
"Metaphysics and Linguistic Relativity"
This is from pp. 246–250 of *The Philosophy of Leibniz: Metaphysics and Language*, Oxford University Press, 1986.

Essays New

Richard L. Epstein

Richard L. Epstein (1947–) received his Ph.D. in mathematics from the University of California, Berkeley in 1973. He began studies in philosophy as a postdoctoral fellow at Victoria University of Wellington, New Zealand (1976–1978). His mentors in philosophy were George Hughes and Benson Mates.

He has published books on mathematical logic, formal logic, logic as the art of reasoning well, and linguistics. He has translated and edited for publication the stories in *The BARK of DOG*. He is now Head of the Advanced Reasoning Forum and director of The BARK of DOG Foundation in Socorro, New Mexico.

The World as The Flow of All

The world is made up of things: rocks, tables, dogs, people, stars. Of this we are sure, for we have words for all these and many more.

We know of process and change, too. But we know of them only through things. For example, suppose I show you an apple. It's round, red, shiny. I take a bite of it. It's changed—no longer round, no longer red and shiny where I bit into it. I take another bite. The apple has changed some more. I take another bite, and another, and the apple has changed a lot. I give the core to my donkey. The apple is all gone.

The apple changed. But is that the apple I started with? If one apple changed, it wasn't what I first showed you, it wasn't what I bit into the second time, it wasn't the core. It must have been something beyond all those, somehow beyond any particular time, something that persists through all "its" changes. Talking of change we find ourselves talking about things beyond any particular time.

Change, we feel, is not real like things are real, like rocks, tables, dogs, people, stars, the sun. The sun? Everything we know about that fiery ball tells us that the sun is a process: nothing endures in it, not shape, not form, not even molecules—only process. A rock, too, is process, changing, never stable, though we don't notice the changes. The difference isn't that the sun is a process and the rock is a thing; the difference is the scale of time over which we note "changes".

Our focus in our language is on the world as made up of things, on stability in the flow of our experience. Still, we have some sense in our lives of flow, of flux, of change, of process. And we have some hints of that in our language.

Suppose you're in my living room with me, and I look out the window and say,

It's raining.

Yes, that's true. But what's raining? There's no "it": the weather isn't raining. The weather is rainy; the weather doesn't do anything. The word "it" is a dummy, there because in English every verb requires a subject. I could have said just,

Raining.

You would have understood me. It's clear I'm talking about now, which is all the "is" in the original sentence tells us. And it's clear

I'm talking about there, outside the window, though in English we don't require any word or phrase to mark that.

On a winter day I might say "Snowing", and you'd understand me. That's complete, clearly true or false, though it doesn't look like a sentence in English. Or I could say, "Sun-ing" or "Breeze-ing", which are odd, but once you've got the hang of my talking this way, you'd understand me.

If we were at my friend's apartment in the city, I might look out the window and say,

Running.

You'd understand me. It sounds odd because I haven't said who or what is running. That seems essential when we talk English because verbs are descriptions of what's happening to or because of a thing. Yet running is running, whether it's one person, a dog chasing a cat, or lots of people in a marathon. I don't describe all when I say "Running", but we never describe all. What I've said is true or false, enough to communicate.

Looking out my window at the patio I could say "Barking" and you'd understand me. On another day looking at my dogs I could say, "Sleeping". These are process words, and used this way they begin to become part of a way to describe process without a focus on things.

After a rain, as I look out at the patio I might say, "Mud". Mud isn't a thing. We don't say "There are three muds out there." We say, "There's some mud" because mud is a mass. Water, gold, snow are masses, too. We know they're part of what the world is made up of, different from things. Every part of mud is mud, while there's no part of an apple that is an apple. Processes are like that, too. Every part of raining is raining—there's no smallest part of raining, for a single drop of water is not raining.

Starting to see the world as process-mass, I look out the window and say, "Dog-ing". You'd understand, though it seems incomplete. One dog or many dogs? What's the dog doing? We need a verb and an indication of singular or plural when we talk in English. Yet if I say, "There's a dog", the verb is just "is". The dog is there, it exists there, that's all. "Dog-ing", understood as about there and now, does that as well, though it doesn't say whether there's one or many, whether alive or dead, whether big or small. Much is left out, but much is left out of our description "There's a dog."

I could turn, and looking around the room say, "Table-ing". You'd understand. An odd way to talk, but true. Or pointing to the next room I could say, "Woman-ing". Odd, too, incomplete, but true. Or I could say "Brown-ing" while pointing in the direction of my old dog Birta. That would be true. Brown is not a color that attaches itself to a thing; "brown-ing" is a description that applies in the flux at that time and place. We are beginning to see the world as made up of processes.

Processes? To say that is to slip back into thing-talk. This process, that process, one process, two processes, a fast process, a blue process. No. To see process in the world there are not processes, just process, the flow of all. Words like "raining", "sun-ing", "running", "dog-ing", "mud-ing" describe the flux at a time and place. They don't pick out separate parts of the flow any more than "Pacific Ocean" and "Baltic Sea" pick out parts separate and distinct from the water that covers the earth.

To say that Zoe is woman-ing is to talk of Zoe as a process-mass, continuing through time not as a supratemporal object but as a way. But Zoe is not a process-mass, for that is to treat her as a thing again, just a different kind of thing. There are no processes, no masses. There is only the flow of all that we describe in various ways, one of which is "Zoe-ing". Still, I'll use the terms "mass-process language" and "mass-process word" because the parts of English that lead us to this other view are words we use in English for processes and masses.

To talk of the world as the flow of all we can borrow and modify some words from English like "raining", "sun-ing", "running", "dog-ing", "mud-ing", "woman-ing". We add "-ing" to remind us of our new way of talking, of seeing. When we specify a context for these words, each is true or false.

We can say "Dog-ing running brown-ing", and that would be true if you had pointed to my dog Birta running in the hills. Better is to use "+ " to indicate that the descriptions are mixed together and not simply applying at a time and place. So pointing to Birta it would be correct to say "Running + dog-ing + brown-ing", while "Running dog-ing brown-ing" without the "+" might be true if there were seventeen white dogs in a room where there is a cockroach running across a brown table (I have to resort to English for my examples).

In "dog-ing + brown-ing" there is no subject or predicate. An equivalent description is "brown-ing + dog-ing". The words "dog-ing" and "brown-ing" have equal status: there is no individual thing that is meant as the subject and no comment on "it" as a predicate. There (pointing) is dog-ing and brown-ing mixed together.

We can mark a description for time and place, like "Raining (yesterday, here)" or "(Running + dog-ing + browning) (today, there)", where the markers are made clear by context. Any of the mass-process words can be marked for time. This suggests that each is a verb. But how can there be verbs without nouns? We could use time marking just for entire sentences, as in "Yesterday ((dog-ing + running) and (raining))". Or we could use only comparisons for temporal ordering, as in "(bark-ing + dog-ing) before (rabbit-ing + run-ing)". In these no part is marked for time, so we have no temptation to classify a part of the expression as a verb.

We can describe more fully by saying:

Not–Raining (here, now)

(Rabbit-ing + Running) (there, now) *and*
   (Dog-ing + Chasing) (there, now)

Coyote-ing (yesterday, there) *or* Dog-ing (yesterday, there)

All the ways we join sentences in English with the connectives "not", "or", "and", "if . . . then . . ." we can use in talking of the world as the flow of all, for those require only that the sentences are (considered to be) true or false, not that they are about things.

In English we get tongue-tied trying to talk of sameness and difference. Is (are?) the apple then and the apple now the same? How can two things be the same? Can there be sameness and difference without talk of things? A visitor to my ranch saw a couple dogs in the corral yesterday. She's standing next to me today and wonders whether those were the same as the dogs that are here in front of us. Is dog-ing then and there the same as dog-ing here and now? We can formulate that question in mass-process talk by asking whether the following is true:

Dog-ing (yesterday, corral) $\approx$ Dog-ing (here, now)

The symbol "$\approx$" is not meant for identity of things but similarity, indicating equivalent descriptions.

We can assert similarity without talk of time and location, too:

(Canine-ing + Domestic-ing) $\approx$ Dog-ing

This is not a universal statement that at any place and time "(Canine-ing + Domestic-ing)" describes the same as "Dog-ing". Rather , the concept, the category, the genus if you will of "Canine-ing + Domestic-ing" is the same (similar to) that of "Dog-ing".

More generally, we can say that dog-ing is part of animal-ing. But that's misleading because for there to be a part, there must be a whole, and animal-ing, just as mud-ing, is not a whole, not a thing. Rather, the conception of dog-ing is *subordinate to* that of canine-ing, so long as we don't think of concepts as things but rather as concept-ing, as I describe in "Language-Thought-Meaning" in this volume. Abbreviating "subordinate to" as "sub", we have that the following are true:

Tree-ing sub Plant-ing

Reading sub Thinking

Pegasus-ing sub Horse-ing

And the following are false:

Cat-ing sub Dog-ing

Barking sub Meowing

We have a simple grammar: base words, conjunctions of base words, base words of specific times and places, sentence connectives, a subordination relation, and a similarity relation.

In the accompanying essay "Language and the World" and essays by others in this volume, we'll see that there are many languages that have the structure and conceptions of this artificial mass-process language: no nouns, no verbs, no partitioning of the world but only describing the flow of all. Those essays explore how this matters to philosophy, to linguistics, to anthropology, to ethics—to our way in the world.

Dedicated to the memory of Suely Porto Alves
in the flow of all, the flow of love

Language and the World

Introduction

There are two kinds of languages: thing languages and mass-process languages.

In a thing language, the grammar leads speakers to look first for stability in the world: the world is made up of things, individual things that persist in time. Words that can be used to pick out that stability are nouns. Descriptions of the individual things in time are verbs. There may be words for mass and process in such a language, but they are secondary, and the grammar forces their use into the syntactic role of nouns and verbs, leading speakers to think of them in some way as things and as descriptions of things in time.

In a mass-process language, the grammar leads speakers to encounter the world as the flow of all. There is no idea of change, for there is nothing to change, there are only differing descriptions of the flow. Every base word can serve as a description and as a modifier. Each can be marked for time, or whole assertions can be marked for time, or assertions can be compared for time as before or after. If stability can be found it is only with secondary grammatical constructions. There are no nouns and verbs, for there are no words for individual things and no descriptions of things in time.

There is good reason for a noun-verb distinction in thing languages. There is good reason for no noun-verb distinction in mass-process languages. This is what I will show in this paper, along with how linguists and anthropologists do or do not take account of such very different grammars.

Thing languages
Languages such as English, German, and French are *thing languages*: the grammar of these directs their speakers to look first for stability in the world as made up of things. For example, in English there are lots of words for kinds of things. We have "dog", "apple", "rock", "chair". We talk of an apple or the apple: the singular with the article indicates we are meaning to talk about an individual thing. We talk of all the apples on the table, indicating with the plural our intention to get someone to pay attention to many individual things of that kind.

We describe things. I take an apple; it's red, round, shiny, firm. I bite into it and put it on the table. It's no longer round, and where I bit it's an off-white color. I leave it on the table for a couple days, and it is no longer red and firm: it's mushy and brown. We say the apple changed. But what changed? Our grammar insists that we are talking about one thing that has gone through changes—the apple. So the apple is a thing that is supratemporal: it persists in time through its changes. We describe the changes with words and phrases like "was red", "is mushy", "softened", "changed color". The grammar of English directs us first to look for stability in terms of things and then to talk of how those things go through changes

We say that a word or phrase for a thing we mean to be talking about is the *subject phrase* of a sentence. In "The apple turned mushy" the subject phrase is "The apple". We might say that the subject of the sentence is the apple itself. The comment we make about the subject is called the *predicate phrase* of the sentence. In "The apple turned mushy" the predicate phrase is "turned mushy". But unlike the subject of the sentence, there is no thing outside the sentence in the world that is the predicate. Some say there must be something outside the sentence that is the predicate: in this example the predicate is the property or abstract thing correlated to "turned mushy".[1] This is an example of how strongly the thing-view of English directs people to find things for our expressions. It can't be only a part of language that is a predicate, but just as the subject of the sentence is a thing, so, too, the predicate is some thing "out there", distinct from our talking. To be clear and avoid this controversy, I'll use *subject* and *predicate* for parts of a particular utterance.[2]

The subject of an utterance is for that particular utterance. But generalizing, we talk about *nouns*, being the words, not the particular utterances, that are used in giving a subject. Thus in the example above, "apple" is a noun, modified by "the" to create the subject of the sentence. In "Dogs bark", the noun is "dog", modified by the suffix "s" to make the subject of the sentence. In "The person I met last week on the plaza was hungry", the subject is "The person I met last week on the plaza", where "person" is a noun; but also "plaza" is a noun because it can be used as a subject by itself, as in "The plaza is rectangular".

What, then, is the subject of "Mud is brown"? In analogy with "This chair is brown", we say that it is "Mud" and call the word "mud" a noun. Yet "mud" is not a word that is meant to direct our attention to one or several individual things. Mud is a mass: every part of mud is mud, and there is no smallest part of mud. But the thing-focus of our language has determined our grammar, and hence we say that "mud" is a noun and "is brown" is the predicate in the sentence.

What is the subject of "Running is good for your health"? Following the pattern we've seen with thing-talk, we say that "Running" is the subject, and then "running" is a noun—even though it can as well be used for a predicate, as in "Spot is running". Yet "Running" does not direct us to some part of the world or our experience that is a thing, not an individual thing. Running is more like mud: every part of

---

[1] Compare the quotes by Radu J. Bogdan on p. 52 below.

[2] Though I say "utterance", I mean to include signs in sign languages and inscriptions in written languages in the discussions that follow.

running is running, and there is no smallest part of running. We treat the word in our grammar as we treat "mud": we talk of some mud and some running, not a mud or a running. Yet running is quite different from mud in that it is not a mass: it is process, for "running" is a word linked to a word that describes changes in things in time, "run". Still, our grammar forces us to use "running" and "mud" as subjects as we do "apple" and "dog".

What is the subject of "Justice is desirable"? On the pattern of thing-talk, it is "Justice", and then "is desirable" is the predicate. We are led to think of justice as if it were a thing. But then is it real or abstract, an idea or a way of being in the world? We are led to these odd questions by the thing-focus in our language because we use "mud", "running", "justice" as nouns following the pattern we have for nouns that we use to pick out individual things.

The predicate of a sentence in English is marked for time. In "The apple was round", the predicate is "was round", and the part that marks time is "was", which is "to be" conjugated to the past tense. In "The apple turned mushy" the predicate is "turned mushy", and the part which is marked for time is "turned", which is the past tense of "to turn". The part of a predicate that marks for time, that indicates the when of the description or how the thing is, or changed, or will be, we call a *verb*. Verbs embedded in predicates, and process words like "running" that come from verbs, are how we talk of process and change in English. They are as fundamental as nouns, for in English we must mark every sentence for time, the "when" of the description. This is how we place supratemporal things into our world of experience.

But in "Dogs bark" what is the mark for time? The verb "to bark" is marked not for the present, past, or future but for all time or an indication of capability, as in "All dogs have the ability to bark". There can be omnitemporal marking for a verb.

Words for individual things like "Birta" or "this dog" cannot be marked for time. To mark them for time would be to see them not as stable but as process. We would have no stability, no thing that continues through its changes, but only another description, like "turned brown".

The classifications we denote with "subject", "predicate", "noun", and "verb" are clear enough in our use of English as well as in German and Romance languages. They are not some arcane talk of grammarians or linguists but come to us from the thing-focus of our language.

We can all recognize them even if we have never been taught grammar in school.

Mass-process languages

There are also *mass-process* languages: the grammar of these directs their speakers to encounter the world first as the flow of all, describing but not partitioning. Since few people who are likely to read this paper speak a mass-process language, I have described in "The World as the Flow of All" an artificial mass-process language.[3]

In that artificial language, it is not simply that there is no noun-verb distinction and no subject-predicate distinction. There is good reason why there should not be such distinctions, at least in the sense of those notions given for thing languages.

Curious, some say, but there could be no human language that does not focus primarily on things with a noun-verb distinction.

They're wrong.

I can't hope to convince you of that, for another way of encountering the world is not a matter of argument. Rather, I'll quote people who have described ordinary languages as having a very similar basis as the artificial mass-process language in the hope that you can see how people can communicate without a thing-focus.

Some mass-process languages

Wintu

In the 1930s and subsequently, Dorothy Demetracopoulou Lee studied Wintu, a Native American language of a tribe living in California along the upper reaches of the Sacramento, McCloud, and Pitt rivers. The language is now extinct. Here are extracts from some of her essays.[4]

> There is evidence that the Wintu Indians recognize or perceive first of all humanity, human-being-ness, and only secondarily the delimited person. They make no distinction between singular and plural, and a cardinal number is never used with this generic, primary form of the word. They individuate, however, making a particular out of the original generic form of the word; out of *nop*—deermeat or venison—

[3] I develop this in *Reasoning and the World as the Flow of All* into a formal language and methods of reasoning that are as rigorous as we have for reasoning about things.

[4] Page numbers in *italics* are to the pages of the essay reprinted in this volume.

they derive *nopum*—(a) deer; out of *se*—handness, hand—they
derive *semum*—finger. Yet here also, unless the Wintu chooses
to use a separate word meaning one or several or giving the definite
number, there is nothing to show whether the word refers to a singular
or plural; *nopum* may be one or many individual deer; *semum* may
be one or several fingers.

"Symbolization and Value", 1954, pp. *160*

To the Wintu, the given is not a series of particulars, to be classed
into universals. The given is unpartitioned mass; a part of this the
Wintu delimits into a particular individual. The particular then exists,
not in nature, but in the consciousness of the speaker. What to us is
a class, a plurality of particulars, is to him a mass or a quality or an
attribute. These concepts are one for the Wintu; the word *red*, for
example, is the same as for *redness* or *red-mass*. Plurality, on the
other hand, is not derived from the singular and is of slight interest to
him. He has no nominal plural form, and when he does use a plural
word, such as *men,* he uses a root which is completely different from
the singular word; *man* is wita but *men* is gis.

"Linguistic Reflection of Wintu Thought", 1944, p. *148*

To the Wintu, generic concepts are primary and the particular is
derivative. I use the term *generic* rather than *universal* advisedly.
To the Wintu, the given is not a succession of particulars, to be conceptualized and classified under universals. Rather, it is immediate
apprehension of qualitatively differentiated being. For the Wintu
speaker, the phrase *there-is-fog,* with a separate word for the subject
and the predicate, is only a grammatical alternative for his other
expressions, *it-fogs.* He prefers an expression such as *it-roes* to
roe exists, it darks to *it-is dark*; he will say *she-soups* instead of
she-makes soup. Round is derived from *to-be-round, thunder* from
to-thunder, nest from *to-build-a-nest.* Actor and result are one with
the act. Substance is one with existence; it cannot be said to be particular, as it is conceived of in European thought. Substances, as for
example roe, fog, deer, are originally differentiated but since they are
not delimited, the particular is a secondary concept.

"Categories of the Generic and the Particular in Wintu", 1944, p. *139*

Salishan languages

Salishan is a family of Native American languages of the Pacific Northwest of North America. In "Salish Evidence against the Universality of
'Noun' and 'Verb' ", M. Dale Kinkade says:

. . . they are predicates in the Salishan languages rather than either nouns or verbs. They are rather like gerunds in English, which are both noun and verb at the same time. Any such simple form may be translated into English either as a simple noun or an equational sentence with a dummy 'it' as subject, with the whole indicating a state rather than an entity. It is difficult for speakers of English to conceive of forms such as *p'oxút* as complete sentences because English requires a subject and predicate in every sentence, but there is no logical reason why one cannot perceive of 'father' (and other nouns) as a state such as 'being a father' (cf. Kuipers 1968). Words such as 'father', 'deer', 'shoe' may even be given imperative inflections in Salish, in which case they mean 'be a X!'

Even names are predicative, although they usually occur as complements or adjuncts rather than as main predicates. But they *may* occur as main predicates. pp. *249–250*

It is readily demonstrable that any full word may constitute the main predicate of a Salishan sentence. p. *248*

Mayan

Mayans are native to the Yucatán peninsula in Mexico, Belize, Guatemala, Honduras, and El Salvador. Michael D. Coe in "Breaking the Maya Code" says:

As English-speakers, we take it for granted that one can speak of, say "four birds" or "twenty-five books," but this kind of numerical construction is impossible in the Mayan languages—between the number and the thing counted there has to be a *numerical classifier*, describing the class to which the object, animal, plant, or thing belongs. We have a glimmering of this sort of construction when we talk of "two flocks of geese" or "a pride of lions," but this is pale stuff compared to the richness of the Mayan classifiers. Colonial Yucatec dictionaries list dozens of these, but only a handful are still in use in today's Yucatán, yet even these have to be interposed even when the number itself might be in Spanish. If I see three horses in a pasture, I would count them as *ox-ytul tzimin* (*ox*, "three"; *-tul*, classifier for animate things; *tsimin*, "horse" or "tapir"). However, if there were three stones in the same pasture, I would have to say "*ox-p'el tunich* (*ox*, "three"; *-p'el*, classifier for inanimate things; *tunich*, "stone"). p. 53

In English, too, we cannot attach a number word directly to a mass word or a process word or a universal word; to say "three muds", or "four runnings", or "two justices" is ungrammatical. We have to add a *classifier* to count: a cup of water, a patch of mud, a piece of meat.[5] For process and "abstract" words, we use very general classifiers — an instance of running, an instance of justice — as if these were events. If there is no obvious classifier, where we do not conceive of the mass as having or possibly having parts, we talk of the mass or process as a thing: "the weather changed", "the fog is lifting". But weather is not a thing, not an individual, though the grammar directs us to think that way.

Stephen C. Levinson in "Relativity in Spatial Conception and Description" talks of "the Mayan (Tzeltal-speaking) Indians of Tenejapa" in Mexico.

> Why does Tzeltal force the speaker into such an arbitrarily detailed geometry of the figure? One answer may be, as just hinted, that the main function of the locative expressions is to provide a means of successful reference. In that case, Tzeltal emphasizes an alternative strategy for achieving successful reference — English does it by telling you where to look, Tzeltal by telling you what to look for. (The Tzeltal locative construction provides equally good answers to 'Where?' questions as to 'How does it look?' questions.) However, another intriguing suggestion has been made by John Lucy [1992B; 73ff] on the basis of work on the related language Yucatec Maya. Like Tzeltal, Yucatec has a developed set of numeral classifiers. The motivation, Lucy claims, is that nominals in Yucatec fail, by themselves, to individuate entities. It is only by collocation with a numeral classifier or some other shape-discriminating phrase that such nouns can come to designate countable entities. This thesis, carried to its logical extreme, would amount to the claim that all nominals in Yucatec are essentially *mass* nouns and that the language makes no ontological commitment to *entities* as opposed to materials, essence or "stuff " at all. In order to individuate entities, a numeral classifier or some predicate is required to impose individuation on the material, metaphorically in much the way that a cookie-cutter cuts up undifferentiated dough.*[see the footnote on the next page]
>
> If the thesis held even partially for Tzeltal, it would help to explain the Tzeltal insistence on specifying the geometrical nature of the figure. Consider, for example, the fact that the Tzeltal nominal *lo'bal* could be glossed 'banana stuff,' because it refers equally to all the parts of the natural kind: to the fruits, to a single fruit, to clusters

---

[5] In "Linguistic Reflection of Wintu Thought" in this volume Dorothy Lee describes a similar feature of Wintu "particularizing forms".

of fruit, to the trunk of the banana tree, to the leaves of the tree, and so on. Now, given a nominal of such a nature, the kind of geometric and shape information encoded in the stative locative predicates we have examined is not as redundant with the information contained within the subject noun as first might seem. Consider the examples in (3).[6]

(3) a. *jipil*   *ta laso*   *lo'bal*
     hanging   AT rope   banana
     'the banana(-fruits) are hanging from the rope'

   b. *k'atal*   *ta*   *s-ba*   *s-k'iyojbil kaipej te lo'bale*
      lying-across   AT   its-top   its-drying   coffee   the banana
      'the banana(-trunks) are situated across the top of the coffee-drying patio'

   c. *palal*   *lo'bal ta   xujk   na*
      attached-in-bunches   banana AT its-side   house
      'the banana(-bunches) are against the inside side-wall of the house'

The figure in these three examples is designated by the nominal *lo'bal*. In each case, the 'banana-stuff' to which it refers gets formed up, as it were, by the positional predicate which indicates the nature of the individuated entities involved. Thus, Lucy's conjecture would go rather a long way to explain why it is that Tzeltal and languages like it have such a wealth of locative (and other) predicates, making such fine discriminations between shapes and dispositions of the figure.

pp. 185–186

* Lucy [1992B] found, for example, that in experimental tasks his Yucatec informants sort entities not primarily according to shape, color, or other surface property, but rather according to the stuff out of which things are made.

Navajo

Navajo is a language spoken by the Diné people who live mostly in central and northwest New Mexico and northern Arizona in the United States. Here is what Gary Witherspoon says in *Language and Art in the Navajo Universe*:

> . . . the astonishing degree to which the Navajo language is dominated by verbs. There seem to be few, if any, nouns that are not either passive forms of verbs or derived from verbal forms. Particles, prefixes, and postpositions are used primarily as verbal modifiers.

---

[6] Levinson says that Tzeltal has only one preposition, which he translates in these examples as "AT".

The dominance of verbs in Navajo also corresponds to the Navajo emphasis on a world in motion. . . . the principal verb in the Navajo language is the verb "to go" and not the verb "to be", which is the principal in so many other languages but is of relatively minor importance in Navajo. This seems to indicate a cosmos composed of processes and events, as opposed to a cosmos of facts and things.

pp. 48–49

[Harry] Hoijer [1951] concludes . . . that Navajo verb categories "center very largely about the reporting of events, or better, 'eventings.' These eventings are divided into neuters, eventings solidified, as it were, into states by the withdrawal of motion."

p. 52

Rik Pinxten, Ingrid van Dooren, and Frank Harvey in *The Anthropology of Space* say:

Navajos seem to stress both process rather than substance and cohesion rather than segmentability of reality.   p. 3

A basic characteristic of the Navajo world view, inherent in all particular phenomena it distinguishes, is the fundamentally dynamic or active nature of the world and anything in it. This feature is indeed fundamental and difficult to grasp, at least in the conceptual framework of the Westerner. It can be illustrated best through its practical, visible consequences. For example, with the static Western view it proved easy and dependable to divide space into segments, to structure the world according to types of objects, units, even atoms, all of which enjoy a certain "objective" status. The segmenting or "slicing" of reality (or at least the continuous stream of phenomenal reality) into chunklike, static units is possible in an easy, intellectually unsophisticated way, only within a static world; only within a world of objects, so to speak. The Navajo world, on the other hand, is essentially dynamic, and in consequence is much less suited for the kind of segmenting required by this part/whole logic which we consider "natural," as it were.   pp. 15–16

The notion of "being" or "existing" is similarly a dynamic concept. In contrast to the Western static and segmentable reality represented in the distinction between "being" and "becoming" or "growing," the Navajo view of "being" implies an essentially dynamic perspective. In this way, "existing" should be understood as a continuous manifestation (or "manifesting"), a series of events, rather than states or situational persistences through time.   p. 18

Maori

Maori is the language of the native people of New Zealand. In the textbook, *Maori Language: Understanding the Grammar* David Karena-Holmes tries to describe Maori grammar in terms of English grammatical categories:

> In Maori there are no words which are used exclusively as adjectives. The word 'big' may be exclusively an adjective in English, but the Maori word *nui* is used as a common noun (*te nui* — 'the greatness'), as an adjective ('big' or 'great' — as in *te tangata nui*) or as a verb, with the sense of 'to be big or great'. p. 25

> But sentences, complete without any verb, may be constructed in Maori simply by using two or more noun phrases in sequence, as illustrated by the examples:

> | *Ko **Tamahae*** | *ahau.* | |
> |---|---|---|
> | Tamahae | I | ('I am Tamahae.') |

> | *Ko tenei* | *te pukapuka* | *a **Tamahae**.* |
> |---|---|---|
> | This | the book | of Tamahae |

> ('This is Tamahae's book.')

> It should be noted that the English translations of these sentences require the use of the words 'am' and 'is' respectively (parts of the verb 'to be') for which there are no corresponding words in Maori. The meaning of each of these Maori sentences, however, is fully and unambiguously communicated in the Maori constructions. pp. 31–32

> Because the sense of 'being' (in some state or other) is expressed in Maori by using words such as *pai* and *nui* as verbs, a case could be made for classifying such words as VERBS OF BEING rather than adjectives. That is, the base words *pai* may be considered to convey the verb sense of 'to be good or fine', rather than the adjective sense of 'good or fine', and *nui* may be taken to mean 'to be big' rather than 'big'. p. 26

Chinese

There are at least three main languages called "Chinese": Mandarin, Wu, and Cantonese. There is also Classical Chinese prior to the Han Dynasty. Authors are not always specific about which of these they are considering, though all are written using (mostly) the same characters or "graphs".[7]

---

[7] As Chad Hansen says in *A Daoist Theory of Chinese Thought*:

> The linguistic diversity of China poses a terminological problem. The ordinary criteria for applying both *word* and *language* in English

Chad Hansen discusses pre-Han Chinese in *Language and Logic in Ancient China* (the symbol ∏ indicates a Chinese character, which I cannot reproduce):

> In most modern Chinese dialects the syntactical parallel with English mass nouns is almost exact for all nouns. Chinese nouns have no ordinary plural. They cannot be directly preceded by numbers or indefinite articles or demonstratives. Each noun is associated with appropriate sortals (called classifiers or measures in most language texts). Thus in (Mandarin) Chinese, one says <one *pen* book>, <three *ko* persons>, and <this *chih* pencil>. The nouns by themselves are complete term expressions.
>
> Another characteristic distinction between the two groups of nouns in English is their association with either *much* or *many* (or the opposites, *little* versus *few*). Mass nouns go with *much* (e.g., much wood, much money); count nouns go with *many* (e.g., many trees, many dimes). Chinese *to* ∏ 'many-much' and *shao* ∏ 'few-little' go with all nouns (and adjectives). Classical Chinese is slightly different from modern Chinese in a few of these respects.   p. 32

Briefly, we can characterize Chinese semantic theories as a view that the world is a collection of overlapping and interpenetrating stuffs or substances. A name (term or predicate—*ming* ∏) denotes (refers to, picks out—*chü* ∏) some substance. The mind is not regarded as an internal picturing mechanism which represents the individual objects in the world, but as a faculty that discriminates the boundaries of the substances or stuffs referred to by names. This "cutting up things" view contrasts strongly with the Platonic philosophical picture of objects which are understood as individuals or particulars which instantiate or "have" properties (universals). . . . Chinese philosophy has no theory either of abstract or of mental entities. The "individuals" in Chinese theories of language are "unit parts" of the "stuffs" picked out by names.   p. 30

---

are linked to the written form. We tend to individuate words mainly by their written form. (When we say, "That is one word, not two!" we are normally giving instruction on how to write, not how to speak.) This criterion partly explains why English speakers refer to Chinese characters as words. We also tend to individuate languages by written form. Where speakers share a written form, ordinary usage terms the spoken variations as dialects. Thus we characterize Chinese regional variations as dialects, despite the fact that the actual linguistic diversity in the spoken languages of China is roughly equivalent to that or Europe.   p. 33

Others say that the division of Chinese base words as nouns and adjectives and verbs is wrong. Marcel Granet said in 1920:

> . . . one cannot set out any particular rule about the different parts of speech; more precisely, there is not, so to speak, any differentiation of the parts of speech. The only distinction that one can make is that which the Chinese make between empty words, *Hiu tseu*, simple oral punctuations and the full words, *Che tseu*, which, alone, connote concepts. The full words (like the empty ones) are invariant monosyllables and no variation of verbal forms indicate if they are employed as verbs, substantives, adjectives or adverbs. Apart from some very specialized words in the use of pronouns or possessives, all the words are susceptible of every use and, rigorously speaking, the fundamental distinction between verbs and substantives does not exist at all.[8]

And Perry Link says in "A Magician of Chinese Poetry":

> The advantages of Chinese characters in avoiding grammatical specificity (advantages to poets, not necessarily to scientists or lawyers) can be analyzed primarily as absences of subject, number, and tense. Each of these three is worth a look.
>
> *Subjectlessness.* It is the norm in classical Chinese poetry, and common even in modern Chinese prose, to omit subjects. The reader or listener infers a subject. . . .
>
> *Numberlessness.* Nouns have no number in Chinese. Weinberger notes that "a rose is a rose is all roses," but that formulation still leaves us too far inside Western-language number habits. "All roses" in English means the summation of individual roses, whereas in Chinese *meigui*, or "rose" is more like "roseness" or "rosehood." (If you want to talk in Chinese about one rose, you may, but then you use a "measure-word" to say "one blossom-of roseness.") . . . (It is worth noting that Western views of Eastern expression as quaint have often originated not in Eastern languages but in the awkwardness that results when rules of Western languages are applied.)
>
> *Tenselessness.* There are several ways in Chinese to specify when something happened or will happen, but verb tense is not one of them. For poets, the great advantage of tenselessness is the ambiguity it opens up. Did I see no one in the hills? Or am I now seeing no one? Am I imagining what it would be like to see no one? All these, and others, are possible. Weinberger's insight about

---

[8] My translation from *Quelques Particularités de la Langue et de la Pensée Chinoises,* pp. 31–32 of the online version.

subjectlessness—that it produces an effect "both universal and immediate"—applies to timelessness as well. p. 50

Chinese languages are quite different from the native American languages discussed above, for they do not incorporate prefixes, suffixes, or infixes in a base word.

But there's no duck

A friend and colleague read this last section yet could not accept that some people talk without a main focus on the world as made up of things without a noun-verb distinction. He said that I and some of these linguists and anthropologists conflate two claims:

A language has a very different grammar.

A language is based on a very different metaphysics.

Or, he said, we are suggesting without establishing that the second follows from the first. He also said of an earlier draft, "[this passage] makes two claims: thing language directs us to see stability, mass-process grammar directs its users to see the flux. These look like empirical claims. Can you cite evidence for them?" This is looking for proof where there can be only insight. The grammar and metaphysics cannot be disentangled. To grasp one is to grasp the other.

The metaphysics is embedded in a language. We cannot use logic to compare different metaphysics because logic is based on metaphysics: different metaphysics yield different logics.

My colleague denies this. There is no different metaphysics, only unusual grammars that talk of things in strange ways.

Suppose I show Rudolfo the rabbit-duck picture (on the next page).[9] He says he sees a rabbit. Then I ask him if he sees a duck. He says, "No". So I point it out to him. He still says he doesn't see it—he's being honest, he really doesn't see it. So I trace it out on the paper with my finger. He still doesn't see it. "There is its bill," I say. He says, "A duck has a bill?" He's never seen a duck in his life, not a live one nor a dead one. He doesn't even know what he's supposed to be looking for. But it's there! "The duck is in that picture," I insist. He says he can't see "it".

---

[9] Anonymous illustrator, "Welche Thiere gleichen einander am meisten?" *Fliegende Blätter*, Braun & Schneider. For history and discussion, see J. Donaldson, "The Duck-Rabbit Ambiguous Figure".

See also E. H. Gombrich, *Art and Illusion* for a discussion and much about meaning and interpretation relevant to this and the other papers in this volume.

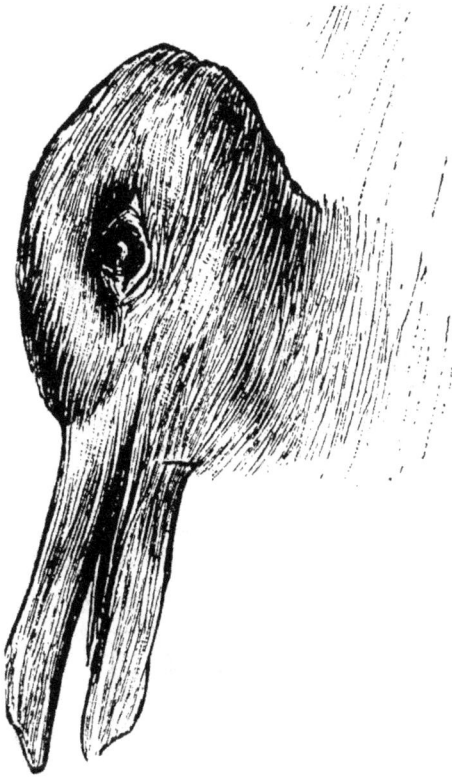

The rabbit-duck picture

But a duck is not in the picture. Nor is a rabbit. There are just some lines on a piece of paper that I interpret as a rabbit, and at other times as a duck. Yet even I can't see both at the same time: now rabbit, now duck, now rabbit, now duck, now duck, now rabbit, ...

There's nothing wrong with Rudolfo's eyes. He just doesn't see the picture *as* a duck.

This is like the problem I have trying to help you see the world as the flow of all. I'm not trying to convince you to see it that way, or trying to convince you that others see the world that way.[10] All the talk about others who encounter the world as flux won't matter

---

[10] The focus on seeing as the central way of encountering the world reflects the dominant metaphor in English: we "see" the world as made up of things; the "view" of language as based on the subject-predicate distinction is in English. I would prefer to speak of *encountering* the world, or *meeting* a different conception of language, but to do so more than occasionally would make this and my other papers in this volume sound very awkward.

if you can't enter that way. They are just wrong, you'll say—there's only a rabbit there. Everything they say about a duck is just some kind of strange way to talk about a rabbit. Yet there is nothing in the world that *is* a thing or *is* the flow of all except as we see it the one way or the other.

When I've given a talk about the world as the flow of all, I ask at the end whether people in the audience can begin to talk in mass-process terms, whether they can begin to see the world with descriptions but not partitioned into things. About half of the people raise their hand. The other half are still insisting that there is only a rabbit. "Curious how you talk of mass-process, but really that's just a funny way to describe the world as made up of things. And you know, the world is made up of things." And there really *is* a rabbit in that picture. It's not just how I interpret the picture. "You have a way to interpret that is so strange," they say, "so far removed from how I talk and see the world, that I can only think of you as confused or trying to be clever. All that kind of talk can be translated into English (or Portuguese when I gave the talk in Brazil). Of course translating isn't always easy, but it can be done since those people do think of the world as made up of things, just as we do. After all, there's only one world, and our language gets it right."

I said that the grammar of English leads us to view the world as made up of things, to thing-ify all our conceptions. Dick comes home and sees that Zoe is mad. "Did I do something wrong?" "Yes," Zoe replies, "you forgot to turn on the dishwasher." Dick did some thing wrong. You can talk all you like about "thing" there being just a place holder, a neutral meaningless word, but Zoe's use of it drives us to think of turning on the dishwasher as a thing and reason about "it" as we reason about individual things.

As speakers of English we can very imperfectly see the world as involving process and mass and have to remind ourselves of the difference. Some try to assimilate talk of masses to talk of things; an inability to see the duck.[11] But our first way to talk, to see, is in terms of individual things. And our grammar is for that and forces that.[12]

---

[11] See "The Metaphysical Basis of Logic: Things and Masses" in this volume.

[12] Benjamin Lee Whorf in "Languages and Logic" says:

> English terms, like "sky," "hill," "swamp," persuade us to regard
> some elusive aspect of nature's endless variety as a distinct *thing*,
> almost like a table or chair. Thus English and similar tongues lead

If you cannot see the world as process-mass, you cannot accept what these linguists and anthropologists say as examples of the kind of view I described. Not one of the languages fits perfectly the artificial grammar I set out in "The World as the Flow of All". Nor should we expect any of them to fit perfectly. We have incorporated into our languages ways to talk of more experience than just things or just mass-process. But the heart of each language is directed either to stability placed into time or to descriptions of the flow of all.

Still, it's not true there are two kinds of language, no more than any taxonomy is true or false. The "claim" is meant as an organizing principle, a way to explain and understand.

Nouns and verbs

By the characterizations I gave, speakers of the languages described above do not make a noun-verb or a subject-predicate distinction. Yet some linguists say they do, and more, they say that all languages distinguish classes of nouns and verbs. Before we can evaluate that claim, we need to be clear how they understand nouns and verbs. In "Noun and Verb in Salish", Jan P. van Eijk and Thom Hess present a survey:

> So many different definitions and descriptions have been given for 'predication', 'predicate', 'complement', 'noun', and 'verb' that it is necessary to explain what is meant by these terms in this article. The definitions which follow are brief but (we hope) uncontroversial in that they encapsulate the basic consensus for the scope of these terms.
>
> *Predication*: a construction in which new information is introduced about a given entity: 'the man works' is a predication.
>
> *Predicate*: that part of a predication that contains the new information: 'works' is the predicate in 'the man works'.
>
> *Complement*: the given entity in a predication: 'the man' is the complement' in 'the man works'. Instead of 'complement', some authors prefer 'argument' or 'term'.
>
> 'Noun' and 'verb' can be defined on three levels, the morphological, the syntactic, and the semantic. The following definitions hold for most if not all Indo-European languages and for a great many other languages as well. In our definitions we use English examples.

us to think of the universe as a collection of rather distinct objects and events corresponding to words. Indeed, this is the implicit picture of classical physics and astronomy—that the universe is essentially a collection of detached objects of different sizes. p. *232*

Noun

(a)   Morphological: a noun is a word that formally distinguishes singular from plural, as in 'box' — 'boxes', 'foot'–'feet'. (We ignore cases like 'sheep' or 'deer'.)

(b)   Syntactic: a noun is a word that can serve as the head of a complement to a predicate.

(c)   Semantic: a noun is the name of a person, place, or thing.

Verb

(a)   Morphological: a verb is a word that formally distinguishes aspects and/or tenses, as in 'work' — 'worked', 'run' — 'ran'.

(b)   Syntactic: a verb is a word that can serve as a predicate.

(c)   Semantic: a verb is a word that indicates action or being.

pp. 319–320

Van Eijk and Hess' definition of predication does not apply even in many English sentences. For example, in "Snow is white" what is the "entity" about which new information is introduced? Snow is not an entity. An entity is some part of the world (of our experience) that we can identify, re-identify, and distinguish from other parts that can be identified and re-identified. My dog Birta is (was) an entity; this rock is an entity; my table is an entity. But snow is not an entity; it is mass. Further, it's not clear what "new information" means, for it's certainly not new to me or I suspect to you that snow is white.

William Croft tried to enlighten me: mud, he said, is an entity. If that's so, what isn't an entity? Is brown an entity? Is running an entity? To talk of actions, processes, and states as entities is to view actions, processes, and states as things, ones we can "talk about", things we can count and supposedly distinguish. But that is exactly what we cannot do, as I show in "Why Event-Talk is a Problem" in this volume. This is why we cannot reason about actions, processes, and states in predicate logic, our best analysis of how to reason about things.[13]

So Van Eijk and Hess' definition of "predication" is either not clear or too restrictive even for English, and with it go their definition of "predicate" and "complement". Yet it is clear enough how to use the terms "subject" and "predicate" in English according to the explanations I gave: we have the standards in talking about individual things, and we extend that pattern to other sentences with similar syntactic structure,

---

[13]   See "The Metaphysical Basis of Logic: Things and Masses"" and "Languages and Logics" in this volume.

even when there is a serious question whether we are talking about individual things.

Van Eijk and Hess' criteria for nouns also suffer from ignoring that there is much even in English that cannot be assimilated to thing-talk. We all believe and have been taught that "mud", "snow", "running", and "sleeping" are nouns, but they are not classified as nouns by the morphological criterion. The syntactic criterion fails because it depends on the definitions of "predicate" and "complement", which have limited application even to sentences in English and would not classify "mud" and "running" as nouns, unless van Eijk and Hess or other linguists can clear up what they mean by "entity". Even if we could understand what is meant, the definition excludes "mud" and "snow" as names, unless mud and snow are things. Some modify the criterion to allow for those words to be classified as nouns by saying that a noun can be a word for a substance. But that is still inadequate because it won't classify "flame", "midnight", or "justice" as nouns.

Van Eijk and Hess' criteria for verbs fare somewhat better for English. What we typically call "a verb" is what we can conjugate for tense or with which we can use a mood word, such as "could". Here is how Robert I. Binnick puts it in *Time and the Verb*:

> As with so many other things, our most basic ideas about the verb go back to the ancient Greeks. Plato defines the verb as that word which denotes action, and it is still often called the "action word." But for Aristotle, "a verb is a composite sound with a meaning, indicative of time"; it is tense which is its essential feature. To this day the verb is thought of as a "time-word"—as in German in which the usual term, alongside the learned *Verb*, is *Zeitwort*. It is that part of speech which is concerned with distinctions of time, that is, with tense. p. 3

By this criterion, Chinese has no verbs, for it does not have tenses that modify words; rather, words or phrases indicating a time preface a whole sentence or even a paragraph. William Croft points out in *Radical Construction Grammar*:

> One might propose that inflection for agreement and tense-mood-aspect will be the criterion for the category Verb across all languages. But why? No reason has been given to do so. And if one does, then one will have to conclude that all words are Verbs in Makah and no words are Verbs in Vietnamese, which is hardly a savory conclusion for a theory that posits Verbs as part of a Universal Grammar. p. 31

These observations about Vietnamese and Makah are what we would
expect of mass-process languages, where each mass-process word
(phrase) can be marked for time in an affirmation, or where no mass-
process word is marked for time, as in Chinese. And there is a reason
to classify as verb what can be inflected for tense: the verb is what
places the description of a supratemporal thing in time.

Returning to van Eijk and Hess, their syntactic criterion for verbs
depends on the thing-based notion of "predicate" and hence is not
always applicable even in English—except that they generalize past
that by saying "can": so if the word can be used in a thing-sentence
construction as a predicate, it's a predicate, even though it can also
be used in a mass- or process-sentence construction.

As for the semantic criterion, long ago Benjamin Lee Whorf in
"Science and Linguistics" noted that it fails for English:

> In English we divide most of our words into two classes, which
> have different grammatical and logical properties. Class 1 we call
> nouns, e.g., "house, man"; class 2, verbs, e.g., "hit, run." Many
> words of one class can act secondarily as of the other class, e.g.,
> "a hit, a run," or "to man (the boat)," but on the primary level, the
> division between the classes is absolute. Our language thus gives us
> a bipolar division of nature. But nature herself is not thus polarized.
> If it be said that "strike, turn, run," are verbs because they denote
> temporary or short-lasting events, i.e., actions, why then is "fist"
> a noun? It is also a temporary event. Why are "lightning, spark,
> wave, eddy, pulsation, flame, storm, phase, cycle, spasm, noise,
> emotion" nouns? They are temporary events. If "man" and "house"
> are nouns because they are long-lasting and stable events, i.e.,
> things, what then are "keep, adhere, extend, project, continue,
> persist, grow, dwell," and so on doing among the verbs? If it
> be objected that "possess, adhere" are verbs because they are
> stable relationships rather than stable percepts, why then should
> "equilibrium, pressure, current, peace, group, nation, society, tribe,
> sister," or any kinship term be among the nouns?   pp. *195–196*

Not one of van Eijk and Hess' criteria can be used to investigate
whether a language has a noun-verb distinction because not one works
even for English. Yet these are the standard characterizations.

Perhaps, though, we've been looking at the noun-verb distinction
in English wrong. Yes, it is the use of thing-words that leads us to the
idea of a noun. We have that "dog", "chair", "rock", "woman", "Zoe",

"London" are nouns according to the semantic criterion of van Eijk and Hess. These are prototypes: we think of them in classifying and extend the classification to other words. But how can these be prototypes for "mud" and "snow" or "running" and "sleeping"? And even if we do extend the notion of noun in some way to these, how can they be used as prototypes for "justice" and "beauty"? There is no extension by analogy or prototype. There is extension by the exigencies of grammar. In English, German, and Romance languages our first focus is on things and what is done by or to them or how they are related. That perhaps drove the creation of the grammar, or perhaps the earliest grammar drove that focus. But talk of prototypes does not illuminate that.[14]

Looking for nouns and verbs

An early crystallization of the view that noun and verb are basic to all languages was by the linguist Edward Sapir:

> It is well to remember that speech consists of a series of propositions.
> There must be something to talk about and something must be said
> about this subject of discourse once it is selected. This distinction is
> of such fundamental importance that the vast majority of languages
> have emphasized it by creating some sort of formal barrier between
> the two terms of the proposition. The subject of discourse is a noun.
> As the most common subject of discourse is either a person or a
> thing, the noun clusters about concrete concepts of that order. As

---

[14] Compare Matthew S. Dryer in "Are Grammatical Relations Universal?":
The view espoused in this paper is that although there is a sufficiently
strong isomorphism between grammatical relations in many different
languages to make it convenient to employ the same label for these
grammatical relations in different languages, the degree of isomorphism between Philippine and more typical languages is sufficiently
weaker that there is not a clear way to assign the familiar labels to
the Philippine languages. The alternative view, which I am arguing
against, is that there exists, in addition to the similarities and differences
noted, a crosslinguistic Platonic concept of 'subject', of which subjects
in English are more prototypical and 'subjects' in Philippine languages
less prototypical. Note that the essential Platonic nature of grammatical
relations as crosslinguistic concepts is not diminished by claiming that
they are prototype categories rather than categories with discrete boundaries. The question of whether they are essentially Platonic is *not* the
question of whether they are discrete categories or not, but whether they
exist at all outside the minds of linguists. p. 133

the thing predicated of the subject is generally an activity in the
widest sense of the word, a passage of existence from one moment
to another, the form which has been set aside for the business of
predicating, in other words, the verb, clusters about concepts of
activity. No language wholly fails to distinguish noun and verb,
though in particular cases the nature of the distinction may be an
elusive one. It is different with the other parts of speech. Not one
of them is imperatively required for the life of language.*

* [footnote] In Yana the noun and verb are well distinct, though there
are certain features that they hold in common which tend to draw them
nearer to each other than we feel to be possible. But there are, strictly
speaking, no other parts of speech. The adjective is a verb. So are the
numeral, the interrogative pronoun (e.g., "to be what?"), and certain
"conjunctions" and adverbs (e.g., "to be and" and "to be not"; one
says "and-past-I go," i.e., "and I went"). Adverbs and prepositions
are either nouns or merely derivative affixes in the verb.

Language: An Introduction to the Study of Speech, pp. 125–126

Sapir is claiming that the thing-perspective of the world is basic
in language, building his definitions around that. Yet his description
of Yana, a now-extinct language that was spoken by the Yana people
who lived in what is now California between the Pit river in the north
and the Feather river in the south, does not show that there is a noun-
verb distinction in that language.

Van Eijk and Hess give their criteria for what constitutes a noun
and verb as a prelude to showing that despite what Kinkade said (p. 15
above), there is a noun-verb distinction in some Salishan languages.

In summation, we can say that there are two basic word-classes
in Salish and these classes are similar enough to the 'noun' and 'verb'
in Indo-European to apply profitably in descriptions of Salish. The
traditional criterion by which nouns are distinguished from verbs
(viz., the idea that nouns are typically complements in a predication
while verbs are typically predicates) fails for Salish, since in Salish
both nouns and verbs freely serve in both predicates and complements. Thus the main criterion by which nouns are distinguished
from verbs in Salish and Indo-European (and many other languages)
is a morpho-syntactic one based on the fact that nouns can combine
with possessive markers while verbs cannot. The fact that only nouns
can take possessive markers is compatible with the fact that nouns
typically refer to things, persons, or places, i.e., to those entities with
which one can enter into a relationship of possession. Verbs typically

refer to actions, i.e., to entities that are too fleeting to be involved in possession relationships. pp. 329–330

They say their categories are given by a morpho-syntactic criterion. But that is not one they started with (pp. 25–26 above). Rather, in their description nouns and verbs constitute what Whorf would call *covert* categories, defined by how they relate to other parts of speech.[15] Moreover, they justify their classifications by the semantic criterion for nouns. Yet from the mass-process view we can describe with "mother-ing" not to pick out a thing, nor a process (though perhaps that might help you see the issue), but as a description of the flow of all. And we can combine that with "my" as a classifier to specify some of mother-ing.

Van Eijk and Hess are engaging in what William Croft in *Radical Construction Grammar* dismisses as "methodological opportunism":

> Language-internal methodological opportunism simply selects a subset of language-specific criteria to define a category when the criteria do not all match. The subset of criteria, or possibly just one criterion, defines the category in question. Mismatching distributions are ignored, or are used to define subclasses or multiple class membership.   p. 41

Michael Tomasello comments similarly in "Universal Grammar Is Dead":

> Just as we may force English grammar into the Procrustean bed of Latin grammar—that is how I was taught the structure of English in grade school—the grammars of the world's so-called exotic languages may be forced into an abstract scheme based mainly on European languages. For example, one can say that all the world's languages have "subject." But actually there are about 30 different grammatical features that have been used with this concept, and any one language has only a subset—often with almost non-overlapping subsets between languages.   pp. 470–471

Worse than unclear or shifting definitions and explanations is that many linguists use the terms "noun" and "verb" with no indication of what those mean, as if there were consensus. For example, Bruce Biggs in "The Languages of Polynesia" says:

> Syntactically the languages [of Polynesia] are characterised by a well-marked division between verbal and non-verbal utterances,

---

[15] See "Grammatical Categories" by Whorf, pp. *175–176*.

and in general, the capacity to frame any utterance in either a verbal or non-verbal way. p. 470

Here is how Biggs applies this to Maori:

> A base is the *sine qua non* of every phrase. Bases fall into five classes according to their compatibility with various particles when filling the head position in the nucleus of the phrase, as follows:
>
> Nouns occur with articles (and other nominal particles), but not with verbal particles, nor with the passive suffix or the noun derivative suffix. Nouns usually denote entities, concrete or abstract, e.g. *ika* 'fish', *whenua* 'land', *moana* 'sea', *takiwaa* 'space', *raakau* 'tree, wood'. p. 476

Biggs does not define "noun". He says that nouns usually denote entities, yet the translations of the examples as "land", "sea", "space", and "wood" are mass-terms. And that *raakau* can mean variously "tree" or "wood" is what we would expect of a base word in a mass-process language.

Georg Hazai in "Altaic Languages" describes Altaic languages, which include Mongolian and Turkish, with talk of verbs and nouns that seems at best strained: verbs being nouns, nouns being verbs, nouns and adjectives not distinguished, all of which would be straightforward if we view Altaic languages as mass-process ones.

How to show there isn't a noun-verb distinction
Kinkade in "Salish Evidence Against the Universality of 'Noun' and 'Verb' " shoots the moving target of what is meant by "noun" and "verb" by showing that none of the characterizations apply.

> It is usually claimed that languages contain at least two major word-classes, nouns and verbs. However, Salishan languages of North-western North America cannot be described in these terms. Instead, only predicates and particles can be distinguished. Nouns and verbs are variously defined for other languages. But whether looked at morphologically, syntactically, semantically, or logically, and whether at a surface or deep level, the notions of 'noun' and 'verb' (as well as other traditional parts of speech) are not relevant in Salish. A Salishan sentence contains at least a predicate, which may be \inflected for pronominal subject and/or object (as well as aspect, control, transitivity, etc.).   p. *246*

But that left open the field to van Eijk and Hess to come up with a new criterion.

In "Grammatical Categories" Whorf showed that even focusing instead on the uses of words as nouns or verbs, what he called "verbations" and "stativations", would not ensure a noun-verb distinction in every language:

> Can there be languages not only without selective nouns and verbs, but even without stativations and verbations? Certainly. The power of making predications or declarative sentences and of taking on such moduli as voice, aspect, and tense, may be a property of every major word, without the addition of a preparatory modulus. This seems to be the case in Nitinat and other Wakashan languages. An isolated word is a sentence; a sequence of such words is like a compound sentence. . . . Of such a polysynthetic tongue it is sometimes said that all the words are verbs, or again that all the words are nouns with verb-forming elements added. Actually the terms verb and noun in such a language is meaningless. . . . In Hopi the verb-noun distinction is important on a selective basis; in English it is important on a modulus basis; in Nitinat it seems not to exist. p. *185*

In "Languages and Logic" Whorf gives examples from Shawnee and Nootka for which it is clear that there is no way to parse them as subject-predicate or noun-verb. No talk of distributional classes or odd definitions of "noun" and "verb" can overcome that. Whorf fixes on polysynthetic languages as lacking a thing-basis. The division of languages into those that are thing languages and those that are mass-process languages gives a more general analysis and applies to Chinese, which is analytic, not polysynthetic.[16]

The search for universals
Many linguists who look for a noun-verb distinction in a language are trying to confirm that the distinction is a language universal. What does that mean?

It's not just that a linguistic feature can be found in every language that has been studied. If all languages other than English were to go extinct along with all records of them, then the word "dog" would be found in every human language. All the linguistic features and categories of English would be universal. No, finding the feature in every human language that has been studied is supposed to be evidence that it will be found in every human language.

---

[16] See Appendix 3 for the distinctions between polysynthetic, synthetic, and analytic languages.

We get this stronger claim, William Croft says in *Radical Construction Grammar*, by induction from the languages we have studied.

> A typologist uses an INDUCTIVE method of analysis, by constructing a sample of the world's languages and seeking language universals via cross-linguistic generalizations. Since diversity is basic, the only safe way that one can discover the range of linguistic diversity is by cross-linguistic research. And it is only through exploring linguistic diversity that one is able to discover the limits to variation, that is, the universals of human language. p. 7

But as Nicholas Evans and Stephen C. Levinson point out in "The Myth of Language Universals":

> Somewhere between 5,000 and 8,000 distinct languages are spoken today. How come we cannot be more precise? In part because there are definitional problems: When does a dialect difference become a language difference (the "languages" Czech and Slovak are far closer in structure and mutual intelligibility than so-called dialects of Chinese like Mandarin and Cantonese)? . . . If we project back through time, there have probably been at least a half million human languages [M. Pagel, 2000], so what we have now is a non-random sample of less than 2% of the full range of human linguistic diversity. It would be nice to at least be in the position to exploit that sample, but in fact, as mentioned, we have good information for only 10% of that. The fact is that at this stage of linguistic inquiry, almost every new language that comes under the microscope reveals unanticipated new features. p. 432

Already in 1938 Whorf and George L. Trager in "Report on Linguistic Research in the Department of Anthropology" observed that generalizing our grammatical categories to other languages is a mistake:

> ["lge" abbreviates "language" and "lgs" abbreviates "languages"]
>
> The task of formal grammar ends when the analysis of all linguistic configurations is completed, but the characteristics of a language are by no means fully accounted for then. It still remains to indicate the type of experience and kinds of referents referred to by different grammatical classes, for lgs may here differ widely. Our ordinary ways of classifying referents, as being "things", "objects", "actions", "states", etc. are quite unsuitable for this work, as they are themselves names for partitionings of experience resulting after it has been grammatically classed, and circular definitions or mere confusion will result from applying them as if they referred to the conformation of reality itself.

Terms like "subject", "predicate", "actor", "agent", "function", "cause", "result", are equally misleading or useless in any other than a strictly grammatical sense, defined for and by each particular lge and referring only to the patterns therein and not to external reality. It is, e.g., quite legitimate to talk about "the agent" in a given lge where the term has been defined or illustrated, but it is not to say that two different lgs of widely different type are alike in their treatment of the "agent". In such a use it is not clear what "agent" means. It is impossible to break up the flow of events in a non-arbitrary manner into "subject", "actor", "predicate", etc. as if there existed external realities of this sort. We, to be sure, may analyze a phenomenon as 'boy runs', but another lge is capable of analyzing it 'run manifests as boy'. p. 258

In any case, as in any science we want more than an induction from a sample; we want a reason for why the generalization should be true. Bernard Comrie in "On Explaining Language Universals" says:

The study of language universals is the study of those properties that are necessarily common to all human languages. It is important to understand that by claiming that a particular property is a language universal, we are not merely claiming that it is true of all human languages that happen to be available to us—all the languages that are spoken today and all those for which we have historical records. Rather, we are making a claim about the human language potential: This is the way human languages have to be. p. 195

Comrie says that there are two ways we can show why a linguistic feature must show up in every language or be in no language. We can look for a *biological* basis. His example is that no language has or could have a sound as the part of its basis that is produced by touching the tip of one's tongue to one's nose. Too few people can do that. If human biology were to evolve so that almost all people in some region could touch their nose with their tongue, that sound might be included in a language. But on the basis of our current biology we can justify that no language can have that sound. There are also *functional* constraints and motives for universals that arise from the purposes for which we use language. As Comrie points out, all languages have greetings that are nearly meaningless in terms of the parts of which they are composed. That's because language is meant for communication between people, and people first have to acknowledge each other.

Some believe that we must experience the world as made up of things due to our biology, and hence that every language must have a noun-verb distinction. But there doesn't seem to be good evidence for that (see Appendix 1 here). Many linguists and philosophers and cognitive scientists just assume that the world is made up of things and that we have to encounter the world that way, as you can see in "On the Genesis of the Concept of Object in Children" in this volume.

Translations

In conversation Melissa Axelrod, who studied Koyukon,[17] agreed with my assessment that linguists who study languages that are very different from Indo-European languages are really only showing how to translate from such a language into our language, how best to describe the grammar of such languages using the grammatical categories of Indo-European languages. Jürgen Broschart in "Why Tongan Does It Differently: Categorial Distinctions in a Language without Nouns and Verbs" concurs:

> I strongly object to Dixon's confident statement that "it is an empirical fact that there is *always* a major class that is aptly termed Noun: there is *never* any doubt as to the applicability of this traditional label, and *never* any question as to which class should be called Noun." Most linguists simply take a practical position implying that whatever translates as a noun in Indo-European will be called a noun. [18]

And Whorf in 1941 in "Languages and Logic" made a similar observation:

> Our [American] Indian languages show that with a suitable grammar we may have intelligent sentences that cannot be broken into subjects and predicates. Any attempted breakup is a breakup of some English translation or paraphrase of the sentence, not of the Indian sentence itself. p. *234*

Suppose we have a grammatical distinction in English and we want to find whether it is "present" in another language. Put that way, it's clear we are trying to find how the other language relates to English; we are not trying to find natural, inherent grammatical categories of the other language. So we should be explicit about this as a basis for finding linguistic features in other languages. For example, we would establish:

---

[17] *The Semantics of Time: Aspectual Categorization in Koyukon Athabascan.*
[18] Note 2, p. 160. The quote is by R. M. W. Dixon in *Where Have All the Adjectives Gone? and Other Essays in Semantics and Syntax*, p. 1.

There is a passive construction in the language.

by showing:

> Particular occurrences of certain elements in the language
> are best translated into English with a passive construction.

We could establish:

> There is no verb "to be" either in the sense of existence or
> as a copula in the language.

by showing:

> There is no word or phrase or afix in the language that appears
> in constructions that we would naturally translate into English
> as a form of the verb "to be".

Now consider:

> There is a noun-verb distinction in this language.

In this pattern of viewing grammatical studies as manuals for
translation, we would establish this claim with:

> Certain words are used regularly in such a way that the most
> natural translations into English of those words in those
> contexts is as a verb, and similarly for other words as nouns.

Then it is the aptness of the translations that is at issue.

A. C. Graham gives a word-for-character literal translation from
Chinese to English in his Introduction to *Poems of the Late T'ang*:

> Dog   bark   water   sound   middle
> A dog barks amid the sound of water.   p. 18

We can see how Chinese works without tenses and pronouns. The
effect, as Graham says, is a "forever", "universal" feel to what is said,
somewhat comparable to using the simple present tense in English.[19]
On p. 25 of that book he gives another word-for-character translation:

WOOD	DARK	GRASS	STARTLE	WIND
GENERAL		NIGHT	DRAW	BOW
DAWN		SEEK	WHITE	FEATHER
LOST	IN	STONE	CORNER	MIDDLE

Here is how he turns this into an English poem:

---

[19] Compare the comments by Perry Link on p. 21 above.

Woods dim, grass startled by the wind;
In the night the general draws his bow.
At dawn they seek the white feather
Lost among the corners of the stone.

Graham's goal in translating is to give some idea of late T'ang poetry
in what we as English speakers would recognize as poems. But it is the
word-for-character translations that allow us to enter into the Chinese
world. The universality, the tenselessness, the lack of nouns and verbs
are all lost when a poem is rendered into "good English".

Linguists have no literary motive for translating. They mean to
show us the nature of the other language. Translating into "good
English" impedes that, for the strangeness, the difference is lost.
Consider again two of the translations from Tzeltal by Levinson:

a. *jipil   ta laso   lo'bal*
   hanging AT rope   banana
   'the banana(-fruits) are hanging from the rope'

b. *k'atal   ta   s-ba   s-k'iyojbil kaipej te lo'bale*
   lying-across AT   its-top its-drying   coffee the banana
   'the banana(-trunks) are situated across the top of the
   coffee-drying patio'

As a guide to the nature of Tzeltal, the renditions into "good English"
mislead. To put "the" and "are" in the translation of (a) is to deny
the mass-nature of the original expression, reading instead nouns and
verbs; to put "are situated" in (b) is to impose a subject-predicate view.

Aert H. Kuipers in "The Categories Verb-Noun and Transitive-
Intransitive" faces this problem:

> The Squamish language lacks a morphological distinction between
> two word-classes which would parallel that between verbs and nouns
> in English.   p. 612

> The translations 'who/which *arrives*' and 'which is *water*'
> suggest the distinction of noun and verb which is absent in Squamish;
> translations which would be more neutral in this respect would be
> '*arrival-manifestation*' and '*water-manifestation*'.   p. 623

W. v. O. Quine in *Word and Object* disagrees:

> Wanton translation can make natives sound as queer as one pleases.
> Better translation imposes our logic upon them, and would beg the
> question of prelogicality if there were a question to beg.   p. 58

Quine's commitment to first-order classical predicate logic as the basis on which to judge translations is another example of reading the thing view of English, German, and Romance languages into other languages.[20]

Only linguists and anthropologists who are fluent in languages such as Navajo or Squamish can try to convey to us a fully different parsing of the world. And then it is their obligation to make as clear as they can the differences, the oddity of the other language by not making translations into good English.

But people do translate all the time between Chinese and English, between Navajo and English, between Maori and English. Surely that shows I'm wrong. It does so only if the standard for a good translation is that the translation is "what I would say if I were in that situation" or "it gets the other to respond in a way that would be expected if he or she spoke our language". Those are behavioral standards. As Joseph H. Greenberg says in "Concerning Inferences from Linguistic to Nonlinguistic Data":

> It would now be generally agreed that meaning is to be understood
> functionally, i.e., that meaning is to be described in terms of a rule
> of use stated in terms of the environment. p. 14

My friend does not like dogs, he has had very bad experiences with them. When we encounter a dog, he walks away, he is clearly frightened, while I approach the dog with coaxing noises. So what does "dog" mean functionally? Does "dog" mean the same to both of us? I think not, unless you have a very impoverished idea of meaning, as I explain in "Language-Thought-Meaning" in this volume.

What is common to thing-languages and mass-process languages?
No language, I suspect, focuses through its grammar solely on the world as made up of things. No language, I suspect, focuses through its grammar solely on the world as the flow of all. How, then, can we discern whether a language is a thing language or a mass-process language?

In trying to orient ourselves we can look for certain features of the language. For a thing language, I look for whether there is a clear noun-verb distinction: words that pick out and words that describe in time. Singular and plural marking on (most of) the nouns is a sign that the grammar is directing speakers to see individuals. Numerals can

---

[20] See "The Metaphysical Basis of Logic: Things and Masses" and "Languages and Logics" in this volume.

be added to (many) nouns. And I look for whether there is a verb corresponding to our "to be" used to connect nouns and descriptions or to indicate existence.

As signs of a mass-process language, I look to see if single word sentences are common. I ask whether there is no clear noun-verb distinction, or at least none that seems fundamental. That numerals cannot be added to a base word except with a classifier suggests a mass-process view. And there is likely no word corresponding to our "to be", either as copula or for existence.

Yet many languages have just some of these characteristics. In the history of Chinese languages, it has varied whether numerals could be added to a base word. English has many words that cannot be preceded by numerals: we call them "mass nouns". It is not the presence of all of these features, or none, or a majority of them that tell us whether a language is a thing language or a mass-process language. It is the main focus of the grammar, toward individuals or toward the flow of all, that we must discern.

The problem linguists encounter is that they look at too much "data", they try to take account of everything. It is clear, once we reflect, that English is primarily a thing-language. Yet if we try to look at all kinds of sentences and take account of all our "informants", we'll never get to that. We'll have to take account of process words like "running" and mass words like "mud". So the linguist would say that English isn't a thing-language, or perhaps not recognize it. Only by ignoring a great deal can we see the thing-basis of English, how we try to force concepts into a thing-mold, using nouns for what cannot be construed as a thing yet are needed for the grammar which is thing-based. If we try to look at all we can find in a language, we see only trees, no forest, blindly stumbling along using a map made for another forest—the grammar of English, German, and Romance languages.

What, though, is common to thing languages and mass-process languages?

Some suggest that the act of reference is universal. A referent is (normally) outside language, some part of the world that the act is meant to get us to pay attention to. That idea is tied strongly to a thing-conception of the world.[21] But it leads to what I think is a key

---

[21] See W. P. Alston, *Philosophy of Language* for the inadequacy of taking referring as basic to language and meaning.

to language: getting others to pay attention to what we want them to. We describe.

We should not confuse describing with referring. To talk of a beautiful sunset, speaking of the colors and the clouds, does not involve referring, unless you think that because "sunset" is a noun it must be a word for a kind of thing and we're talking about this particular one. From the mass-process view, there is no distinction between concrete and abstract. The words "dog", "run", "mud", "justice", and "white" are used for describing in the flow of all. There is nothing abstract in our conception of justice. We do not abstract from experience to use the word "justice" any more—or any less—than we abstract from experience to use "dog". We describe using that word.

The spoken "dog" evokes all of that concept ready to be used in many ways within the grammar of English. For example, we have:

dog   a singular noun, as in "A dog is barking."

dogs   a plural noun, as in "The dogs are barking."

dog   a mass noun, as when a person in a country where dogs are eaten might say, "Let's have dog for dinner tonight" (and be damned to eternity for that).

to dog   an infinitive, as in "He set out to dog her steps."

dogs   the present tense of a verb, as in "He dogs her steps."

dogging   the progressive of the verb, as in "He was dogging her."

dogged   the past tense of "to dog", as in "He dogged her steps."

doggéd   an adjective, as in "She had doggéd determination."

doggy   an adjective, as in "Birta coming out of the river has a wet doggy smell."

doggedly   an adverb, as in "She doggedly pursued the subject."

doggieness a noun, a mass word.

Though the last seems like a mass-process word, it is a genus or universal word, an essence word. It is "dog" by itself that is like a mass-process word. Alone, without modification, without use in a sentence, it conjures up all of the notion of dog: one animal; many animals; dogging; the nature of doggieness; the way dogs act; the way other concepts are likened to dogs; . . . .

Similarly, only by modifying and using "run" do we have a word that fits into a grammatical category:

to run   an infinitive, as in "He likes to run."

runs   the present tense of the verb, as in "She runs well."

running   the progressive of the verb, as in "She is running."

run   a singular noun, as in "I had a good run around the block."

runs   a plural noun, as in "They won by five runs."

runner   a singular noun, as in "There was only one runner on the street."

runners   a plural noun, as in "All the runners finished the race."

runny   an adjective, as in "She likes her eggs runny."

running   a mass noun, as in "Running is good for your health."

And we have:

white   an adjective, as in "This is a white piece of paper."

white   a noun, as in "This restaurant serves only whites."

whiten   a verb, as in "Whiten his face for the show."

whiter   a comparative, as in "This dress is whiter than that one."

whiteness   a noun, a mass word

Such base words, such roots, are what all languages must have. How those words or roots are used, how they are placed into a grammatical system, varies from language to language. But in each language we can find such words, such basic symbols that evoke a concept or category.[22] We start with those words when we translate.

Learning Arabic, if someone points to a dog and says "kalb", I have a way to begin to understand the word, though not whether what is meant is one dog, a dog as part of the mass of doggieness, the essence of doggieness, or some other, for I do not know how it is used in the grammar. Only by application, by learning to speak and use the grammar, do I begin to see with the language as a thing language or as a mass-process language, though with "kalb" the doggy smell, the pleasure of petting a dog, the barking, the howling, the whimpering, the running and chasing are all there ready to be fit into the grammar or adjusted to include, perhaps, uncleanness, once I have seen the person point.

---

[22] In "Language-Thought-Meaning" in this volume you can see that "concept" and "category," even "idea", are too rigid for describing how we mean.

Words we use to describe are part of both thing languages and
mass-process languages. Except that "word" is a bad term. Is "run"
a word in English? As we saw above, it is a stem, a base, that we
modify and whose role we understand in the context of an utterance.
To talk of a word in Makah where it can be modified by a prefix, suffix,
and/or an infix to be a complete utterance, makes the idea of word even
more suspect. We should talk of *stems*, of basis parts of a language.
But bowing to convention and ease of discussion, I'll talk of "base
words", or better, *concept words*. We use concept words to describe;
they are the bases for our descriptions in both mass-process languages
and thing-languages. They are the *categorematic* parts of speech.[23]

I am not suggesting that there are any particular concept words
that are shared by all languages, only that each language has some.[24]
Nor am I suggesting that any concept word has a (possibly complex)
correlate in the other language. It may be that the smallest unit of
a language that can be translated into English is a sentence. Whorf
in "Languages and Logic" says:

> When we come to Nootka, the sentence without subject or predi-
> cate is the only type. The term "predication" is used, but it means
> "sentence." Nootka has no parts of speech; the simplest utterance
> is a sentence.   p. *234*

The only idea of "predicate" I can find that makes sense in the
writings of the linguists above on mass-process languages is that of
description, the use of a (possibly complex) concept word modified
to work in a grammar. But that doesn't mean that a concept word in
another language that is best translated into English as "red" could not
be used in that other language in differing grammatical ways: we've
already seen that with Wintu (pp. 13–14 above). When Kinkade talks
of predicates in Salishan languages (p. 15 above), we can understand
that as uses of parts of speech for describing.

In English and other thing languages, we divide uses of categorematic words — not the words themselves — into various classes: noun,
verb, adjective, and more. Mass-process languages do not so clearly
divide uses of their concept words into classes, though they may. But
the classes into which a language divides uses of categorematic parts
of speech need not apply to any other language, though there may be

---

[23] Borrowing the term from the medieval logicians.

[24] Anna Wierzbicka does believe there are some universal concepts; see Cliff
Goddard in "Whorf Meets Wierzbicka".

similarities that will help us find our way in understanding a particular language. Yes, we might say, that is a kind of verbal use of a stem since it is marked for time in Makah. But those "correlations" are as likely to mislead.

Both kinds of languages also have parts of speech or markers that are meant to help us understand the way in which a concept word is being used to get us to pay attention. There are prefixes, suffixes, and infixes, as in English "man*ly*" and "*ir*reverent". There are connectives, as in English "not" and "if . . . then . . .". These have significance only when used with one or a combination of categorematic parts of speech. So we call them *syncategorematic*.[25]

Descriptions can be good or bad, right or wrong, true or false. *Affirmations*, in the widest sense as indicating that an utterance is in the part of the dichotomy for good, right, or true, seem to be an essential part of communicating, too.

Both kinds of languages also have parts of speech for *punctuation*. It might seem that these appear only in written language: commas, periods, question marks. But they are an integral part of our talk, indicated by pauses or tone, or other means in sign languages.

So in thing-languages and in mass-process languages we have the following ways to divide speech:

categorematic

syncategorematic

affirmations

punctuation

Now we can ask whether these are universals of language. As a prelude to that we should look for whether there are other kinds of languages besides thing languages and mass-process languages.

Metaphysics and language relativity
It's often said that metaphysics consists of claims that are in some sense fundamental. So consider:

The world is made up, at least in part, of things.

---

25 Again borrowing from the medieval logicians ("syn" = "with"). This division of parts of speech into categorematic and syncategorematic seems to be what Marcel Granet says that Chinese speakers make between whole words and empty words (pp. 21 above).

Is this a claim? There is no way we can show that it is true or show that it is false. It summarizes how we encounter and understand the world, and as such is fundamental to our way of life. But rather than "summarizes" perhaps we should say it serves as a guide, directions in our lives. It is relative to this sentence that a very large part of what we put in propositional form is evaluated. It is assumed, not shown, for it cannot be shown.

We assume that the world is made up of things, but when we try to be clear about this we must work very hard, writing books, debating, looking for form in both language and reasoning. We do not show how it is true, but how it underlies our beliefs.[26]

Some say that language shapes how we see the world. Surely it does—it is hard for us to distinguish different kinds of snow for which there are distinct words in Eskimo languages. That kind of shaping due to vocabulary is not very significant, for we can, with little effort, learn the other vocabulary and begin to use it.

No, the claim of linguistic relativity is a claim about differing metaphysics, about how different languages shape how we see, live in, encounter the world. Grammar—what must be said and what cannot be said—is what shapes a speaker's view of the world. For thing language speakers, our grammar directs us to see stability—things continuing in time despite their changes—that shapes how we live. For mass-process language speakers, their grammar directs them to see the flow of all described but not partitioned that shapes how they live. Note that I say that the language shapes, not determines. If English determined how we can see the world, I could never have led you to understand the mass-process view. If a language determined how we understand the world, we could never have new insights that initially seem like mysticism but with time lead us to modify our language.

Max Black in "Linguistic Relativity: The Views of Benjamin Lee Whorf" dismisses the idea of linguistic relativity:

> Were we able, as we are not, to infer from a given vocabulary to corresponding cognitive capacities, a further inferential leap would be needed to show that different languages incorporate different conceptual systems. The admitted possibility of translation from any language into any other renders the supposed relativity of such systems highly dubious. p. 231

---

[26] As I have tried to do in my works in logic, as described in "Languages and Logics" in this volume.

What makes Black think that the translations are good, that they preserve meaning? And Black misses Whorf's most important point that it is not the vocabulary, or at least not the vocabulary alone, that shapes thought so much as the grammar. As Whorf says in "Science and Linguistics":

> We cut nature up, organize it into concepts, and ascribe significances as we do, largely because we are parties to an agreement to organize it this way—an agreement that holds throughout the speech community and is codified in the patterns of our language. The agreement is, of course, an implicit and unstated one, *but its terms are absolutely obligatory*; we cannot talk at all except by subscribing to the organization and classification of data which the agreement decrees. p. *194*

And Dorothy Lee says in "Conceptual Implications of an Indian Language":

> It has been said that a language will delineate and limit the logical concepts of the individual who speaks it. Conversely, a language is an organ for expression of thought, of concepts and principles of classification. True enough, the thought of the individual must run along its grooves; but these grooves, themselves, are a heritage from individuals who laid them down in an unconscious effort to express their attitude toward the world. Grammar contains in crystallized form the accumulated and accumulating experience, the Weltanschauung of a people. p. *124*

And Harry Hoijer in "The Relation of Language to Culture" says:

> The fashions of speaking peculiar to a people, like other aspects of their culture, are indicative of a view of life, a metaphysics of their culture, compounded of unquestioned, and mainly unstated, premises which define the nature of their universe and man's position within it . . . It is this metaphysics, manifest to some degree in all the patterns of a culture, that channelizes the perceptions and thinking of all those who participate in the culture and that predisposes them to certain modes of observation and interpretation. The metaphysics, as well, supplies the link between language as a cultural system and all other systems found in the same culture. p. 561

In "The Scope of Linguistic Relativity: An Analysis and Review of Empirical Research" and in *Linguistic Diversity and Thought*, John A. Lucy describes how linguists look to other languages, see how those differ, infer metaphysics from that, and then look first for linguistic consequences and then cultural and behavioral consequences. Perhaps that can be done, but looking at number or gender or tense, though interesting, is not likely to lead to the thesis that language shapes how we encounter the world. If a Portuguese speaker has six aunts and one uncle, he or she will say "meus tios", the masculine form, not "minhas tias", the feminine form, and all the adjectives must agree and be masculine. No doubt this encodes a view that men are more important than women. But this can be pointed out easily to a Portuguese speaker. Learning English, that person will have to say, "My aunts and uncles" which is not a hard stretch to make.

In contrast, some speakers of English and Portuguese, in my experience at least, cannot imagine seeing the world first as the flow of all and not as composed of things. It is not a habit. It is not an emphasis. They cannot adjust to conceive of the world as the flow of all, not even as a mystical vision. This is the deep way that language shapes our thought.

Lucy and others look to those parts of the language that are hardest for speakers to recognize as significant as the key to the metaphysics that shape their experience. But every speaker of English is aware or can be easily shown that the language has words for things. The notion of thing is not hidden, yet we can see that it is a fundamental part of our language experience because it is so extraordinarily hard for us to conceive of an alternative.

Moreover, that language shapes how we see the world is not an issue of relativity, for it could be true and demonstrated even if no other language embedded a different way to see the world, for example, if there were no mass-process language other than the artificial one I devised.

Language and culture

Many look for behavioral differences to justify a linguistic relativity. But small behavioral differences, such as how you or I respond to dogs, unless generalized to a whole population from a careful study, can be idiosyncratic, arising from our personal experiences. If there are behavioral differences, then they must be culture-wide, seen in the large. Here are some cultural differences that seem to flow from whether a culture is based on a thing-language or a mass-process language. But whether they do I'll leave to others to investigate.

Owning

Birta is my dog, I own her. Hence I can do what I like with her, constrained only by laws that require humane treatment. I can sell her,

I can kill her, or I can give her a doggy treat every morning. To think of owning Birta, though, is to view her as a thing, and me as a thing, too, for owning is a relation between things. As process I can only interact, intermingle, flow with her, perhaps controlling her flow but as much controlled by her flow.

I own my ranch Dogshine. Hence I can do with it what I like, subject only to laws that constrain the impact on others of what I do. I can sell it, I can divide it into parts, I can plant trees, or I can graze sheep until there is not a single bit of green on the land. It is mine. I own it, which is to say that this piece of land is a thing, and I am a thing, and I have a special relation to it. But as process I can only interact, intermingle, flow with the process of the land, perhaps controlling its flow but as much controlled by its flow. In process-mass grammar we think principally of being with the land, of inter-acting. Conservation is not a foreign idea to be reconciled with ownership but is natural, for the relation is not owning but at most modifying the flow.

Can we even talk about owning in a mass-process language? Some individuating operator or classifiers would be needed. But what is natural for us as we speak such a language is to see my flow intermingling with the flow of dog-ing and land-ing here and now and through time.

Counting

To someone raised on a mass-process language, the idea of the world as made up of things must be a mystical vision. Counting would be an alien notion, for it is only things that are counted. Perhaps one, two, many — but not seventeen sheep and eight children.

Compare how Franz Boas in his Introduction to *Handbook of American Indian Languages* explains the lack of numerals in some cultures:

> As is well known, many languages exist in which the numerals do not exceed two or three. It has been inferred from this that the people speaking these languages are not capable of forming the concept of higher numbers. I think this interpretation of the existing conditions is quite erroneous. People like the South American Indians (among whom these defective numeral systems are found), or like the Eskimo (whose old system of numbers probably did not exceed ten), are presumably not in need of higher numerical expressions, because

there are not many objects that they have to count. On the other hand, just as soon as these same people find themselves in contact with civilization, and when they develop standards of value that have to be counted, they adopt with perfect ease higher numerals from other languages and develop a more or less perfect system of counting. . . . It must be borne in mind that counting does not become necessary until objects are considered in such generalized form that their individualities are entirely lost sight of. p. 62

Crime and punishment

Higaberto is an evil person, a murderer. We put him in prison for his crime. He is a thing with a label "evil". So we isolate him from our society. We are punishing, isolating a thing. But seeing the world as process, putting Higaberto in prison we are mixing the flow that we describe with "Higaberto-ing" with the process of prison-ing, and we think of how those intertwine, how they may affect one another and all the flow they encounter. The possibility of change in the process of Higaberto comes to the fore, rather than as an afterthought with a notion like "reform" or "degrading".[27]

Time

In English we talk of times and locations as things, ordering them as bits. Benjamin Lee Whorf in "Science and Linguistics" and "The Relation of Habitual Thought and Behavior to Language" has shown that this view of time and space is not shared with the speakers of the mass-process language Hopi, and that broad cultural differences follow from how we and the Hopi take account of time in our talk.

Linguistic relativity is now well-established — at least if you can understand how differently speakers of thing-languages and speakers of mass-process languages encounter the world. Language shapes thought, no doubt. But outside the large cultural differences that come from speaking very different languages, it is hard to know to what degree. When I am sitting outside my home with my dogs, content, stroking one, looking at the sunset, seeing the tree large and full with green leaves, with no sentence, no words in mind, is that perception or experience shaped by my language? I do not know, and I do not know how I could ever know.

---

[27] See "Life Comes from It: Navajo Justice Concepts" by Robert Yazzie, Chief Justice of the Navajo Nation.

Linguistic imperialism

Many linguists who study languages of people who live and speak very differently from how we in the West live and speak claim that their data is objective, scientific, there for anyone to see and understand.[28]   But data is or should be recorded to illustrate, or confirm, or challenge a theory. The idea that the researcher provides "raw data" to be mined by anyone is a bad way to do research, as any scientist will tell you.[29]

Often linguists have a theory of universals they are testing. Those theories are tied to a thing-view of the world, invariably derived from the grammar of English, German, and Romance languages. So they look for and find nouns, verbs, subjects, and predicates, not even aware that they are imposing the thing-view of their own language on the other language and culture. But some linguists and anthropologists are sensitive to the language and culture of other people. Dorothy Lee, Benjamin Lee Whorf, M. Dale Kinkade, Jürgen Broschart, and others step outside their own language habits. They find no nouns and verbs, no subject and predicate; they find a different world-view embedded in a different grammar. Linguists who ignore their work are not just wilfully ignorant; they are enforcing a linguistic imperialism of Western languages.

And in the end . . .

What seemed a mystical vision, the unity of all, the world as flux, is accessible to us now not as revelation, not as mystical insight, but through learning a different language. It is not mysticism but a habit of grammar.

They're not like you and me. They think that the broad divisions of our language correspond, however imperfectly, with what is "out there" in the world. There are things and masses, substances and what is done by or to them. We know that the world is not so static, so fixed, so correctly classified. These are our ways of encountering the world, but there are other ways that are just as "real". Those do not lead us to become aware of different aspects of reality. They lead us to different ways to experience, not better, not worse.

Our language is a template we hold up to the world. We see through the holes that make the pattern and think this is the world.

---

[28] See the criticism of that view in "North-South Relations in Linguistic Science" by Colette Grinevald and Chris Sinha.

[29] See my *How to Reason + Reasoning in the Sciences*.

But we can, with some effort, put that pattern down and pick up another. What we cannot do is see the world without such a pattern — or if we can, we cannot communicate what we see. That is where mysticism begins and grammar ends.

*   *   *   *   *   *   *

Appendix 1: A biological basis for a thing-focus?
In the only paper I have seen that attempts to show that there is a biological basis for a thing-view of the world, "Objects Limit Human Comprehension", Philip Richard Sullivan says:

> A type of nerve cell in this area responds to a reporting cluster of retinal ganglion cells that forms a line of stimulation along a given slant. And since a line of such activated ganglion cells will chart the direction of relatively abrupt light-intensity change formed by a partic- ular "edge" (as we perceive it) within the visual field, brain cells that respond to this sort of stimulation are referred to as "edge cells"—edge cells because they chart the edges of objects that exist in our surround- ings. That, at any rate, is the commonsense conclusion: the computa- tional process just described will assure that we detect the edges of the discrete objects that actually exist in our surroundings.
>
> But what if there were no actual "discrete objects?" What if there were only "regions in space where the field is extremely strong?" Our visual system would, under those conditions, structure the strong fields so as to form "edges", thus representing those regions as the perceptual objects that we ineluctably experience. p. 74

The argument then is: the human visual system responds most strongly to differences of intensity of light, therefore we cannot help but experience the world as made up of objects. Let's assume that the premise is true. So instantaneously we see edges. It doesn't follow that we have to conceive of those edges as delineating a thing: an individual that persists in time. After all, "the edges of this apple" move and vary considerably over even short times, and move a lot if "the apple" is on a branch of a tree. And what about hearing or smelling? Do our physical systems for those lead us to conceive our experi- ence in terms of things? What about touch? Are blind people predisposed to parse their experience in terms of things? Certainly much of our experience can't be parsed in terms of individual things: think of the last time you had diarrhea.

Evans and Levinson invoke evolution for a noun-verb and subject- predicate division in (almost) all languages:

> In short, there are evolutionary stable strategies, local minima as it were,

that are recurrent solutions across time and space, such as the tendency
to distinguish noun and verb roots, to have a subject role, or . . .   p. 444

Radu J. Bogdan in *Predicative Minds* more strongly invokes evolution to
explain why there has to be a subject-predicate division in every language.

> When conscious and explicit, human thoughts have a number of singular
> properties. One of them is being predicative. In a predicative mode, one
> can think and say of a house that it is big, a car that it is to the left of the
> house, a cat that it is about to jump, a hypothesis that it is plausible, this
> book that it is worth reading, or the like. The idea, in this formulation,
> is that a predicative mind singles out and represents an item (thing, agent,
> event, situation, and so on) in order to attribute to it—or to direct at it,
> as I prefer to put it—the representation of another item (be it property,
> relation, action, evaluation, and so forth).   p. xv

> Predications are the bread and butter of human propositional thinking
> and language use. When I think or judge, and say, that this pig is fat,
> I predicate—mentally and linguistically—a property (fatness) of an
> individual (this pig). p. 3

> There are several reasons why human ontogeny appears to be an
> evolutionarily unique incubator of predicative thinking.   p. 46

Yet even as thing-language speakers we have lots of thoughts that have no
linguistic structure, such as when I sniff and know the smell as that of sheep,
without any language or reasoning, just knowing. If there were an evolutionary
basis for predication, it would seem that people who speak languages without a
subject-predicate distinction must have evolved differently from speakers of
English. Yet we can interbreed!

Appendix 2: An example of linguistic imperialism
John A. Lucy in *Linguistic Diversity and Thought* describes an experiment:

> Bloom [1981. p. 31] administered a second experimental procedure
> involving counterfactual questions. Chinese and English speakers
> were presented with the following question written in their respective
> languages:
>> "If all circles were large and this small triangle '▲'
>> were a circle, would it be large?"

> Most Chinese speakers answered "no," whereas most English speakers
> answered "yes." This result was consistent with the hypothesis that
> the Chinese speakers have trouble working with the counterfactual
> mode. Bloom also reported that whenever the same question was
> given orally, even to highly educated speakers (for instance, to Hong

Kong University faculty members), most Chinese responded with the
following sorts of remarks:

> "No! How can a circle be a triangle. How can this small
> circle be large? What do you mean?"

Some subjects elaborated further, as did one who said:

> "I know what you Westerners want me to do, you always
> want me to assume things, even when they don't make sense.
> But we Chinese don't do that."   pp. 214–215

The experimenter viewed this as a deficiency of Chinese compared to English.
But in my paper "Conditionals" in *Cause and Effect, Conditionals, Explanations*, I point out that most uses of counterfactuals in English are too vague
to be considered claims. We can't guess what's being held constant and what
different in an imagined way the world could be. The example with the circle
and triangle is perfect for showing that: if a triangle can be a circle, maybe
small can be large, maybe pigs could fly. After all, supposedly triangles are
part of mathematics, and what is a triangle can't be anything else. I suggest
that this shows that Chinese speakers aren't given to crazy flights of fancy
that they can't make any sense of. Good for them!

Appendix 3: *Analytic, synthetic, and polysynthetic languages*
Joseph Greenberg in *Anthropological Linguistics*, explains those terms.

> These possibilities can be illustrated by reference to one aspect of
> a typology of language that was popular in the nineteenth century.
> Languages were at that time classified as either analytic or synthetic.
> An analytic language was one in which grammatical categories were
> typically expressed by individual words; a synthetic language, one in
> which grammatical categories were incorporated within the word as
> inflections. Thus, the English construction *I shall go*, in which the
> first-person singular subject (future) and the concrete verbal meaning
> are each expressed by separate words, would be regarded as analytic,
> by contrast with the Latin translation equivalent $\bar{i}b\bar{o}$ (I shall go),
> in which the root $\bar{i}$ (to go) and $b\bar{o}$, the future first person singular
> inflection, are contained in the same word.
>
> When certain American Indian languages were discovered—for
> example, Aztec—in which certain concepts, notably the noun object
> of a verb and the verb itself, were expressed as parts of the same word,
> so that concepts that were expressed by separate words even in a
> synthetic language like Latin were incorporated into the same word,
> the term *polysynthetic* was invented, to designate this still higher
> degree of synthesis.   p. 128

The mass-process language vs. thing-language division cuts across these typological classifications. Both Nitinat , which is polysynthetic, and Chinese, which is analytic, are mass-process languages.

Appendix 4: Distribution of mass-process languages
In my reading I noticed that native people in New Zealand, Polynesia, Tonga, Southeast Asia, China, and across the Bering Strait to North and South America speak or spoke mass-process languages. I wondered whether there was a connection among these, some common ancestral language. But that seems unlikely, since Chinese is analytic and Nitinat is polysynthetic. Indeed, that question shows my bias that thing languages are the standard.

Now it seems to me more natural to ask about the distribution of thing languages. Can all of them be traced back to the ur-language of Indo-European, across a swath from India to Europe? Are thing languages, not mass-process languages, the outliers?

REFERENCES
For articles reprinted in this volume, page numbers cited in this essay are to that version.   Works cited in the text without attribution are by Richard L. Epstein.

ALSTON, William P.
    1964   *Philosophy of Language*
           Prentice-Hall, Inc.
AXELROD, Melissa
    1993   *The Semantics of Time: Aspectual Categorization in Koyukon Athabascan*
           The University of Nebraska Press.
BIGGS, Bruce
    1971   The Languages of Polynesia
           In *Current Trends in Linguistics*, volume 8: *Linguistics in Oceania*,
           ed. Thomas A. Sebeok, Mouton, pp. 466–505.
BINNICK, Robert I.
    1991   *Time and the Verb: A Guide to Tense and Aspect*
           Oxford University Press.
BLACK, Max
    1959   Linguistic Relativity: The Views of Benjamin Lee Whorf
           The Philosophical Review, vol. 68, no. 2, pp. 228–238.
BLOOM, A. H.
    1981   *The Linguistic Shaping of Thought: A Study in the Impact of
           Language on Thinking in China and the West*
           Lawrence Erlbaum.

BOAS, Franz
  1911 Introduction to *Handbook of American Indian Languages*
         Vol. 1, Smithsonian Institution Bureau of American Ethnology,
         Bulletin 40. Washington: Government Printing Office, pp. 1–83.
BOGDAN, Radu J.
  2009 *Predicative Minds*
         The MIT Press.
BROSCHART, Jürgen
  1997 Why Tongan Does It Differently: Categorial Distinctions
         in a Language without Nouns and Verbs
         Linguistic Typology, vol. 1, pp. 123–165.
COE, Michael D.
  1999 *Breaking the Maya Code*
         Thames and Hudson, revised edition.
COMRIE, Bernard
  2003 On Explaining Language Universals
         In *Volume 2: Cognitive and Functional Approaches to Language
         Structures*, ed. Michael Tomasello, Psychology Press, pp. 195–210.
CROFT, William
  2001 *Radical Construction Grammar*
         Oxford University Press.
DIXON, R. M. W.
  1982 *Where Have All the Adjectives Gone? and Other Essays in
         Semantics and Syntax.*
         Mouton.
DONALDSON, J.
  2016 The Duck-Rabbit Ambiguous Figure
         In F. Macpherson, ed., *The Illusions Index*, July, 2016. Retrieved
         from http://www.illusionsindex. org/i/duck-rabbit.
DRYER, Matthew S.
  1997 Are Grammatical Relations Universal?
         In *Essays on Language Function and Language Type*, eds. J. Bybee,
         J. Haiman, and S. A. Thompson, John Benjamins, pp. 115–143.
EPSTEIN, Richard L.
  2011 *Cause and Effect, Conditionals, Explanations*
         Advanced Reasoning Forum.
  2019 *How to Reason + Reasoning in the Sciences*
         Advanced Reasoning Forum.
  2022 *Reasoning and the World as the Flow of All*
         To appear, AdvancedReasoningForum.org.

EVANS, Nicholas and Stephen C. LEVINSON
   2009   The Myth of Language Universals: Language Diversity and Its
             Importance for Cognitive Science
             Behavioral and Brain Sciences, vol. 32, pp. 429–492 (includes
             commentary pieces by other researchers and reply from the authors).
   See also LEVINSON.
GODDARD, Cliff
   2003   Whorf Meets Wierzbicka: Variation and Universals in Language
             and Thinking
             Language Sciences, vol. 25, 2003, pp. 393–432.
GOMBRICH, E. H.
   1961   *Art and Illusion*
             Princeton University Press. 2nd revised edition.
GRAHAM, A. C., translator and introduction by
   1965   *Poems of the Late T'ang*
             Penguin Books.
GRANET, Marcel
   1920   *Quelques Particularités de la Langue et de la Pensée Chinoises*
             Librarie Férie Alcan, 1920. Also in *Revue Philosophique*,
             mars-avril 1920, pp. 98–129 and 161–195. Accessed August, 2019
             via chineancienne.fr (Google Scholar).
GREENBERG, Joseph H.
   1954   Concerning Inferences from Linguistic to Nonlinguistic Data
             In *Language and Culture*, ed. H. Hoijer, Univ. of Chicago, pp. 3–19.
   1968   *Anthropological Linguistics: An Introduction*
             Random House.
GRINEVALD, Collette and Chris SINHA
   2016   North-South Relations in Linguistic Science: Collaboration or Colonialism?
             In *Endangered Languages and Languages in Danger: Issues of Documen-
             tation, Policy, and Language Rights*, 42, pp. 25–43. Available at
             DOI 10.1075/impact.42.02gri.
HANSEN, Chad
   1983   *Language and Logic in Ancient China*
             The University of Michigan Press.
             Reprinted Advanced Reasoning Forum, 2020.
   1992   *A Daoist Theory of Chinese Thought*
             Oxford University Press.
HAZAI, Georg
   1990   Altaic Languages
             Volume 22, *Encyclopedia Britannica*, 15th Edition, pp. 711–715.

HOIJER, Harry
  1951 Cultural Implications of Some Navaho Linguistic Categories
        Language, vol. 27, pp. 111–120. Reprinted in *Language in Culture
        and Society*, ed. Dell Hymes, Harper & Row, 1964, pp. 142–151.
  1953 The Relation of Language to Culture
        In A. L. Kroeber (ed.), *Anthropology Today*, University of Chicago
        Press, pp. 554–573.
KARENA-HOLMES, David
  2006 *Maori Language: Understanding the Grammar*
        (*Te Reo Maori: He Whakamarama Wetenga Reo*)
        Reed Publishing (NZ) Ltd., revised edition.
KINKADE, M. Dale
  1983 Salish Evidence against the Universality of 'Noun' and 'Verb'
        Lingua, vol. 60, pp. 25–40. Reprinted in this volume.
KUIPERS, Aert H.
  1968 The Categories Verb-Noun and Transitive-Intransitive
        Lingua, vol. 21, pp. 610–626.
LEE, Dorothy Demetracopoulou
  1938 Conceptual Implications of an Indian Language
        Philosophy of Science, vol. 5, no. 1, 1938, pp. 89–102.
        Reprinted in this volume.
  1944 Linguistic Reflection of Wintu Thought
        International Journal of American Linguistics, vol. 10, no. 4, pp.
        181–187. Also in LEE 1959, pp. 121–130. Reprinted in this volume.
  1944 Categories of the Generic and the Particular in Wintu
        American Anthropologist, vol. 46, no. 3, 1944, pp. 362–369.
        Reprinted in this volume.
  1954 Symbolization and Value
        In *Symbols and Values, an Initial Study*, Thirteenth Symposium of
        the Conference on Science, Philosophy, and Religion. Also in LEE,
        1959, pp. 78–88. Reprinted in this volume.
  1959 *Freedom and Culture*
        Prentice-Hall, Inc.
LEVINSON, Stephen C.
  1996 Relativity in Spatial Conception and Description
        In *Rethinking Linguistic Relativity*, eds. John J. Gomperz and
        Stephen C. Levinson, Cambridge University Press, pp. 177–202.
  See also EVANS and LEVINSON.
LINK, Perry
  2016 A Magician of Chinese Poetry
        A review of *19 Ways of Looking at Wang Wei* (*with More Ways*)

and *The Ghosts of Birds*, by Eliot Weinberger, New York Review of Books, vol. LXIII, No. 18, pp. 49–50.

LUCY, John A.

1992A *Linguistic Diversity and Thought: A Reformulation of the Linguistic Relativity Hypothesis*
Cambridge University Press.

1992B *Grammatical Categories and Cognition: A Case Study of the Linguistic Relativity Hypothesis*
Cambridge University Press.

1996   The Scope of Linguistic Relativity: An Analysis and Review of Empirical Research
In *Rethinking Linguistic Relativity*, eds. John J. Gomperz and Stephen C. Levinson, Cambridge University Press, pp. 37–69.

PAGEL, M.

2000   The History, Rate and Pattern of World Linguistic Evolution
In *The Evolutionary Emergence of Language*, ed. C. Knight, M.Studdert-Kennedy & J. Hurford, Cambridge University Press, pp. 391-416.

PINXTEN, Rik, Ingrid VAN DOOREN, and Frank HARVEY

1983   *The Anthropology of Space*
University of Pennsylvania Press.

QUINE, W.v..O.

1960   *Word and Object*
The M.I.T. Press.

SAPIR, Edward

1921   *Language: An Introduction to the Study of Speech*
Harcourt, Brace and Company.

SULLIVAN, Philip Richard

2009   Objects Limit Human Comprehension
Biology and Philosophy, vol. 24, pp. 65–79.

TOMASELLO, Michael

2009   Universal Grammar is Dead
Comment in EVANS and LEVINSON, pp. 470–471.

VAN EIJK, Jan P. and Thom HESS

1986   Noun and Verb in Salish
Lingua, vol. 69, pp. 319–331.

WHORF, Benjamin Lee

1940   Science and Linguistics
Technology Review (Massachusetts Institute of Technology), vol. 42, no. 6 (April), pp. 229–231 , 247–248. Reprinted in this volume.

1941 Languages and Logic
Technology Review (Massachusetts Institute of Technology), vol. 43
(April), pp. 250–252, 266, 268, 272. Reprinted in this volume.

1941 The Relation of Habitual Thought and Behavior to Language
In *Language, Culture, and Personality: Essays in Memory of
Edward Sapir*, Sapir Memorial Publication Fund, 1941, pp. 75–93.
Reprinted in this volume.

1945 Grammatical Categories
Language, vol. 21, no. 1, pp. 1–11 . Reprinted in this volume.

WHORF, Benjamin Lee and George L. TRAGER
1938? Report on Linguistic Research in the Department of Anthropology
of Yale University for the Term Sept. 1937–June 1938
Printed in Penny Lee, *The Whorf Theory Complex: A Critical
Reconstruction*, John Benjamins Publishing Company, 1996,
pp. 250–280, with a history of the work on pp. 129–130.

WITHERSPOON, Gary
1977 *Language and Art in the Navajo Universe*
University of Michigan Press.

YAZZIE, Robert
1994 Life Comes From It: Navajo Justice Concepts
New Mexico Law Review, vol. 24, 1994, pp. 175–190. (available at
https://digitalrepository.unm.edu/nmlr/vol24/iss2/3). Reprinted in
Navajo Nation Peacemaking: Living Traditional Justice, eds,
M. O. Nielsen and J. W. Zion, Univ. of Arizona Press, 2005, pp. 42–58.

Language-Thought-Meaning

Apology

For many years I have been thinking about logic. I've been writing, trying to understand, and I've been putting the human back into logic. To me it's not some formal game, nor a study of abstract things, but a serious project to give us guides for how to reason well. We need to reason well in our ordinary lives. We need to reason well for our deepest worries and fears, which include our worries about the way the world is. Doing so I have had to relate language and how we mean to reasoning and how we give rules for reasoning. Now it's time for me to try to write up a summary of my ideas, ideas that I've developed here and there throughout my work, a little piece made explicit in one place, used and lightly commented on in another.

What I write here is only a report of how I view this large subject now. I have no thesis, no set view that I develop clearly from beginning to end. The duplication, the repetition of certain ideas in slightly different contexts doesn't seem bad to me now. I'm still finding my way, and at best this can be stimulating to others. At times I may sound dogmatic. It is better to state strongly a position so you can disagree, and disagreeing we can learn together. But all that I say here is only what seems to me. I organize, I try to understand, but at heart I am a pyrrhonist.

Over 40 years I have read a lot. I have notes and notes and notes of works that I have read along with my comments on them. Sometimes I remember that a book I read was important, and I'll go back and re-read it. Sometimes I'm surprised to find that a paper I just discovered is one I read long ago. It's hopeless for me to try to trace the development of my thought. It would be misleading to try to relate my conceptions now to what others have written; any quote or citation would be from only what I happen to remember or have good notes on recently. Those familiar with the subject will find that much of what I say is commonplace in a certain trend of thought in linguistics, psychology, ethology, and anthropology if not in philosophy and logic. I do not claim originality, except perhaps in relating those trends to a view of logic as the art of reasoning well.

Language-Thought-Meaning

Language, thought, meaning. These are not three things, not even three subjects. There is just the flow, the process we live in with talking, thinking, and meaning. We don't have language; we talk and write and read. We don't have thoughts; we think. We don't convey meanings; we mean. There is the whole, a fabric of our life that cannot be taken apart without destroying the design. But we can focus on talking, or on thinking, or on making meaning in that fabric, never forgetting that it is only a part, not even a part but a flow that we are attempting to pay attention to in one way.

Introspection

To discuss thinking, I must first look to my own mental life. That's the only route I have to thinking that I can rely on. Reports by others about their own mental life cannot be illuminating to me unless I assume some correlation between spoken or written language and mental life. It is only through reflection on my own speaking and writing and thinking and meaning that I can justify such a correlation.

Language

We talk, and we hear in the stream of sounds separate units. We intend to make separate units: words, sentences—more or less. But it is a stream of sound.

Language, what is linguistic, is any form of symbolic communication: a learned, shared system of acts we agree are symbolic.

But we have no language, only talking and, in imitation of that, writing, and interior talking, talking "in our heads".

Gesturing, too, is linguistic. A woman gives me a present with a little kiss on my cheek, and I'm embarrassed, I turn away slightly, smiling, and wave my hand palm outwards towards her, saying, "Aw, shucks." There are no words spoken, and there are no words equivalent to either gesture, but I understand her kiss and she understands my pleasure and embarrassment. People from another culture are not likely to understand, which is how we know that the movements are symbolic.

Comics, too, are based on a shared system of symbols: we read from left to right, or top to bottom, the succession meant to indicate time.

Perhaps paintings and sculptures could be said to be based on a shared symbol system, but to investigate those would take us too far from my worries here.

Categorizing

We understand by categorizing, abstracting: this is like that and unlike that. We compare. Analogy is how we live.

We are not so different from other sentient creatures, other creatures that can move and find and avoid. This is hot—avoid. How hot? As hot as what hurt me before? Just hot. This smells like what I ate that made me sick—avoid. Whether a cockroach, a dog, or a human, we perceive our experiences through categories.

Yet aren't humans different in that we create our categories through language? Animals just have categories. But consider my dog Chocolate. He's a Catahoula, very athletic. I brought him home to live with me when he was just weaned. When he got big enough, he could jump over the fence that surrounds the patio. I had to keep him in so he wouldn't chase the sheep in the corral because he could jump that fence, too. So I put up an electric wire along the top of the patio fence about 3 inches (8 cm) above the top. I picked him up and touched him to the wire—he yelped. Later when I was inside I heard him yelp again. Then I offered him some food next to the wire; though it was food he loved, he wouldn't take it. Wire—avoid. Later in the summer, around the pastures for my sheep about a quarter mile (four-tenths km) from my home, I put up a single strand of barbed wire above the wire mesh fencing. When I went there with Chocolate and climbed over the fence to an empty pasture, I expected him to jump over the fence and follow me. He always had in the past. I called to him. He sat looking up at the fence, then at me, then at the wire. He wouldn't jump. This wire is like that wire—though he could have no innate category of wires. They are the same—for his purposes of not getting shocked. Surely he could see that the electrified wire was smooth and thin and the wire above the fencing at the pasture was thick and had barbs on it. But he made the analogy; the risk was too great.

Risk? Analogy? He had developed a new category for his world, however he conceived that. We do the same. The difference is that we can give a word or a grammatical form for that new category and so share our categories. Yes, animals, or at least social animals, can share new categories too, though less easily and more rarely. We do it constantly, directing each other's attention to this or that. Both animals and we can and do make categories without language. But we are so much more ready to share categories, to direct attention, to try to get others to act and react in concert with us by our talking, by our gesturing.

We do not group similar things or similar masses or similar experiences in a category, not even similar types of things, masses, or experiences. Categories are not in the world—they are the result of us categorizing. We do not recognize similarities and differences; we make similarities and differences. This experience is like that experience, though we may not be aware that we have drawn an equivalence until we use it later. If categories were in the world, languages would all pretty much agree and translation would be easy.

My friend says that's crazy. Dogs exist whether we have a category for them or not. Our categories arise as we recognize the similarities and differences in the world. What is there is there.

But someone who's never seen a dog would be shocked to learn that this tiny hairless Chihuahua and this giant hairy Great Pyrenees are "the same"—kind of animal. They can't breed, at least not naturally. We can't invoke similarity of their DNA to show that the category of dogs is in the world, for it is because we classify them both as dogs that we ignore what is different in their DNA.

Still, I agree that with our background—which includes our language and culture—it is incoherent to say that dogs do not exist. But it is not incoherent to have another background in which when you say, "There's a dog. Can't you see it?" the other person gets hung up on understanding the words "a" and "it". Seeing the world as process there is dogging, but no dogs.

Nothing is ever repeated except as we draw equivalences to say that there is repetition. The red in this rose is not repeated an instant later, for the sun shines a bit differently, the intensity and saturation, all change. The red in this rose most definitely is not repeated in another rose, nor in the color of a car that is driving by. Yes, something like that color is there, but the "like" is our classifying. Other cultures and languages classify colors differently than we do: they classify as the same, and hence a repetition, what we classify as different. We classify as the same, and hence a repetition, what they classify as different. With sounds, too, we classify differently what counts as a repetition.

Japanese speakers don't distinguish our "l" and our "r" sounds: they're the same for them. We don't distinguish our glottal "l" sound and our tongue "l" sound, classifying them as the same. We could distinguish them if we wished, but we don't. Most certainly the same shape never recurs again: each potato is different, each tomato is different. And the shape of each cell phone is different: though millions are meant to be identical, they are not exactly the same shape. Even the idea of shape is an imposition we make on our experience, surely different from the impositions that a frog makes.

But, my friend insists, rectangles and rhomboids are in the world. We recognize them; we don't create a category. Me, I've never seen a rectangle except in a drawing in a book; I've seen rectangular things. I take the various rectangular things to have "something in common", to be in some way similar. Would a person who grew up in a rain forest, living how her ancestors lived 2,000 years ago, "perceive" rectangular things as similar? Would she even encounter rectangular things? But suppose she does. Do chimpanzees "see" rectangular things as similar? We can do experiments for that. Do dogs "see" rectangular things as similar? Perhaps they would if we gave them a task that would require them to make distinctions, that is, give them a purpose for making that classification. What about donkeys? If there is even one creature to which we ascribe intelligence and which has sensory capabilities of noting edges and angles (eyes, touch, echo-location) that does not "recognize" that similarity—and I would suggest octopuses as a possible example—then it is hard to say that the similarity is "in the world". But, my friend says, those creatures just aren't intelligent enough to recognize the similarity. You have to be as intelligent as (perhaps) a donkey to "see" that similarity. But that's the point. You have to be like us to recognize the similarity, to draw that classification.

What counts as "the same" is never the same except as we choose to call it, to think of it as the same. And that depends on our biology, our experience, our culture, and our language. Until we learn this lesson we will chase after universals and certainty like a child running for the a flickering light in the trees that she thinks is a butterfly.

Categorizing and our purposes
Categories are made for our purposes. But that's too strong, for often we just find that we have a new category; somehow we have brought

together separate experiences without even noticing. Only rarely do we intentionally devise a new category for a particular purpose. No more than Chocolate said to himself, "Watch out for that sort of stuff, I'll call it 'wire' ", do we more than rarely say anything like, "I'll call that 'jackrabbit', which I'll be able to use to describe those things."

Categories serve our purposes. Those purposes, which we recognize almost always in hindsight, are relative to our bodies, including our wants, desires, hopes, fears—all our emotions that secure our experiences to our lives. That others have similar bodies, similar wants, similar desires, similar hopes, similar fears—we think— helps us share our categories.

Categories not only serve our purposes, they direct us to purposes. We have a category of romantic love, so we look to have that kind of experience to fulfill our lives. The purpose of that category is lost in the time when people first began to use that kind of talk.

Wires, snakes, those were new categories for Chocolate that summer. Different? The same? Categories for him, as for us, change as we use them, relating one to another, extending, contracting. It wasn't long before he began to jump over the barbed wire fence.

If our categories didn't change, we could never respond to new experiences except to try to stuff them into the categories we have. And we learn soon enough as we grow up that the world will not always fit into the boxes we have. But the changes are constrained by our grammar: things, masses, relations, ... New categories outside that require a new language.

With categories we organize our experience, or rather, we have experiences. We organize further by relating our categories. We distinguish them, we compare them. We conceive of relations among categories: parent of, taller than, more abstract than, more intense than—these also are ways of categorizing.

Language is good for helping us fix our categorizing and share that with others in a way that animals cannot. Language is bad in misleading us to see an experience as similar that is different, freezing with a word or phrase a way of seeing that leads us to deal with the world in a way that makes it harder for us to reach our goals. Is light a wave or a particle? It is what it is; sometimes we see it as a wave, sometimes we see it as a particle because those are the only

categories we have for it. It's got to be a dog because it's too small
to be a wolf; but it's a coyote, a kind of animal my friend from
Switzerland had never seen. Frozen categories distort our experience.
But that's not right, because often there's no experience to distort prior
to our categorizing. Once we have the categories, perception follows
unless we make an effort to escape. Even a baby, turning its head to
a sound, smiling at her mother's face, has categories that organize
some of what she encounters. It is because as infants we have so
few categories that all is a blur when we try to recall those times.

Thinking

We think, a process for sure. We imagine in the stream of thinking
separate units we call thoughts. They are picked out from that stream,
having no separate reality until we recognize them as separate.

We try to separate out parts of our thinking as things: thoughts. But
we are very unsuccessful in doing so. What thought am I having now
as I write?

The answer is easy if we identify thoughts with pieces of language.
Why, you're thinking "What thought am I having now as I write?"
We describe and name the thought with the piece of language that is
—what? That is the thought itself? But I wasn't thinking that piece
of language as I wrote, I can tell you that. I was just writing, and that
came out. Now (right before I write this), I am thinking in language:
I thought "Ralph is a dog." That's a sentence. Then I wrote that down.
Sometimes we do have thoughts that are linguistic. I look out the
window and say to myself "Sunny". Or on another day I look out the
window and say to myself "Raining". The phrase "say to myself" is
misleading, as if I were having a conversation with myself. No, the
word or phrase or sentence is just there. Is that all there is to the
thought? I very much doubt it. I can often note a small delay from
perceiving and then the word or phrase in my thinking. I perceive
in terms of a category and then say the category internally.

To say that all thoughts are linguistic is to say that all thinking is
talking and writing and reading. Except that we also gesture and
often have no words for that.

Besides talking and gesturing in my thinking, I dream. I woke from
a dream and had a complete story, the whole from beginning to end,
coherent, filled with emotion, yet not a linguistic thought around.

By "coherent" I guess I mean that it "made sense"; I could and did re-create it. I don't know how to say more what I mean by "coherent", for it definitely isn't that I could have put it into words and the resulting sentences were logically consistent. I can still remember the entire story, but I doubt that I could ever put that story into words: any attempt would be lacking so much of what constituted the story, the emotions, the connections of the parts to the rest of my emotional and historical life.

I also have thinking in mental images connected to my emotional life and indeed to all of my life in some way. These include not only visual images, but sound images, smell images, taste images, touch images. These are definitely not linguistic. I think of cooking a steak on the grill, and my whole body is involved in the thinking: my hands as if to grasp tongs to turn it; my mouth with the taste of the fat and beef; my eyes as if I were seeing the steak and the smoke smarting them; my feet positioning myself relative to the grill; and the meaty smoke-flavored smell.

All those are here "in" me, part of my thinking. Indeed, the single word "steak" creates much of that "in" me only less powerfully than when I am thinking of me cooking a steak on my outdoor grill.

And I have images from my own interior, where I am, the position of my feet, my balance, my breath, my digestion, my joy, my fear. Sometimes I can find a verbal equivalent, but only rarely do I try.

We have linguistic thinking in spoken or gesturing language. We have dreaming. We have imagistic thinking. We have sensing our own bodies in the world. We try to break those processes into bits to talk about them, to convey them to another, but they are a flow within us and us within the world with them. Beyond these, I have no idea what is meant by "thoughts".

During the day when I am working outside with my sheep, putting out hay, fixing a fence, leading my donkey out of the corral to graze, I often have nothing I could call "a thought". Worried as I am about the nature of thoughts and language, I have recently begun to stop myself and consider whether I am thinking. I shovel manure and all I am doing is shoveling manure. No linguistic thoughts. No images. I just do it. From the outside it must certainly look like I'm making decisions: I rake the manure and straw and throw it over the fence, the wind blows some of the straw back, I then rake the rest of the straw and manure towards a different area of the corral and throw it over the fence in a way that it doesn't blow back. But introspecting afterwards I know that I made no decision: I just did that. I had no linguistic thought, I did not weigh alternatives. Now you may say that I had unconscious thoughts, or that subconsciously I did make a decision. But that is just a way for you to preserve your interpretation of what I did as making a decision.

It is my noting that I often act with no thought that makes me so uneasy about ascribing thoughts or decision-making or intentions to animals based on our observations of them. I am willing to grant that my dogs have mental images, especially mental smells. That I can understand their actions in the sense of predicting what they will do and describing what they do by invoking intentions they have is not any evidence that they have intentions and are making decisions any more than your watching me shovel straw and manure and describing me as making decisions accurately describes my thinking.

Perhaps, though, my raking manure is like driving a car: I once made decisions, once thought about what I was doing and should do, and now it's automatic. But consider: Winter at my ranch. It's cold. I go out every morning to the corral to the sheep. The first thing I do is break the ice on their water. One morning it didn't seem very cold. I went to the corral, felt the wind, and saw ripples on the water. I said to myself, "The water isn't frozen this morning." I did not conclude that; I simply recognized. If you say that nonetheless I did make an inference, then I am at a loss to know what you mean. I had no recognition of thinking in a chain, of thinking at all beyond seeing the ripples on the water and saying, "The water isn't frozen this morning." Is there any reason to believe that this is more sophisticated, more peculiarly human than what my dogs do?

It's not that we underestimate animals' (particularly dogs') abilities to think. It's that we overestimate our own.

Much of my life is spent just doing. You might think that by this I am talking about those times when we say someone is on automatic pilot. When I drive my car and somehow find that I've driven several blocks without any memory of having done so, without having paid attention to any of it, that might seem like what I am talking about. But usually at those times I am having thoughts, daydreaming—it's just that those thoughts have nothing to do with the actions I am making. No, I am talking about those times where I just do.

It's a puzzle how we act without language-thinking or image-thinking or sensing-thinking. But we do. Or at least I do.

We act. And the only way someone can describe it is to ascribe intentions and thoughts to us. But what those thoughts are is hard to say. I look at the straw and manure, I rake it, I put my shovel under some of it, I throw it over the fence. I am looking, and I am, in computer terminology, processing. But what is meant by "processing" I cannot say.

If by "thought" you mean something other than language-thinking or image-thinking or dreaming or sensing-thinking, I am at a loss to know what it is. Mentally uttered words, phrases, sentences, these I can identify, I can re-identify, I can treat as things and reason about them as things, using the most developed logic we have: predicate logic. Mental images and dreams are harder to conceive of as things; they are more like masses. But I know how to talk and reason about masses, as we do every day in discussions about water and mud. Sensing-feelings are harder still to reason about, but I know how to think of them again —if I can categorize them.

Am I having the same thought now as I had an hour ago? Ten minutes ago? Forty seconds ago? Even with linguistic thoughts that's hard to say, for we don't remember them except as we write them down or repeat them to ourselves to try to commit them to memory.

Whatever else someone might mean by "thought" is so unclear to me that I cannot tell if I have had one. I cannot recollect it in order to talk about it or reason about it. Recourse to describing thoughts as unconscious is not helpful, even if we could make that clear, for that just certifies that I cannot talk about those experiences nor pick them out in any way, though you in your omniscience about my mental life feel that you can.

It seems to me that no thinking can be completely linguistic. Yes, the word or phrase may be what I am thinking, for example, "Ralph is a dog." But that is not all that I am thinking. With those words, that phrase, comes all the meaning of it.

Meaning

We respond to the sounds, to the thinking—though there is no response just the doing—and call our response, part of the whole experience, meaning. But meaning is not a thing; it is a process. This is not meaning; it is us meaning. Not meaning this or meaning that.

Not giving meaning. Not having thoughts, not saying words. But language–thought–meaning in a grand process, in the grand process of our lives that we break into parts, focussing our attention, so we can more easily understand, more easily cope, just as we break up the flow of all, the flux of experience into parts: dogs, cats, lightning, running, water, gold, ...

One way people talk about meaning is to say that language expresses thoughts. You can see from the previous discussion how unsatisfactory I find that view. What good is it to say that my saying "Ralph is a dog" expresses my linguistic thought "Ralph is a dog"? When I say "Ralph is a dog" it is concomitant with my mental utterance of that, if I do have a mental utterance of it. But often I do not have a mental utterance. I simply speak or write, and I find out what I'm thinking by noting what I say or write, as I am doing at this very moment. But, you'd say, I must have some linguistic thought or some thought prior to my speaking or writing. If so, it must come very close before that overt action, and often must come and go so quickly that I cannot note it. Such thoughts seem unlikely as candidates for what language expresses. But if I formulate what I am to say before I say it, then saying that "Ralph is a dog" expresses that mental saying of "Ralph is a dog" is not much help in understanding talking-thinking-meaning. By "Ralph is a dog" spoken I mean "Ralph is a dog" mentally spoken tells us too little. If you say that when I speak or write "Ralph is a dog" the thought it expresses is that linguistic thought that I wasn't aware of, we are back to unconscious thoughts and your ascribing mental clarity and relations to me that I cannot perceive.

On the other hand, when I try to put that story I dreamt into words, you could say that the words are expressing the mental imagery thoughts. That may be, though we have to consider what we mean by "expressing".

If you say "Arf decided to rake the manure and straw to that side of the corral so that the wind wouldn't blow it back when he threw it over the fence" expresses the thought I had, then I am at a loss to know what you mean. I can understand it as expressing a thought you had, but not one I had, for I was not and still am not aware of having had any thoughts at that time.

What is this idea of a piece of language expressing a thought, then? Anyone who has tried to write poetry or tried to describe to a doctor the pain in her gut must have had the feeling of trying to put into words some thought. I would say that they are trying to put into words some mental imagery. What is the relation between talking and mental imagery?

Yesterday I conjured up an image of a woman I'd met recently, and I had a sensation vaguely like lust—perhaps "wanting" might be a better word. But that's the point: what is the word? I classify that experience as having been thinking (having a thought), but I cannot find any verbal equivalent of it. It's not just that I can't find a good one or the right one; I can't find anything that approximates describing or categorizing or expressing that sensation/thought. This is the problem all poets face: they cannot find the right words to "put down their thoughts". When I used to write poetry, I would spend a long time trying to capture just the right phrase to express a sensation/thought, but even when I felt I was successful, I knew that it fell far short of being full enough.

I have some mental imagery. It is not just a picture or a sound or a smell or a taste or a touch-feeling in my mind. It is a coherent picture that connects to my emotional life and to all of the history of my life. I feel the imagery and how it connects, and how it connects can lead me to further imagery, speech, or action. The thought, that is, the mental imagery, is not a piece that is separate and separable from the process of my life as a whole. We can and do, however, separate it to talk about it. By doing so, we are abstracting. We pay attention to some aspects of that imagery and ignore others. That is what we do when we when we try to "put into words" what we have experienced. I have a memory of what I did many years ago, and that memory is entirely in mental images, not just visual images but hearing images, smell images, taste images, touch images, as well as sensations. I try to put it into words and find that I cannot capture all of it, all the links and connections with the process of my life. I "capture" only some small part of it, not all of the whole, and each such rendering of some mental imagery always seems pale in comparison to the fullness of the imagery itself. It is not that what I say is not what I meant, for I did not mean before I said. It is that what I say is not all of the fullness of the imagery but only describes some aspects of it, perhaps getting right the temporal progression of the images, the feeling of one or two parts of it, but lacking so much else.

It isn't just images but the organization, the posture we take to experience that is key to comprehension: how the utterance connects not just to the web of our associations but to how we perceive, the categories that are activated and sometimes newly related one to another. "Now I see what you are saying", "Now the situation has become clear", "You've convinced me", "Now I will act differently, remembering the stories of Juney and Fido and Feral."

What do I mean by "dog"? I have learned that word, and I know how to use it. I know that I can pick out things by using the word, and I can describe someone as a dog, and I can talk about dogs generally. How I learned to use that word is certainly not identical to how you learned to use that word. We have different experiences to draw on in our original learning. And we have different experiences that we draw on in connecting that word to the rest of our lives, both exterior and mental. When I say "dog" I think of a creature—no, many creatures—that has a particular shape and look, I think of the warmth and succor such a creature brings to people, I think of the doggy smell, I think of life after death where I could be re-united with my dog Juney and where every-one who has lost a dog could be re-united with their dog and be forever happy wandering through the fields, I think of . . . . By "think of " I mean I have those mental images or I mentally utter phrases like those. All of that, all of those mental images and mental utterances that the word "dog" conjures up—some on one occasion, others at a different time—all the sensations, all the links it has to not only how I learned it but to all of my life where I have used that word and encountered dogs, is part of the meaning of "dog" to me.

Some would say this is too broad a construal of the meaning of that word. It's meaning, they say, is those things that are dogs. Certainly I could agree to talk about the meaning of "dog" in that way. But it would be an abstraction from what I do mean when I use the word. It leaves out a great deal, just as my description of the dream I had leaves out a great deal.

We abstract in this way for a good reason. I have no reason to believe that you understand the word "dog" the same as I do, and I have good reason to think you don't. Your life has been different from mine: you learned the word in different circumstances, you have had different experiences with dogs, you have invested those experiences with emotions that make them part of your long-term memory differently than I have. If "dog" expresses a thought you have, then it is a very different thought than I have.

However, we can and do use the word "dog" to communicate. You say, "Do you see that dog there?", and I say, "The one that's pissing on the bush?", and you say "Yes." We have communicated. We have picked out one thing, directing our attention to that one thing. We think about that thing differently. We use little of our understanding of the word "dog" in that communication. The little we use is what is needed to direct each other's attention to the one object. It doesn't matter that "dog" to you conjures images of an animal barking ferociously and the sensation of fear, far different from images and sensations I have when I use "dog". We use so little of our understanding of the word "dog" that we feel justified in abstracting from our mental imagery and the web of relations to say that the meaning of the word is those things that are dogs. But that is not the meaning of the word either to you or to me. It is the abstraction of the meaning of the word, the common part of the meanings of the word that we share, if you like. But that is a bad way to describe it. We do not share a common part to our meaning. There may be nothing at all common to the meanings we have for the word "dog"—nothing truly identically the same for both of us. Rather, the abstracted "common meaning" of the word "dog" is just the externalization of how we act and use that word.

We communicate. You talk, I talk. We use our talk to direct each other's attention to things, to processes, to masses, to feelings, to smells, to . . . . By doing so we hope to give each other some sense of the mental imagery each of us has or to give each other some sense of how what we are saying connects to all of our life. We must, perforce, do so imperfectly, for I can never convey to you all that I mean by "dog", for to do so would require you to have had the same experiences and to have invested those with the same emotions as I. Nonetheless we can count on our both being human, and we believe that both of us being human we go through life interacting with others and all the rest of the world in roughly similar ways. You grasp with your hand much as I do, so you can understand what I mean when I talk about using a hammer. But we share no meanings. We know as well as we know anything that each of us has an entirely private language. But our private languages have enough in common through our all being human and having learned the languages in roughly the same way for us to communicate. And by "communicate" I do not mean understand each other completely, convey to each other the exact meanings each of us has. By "communicate" I mean something like directing each other's attention in such a way that we can predict each other's actions, in such a way that our understanding of how others act and react can fit into the general picture of the world we have. That is, we can integrate our perceptions of those actions and reactions to the rest of our mental life based in part on how you and I use words.

Meaning does not reside in a piece of language; it does not reside in us; it does not reside in the world. Meaning resides in us using language to talk about the world and our experience. Meaning is made in a particular use of language, in a particular context, among particular people. Meaning is not fixed, not for us individually and most certainly not among ourselves when we talk. We negotiate meaning.

We negotiate meaning to try to understand each other better, or perhaps at all. I, you negotiate meaning with ourselves each time we use language in a different way, or in a different context, or just when we reflect on what we say. We negotiate meaning with others, trying to fix more closely how we understand what we say so that we can have some confidence that we are communicating, that we understand together. The need for such negotiation may be evident only from our actions and disagreements. When we negotiate meaning with ourselves, we may do no more than think about what we are saying.

We share meanings with dogs, too. I say "Sit" and Chocolate understands. Chocolate comes up to me on a walk and looks up at me and then sits, and I understand he wants a doggy biscuit. We count on our both being living, moving, animals, creatures that encounter and deal with experiences that are sufficiently similar that we can share some small part of our meanings. We negotiate meaning with our dogs, too.

Negotiating meaning depends on our recognizing, our using the most basic of our categories: good/bad, beautiful/ugly, nice/not nice, like/dislike. If we have no sense that the other shares these categories with us, we cannot communicate. It is these that link all our other categories to our lives and the world. It is not truth and falsity that are essential to communicating. I don't share that idea with Chocolate, but he and I have learned to recognize enough of what the other classifies as good and as bad. Wires bad. Cats bad. Dogs good. Steak good.

Speaking and dialogue are action, and just as we adjust our actions as we try to hammer a nail or turn a screw that resists our first attempts, we adjust our actions—our speaking—when the situation, the blank stare of incomprehension of the other, demands it, if we wish to be "successful", to do what we set out to do. We do not, therefore, need to reflect on our meanings, though sometimes we do. We just talk and adjust, and in the process modify our meanings.

We are successful in using language, communicating if you like, by getting others to act in ways we intend to direct them to by our words and by being able to understand the actions of others using words we both employ. We would like to believe that we are successful in communicating when we "communicate our thoughts". But that is something we never do: nothing I say can be understood by you in the fullness of how I understand it. But often, perhaps almost always, we use much less than the full meaning of words and phrases, we intend to convey much less, and we can, more or less communicate. The less we hope to communicate, the more likely we are to communicate well, though again, never completely if by that is meant eliciting in the other the exact same pared-down thought.

We direct each other's attention to that pared-down meaning by picking it out as "the meaning" of the word or phrase or sentence. We abstract, as we do in all of our communicating, even with ourselves. When I say to myself "My dog is outside the window wagging her tail" I do not conjure up all of the meaning of the words "dog" and "wagging" but only some small part that I need in that context.

When we are unfamiliar with a word or are learning a language, a dictionary definition is a hook on which to hang our own analogies and use and experience, continuing until we make the word our own. It is a reference point to orient our analogies.

It is not just logicians who balk at taking meaning to be so ample to include all these bodily sensations and memories and reactions we have as we use words. When a student tells his literature professor that a poem about ravens reminds him of his grandmother, the literary critic will say that's a mnemonic irrelevance. It is not what the poem means, she'll say, but only what the poem happened to jiggle in your memory. How wrong that critic is. That you have images of your grandmother, smell the cookies baking by reading that poem, is part of the meaning of that poem to you. But it is not part of the meaning of that poem to other people. What the critic wants to focus on is the meanings that can be shared by us generally which the poem evokes. Yet the critic, too, will try to expand that, showing more meaning in the poem than you or I had originally perceived. Whether that is just his or her own mnemonic irrelevancy depends on how many of us can share that; the poem begins to mean more.

A poem has no fixed meaning. It is directions. Like a computer program, it is meant to be instantiated: the poem in someone reading or hearing it, the program in being run on a computer. Similarly, a mathematical proof is directions, a guide. It is instantiated by us understanding and using it.

The purpose of speech is to help the other focus on what we intend or want or . . . . To help us focus on what we intend or want or . . . . Our talk only has to say what the context does not make clear. We're building a fence, and I run out of screws. I say, "Can you go and get me some?" Not noticing we're out of screws, you look around and ask, "Some screws?" "Yes," I say, "screws." I don't say the size of the screws, nor whether they are brass coated, nor whether they have a slot head or a phillips head. I don't convey all of the web of meaning of that word in my life. Is my language too vague? Not at all. I've communicated because you know what screws we're using. We mean differently in all we say, but here we can use language clearly enough to have agreement: you'll get me the right screws, I'm sure. If you bring back the wrong screws, I'll say more, we'll negotiate meaning. Meaning is relative to context, whether that be building a fence or reading a book. Or rather, how much meaning is relative to context, how much we intend or want to share, or simply how much we are likely to share is relative to context.

I say to my friend, "Come to my home, and we'll have ribs and beer and coleslaw." He comes, and I'm grilling beef ribs. What's this? He thought we'd have pork ribs with barbecue sauce. Is "ribs" ambiguous? No, "glasses" is ambiguous: eyeglasses and drinking glasses. With "ribs" there is a more profound difference in "meaning". To you, "ribs" means . . . you think of pork ribs with sauce. To me, "ribs" means . . . I think of grilled beef ribs. I didn't give a full description. But we never give a full description. I didn't give a full enough description. I was egocentric: my meaning is what everyone has. I should have negotiated meaning.

My friend from Colombia stops me when I'm talking about my cousin: "Is it a male or a female?" What I was saying was incomplete, not a full enough description by her standards because in Spanish "cousin" has to be marked as male or female. Yet what I was saying was full enough in English. But never a full description. No, never. All we say is vague, for that is the only way we can communicate. It is the most vague words—good/bad, beautiful/ugly—that link us most closely together and most closely to the world.

When I go walking with my dogs and I see—in the terms you would say—a rabbit or a jackrabbit, I yell "Gavagai." What do I mean with that? There is no noun nor noun phrase that is equivalent, not rabbit, not rabbit part, not rabbit departing; there is no verb or verb phrase that is what I am thinking, not rabbiting for sure. There is no "thought" it is meant to express. Stimulus-response: I see, I yell out, the dogs look around and, if they see, they chase. We communicate. That is the whole meaning of my yelling "Gavagai."

Universals
We search for universals in our experience and our language, some hook we can hold on to while we are standing and swaying on the trolley-car of life. There must be some meaning, some significance, some ideas out there—as much out there as the rocks and trees and dogs we encounter—that were we to grasp them fully would illuminate so much. It can only be by our grasping those meanings, each of us individually holding on to them, that we can communicate.

This, I believe, is the fear of being alone in the universe. Each one of us wants to believe that he or she is an individual, different from all others. Judge me not as one of a type. But we fear even more greatly that we are each of us so distinct, so individual, that we can never communicate fully with someone else.

Yet it is the most common and daily of our experiences that no one ever fully understands us. No one can understand exactly my thoughts. "That is not what I meant" is what we encounter all day long. We never get someone else to understand exactly what we mean—more or less, yes, well enough, yes. But it is shocking how often we are shocked to find that someone didn't grasp at all what we meant. Yet in the face of this constant experience of not being understood, we continue to search for universals in meaning and for meaning standing apart from us.

Intentions

To communicate, to even want to communicate, we have to believe that the other person, or dog (or even cat) has a mental life. We ascribe intentions to them: they intend to understand me; they intend to disregard me; they want to eat; they want to sleep; they want to urinate; they're looking for ice cream; . . . . Yet often enough the other person has no thought, no intention that he or she is aware of. We ascribe intentions to others; they ascribe intentions to us; but that is our way of seeing each other. It need not be how the other is in the world at that time.

Our categorizing is built on our conceiving of others' intentions, too. A chair is an object that is useful for sitting on—but that's not enough. It is a man-made object that the maker or designer intended to be useful to sit on. We find a rock in the woods that's perfect for sitting on; it's just a rock that can be used as a chair, it's not a chair—unless we haul it home and say it's a chair. It's the saying, the intention, that makes it a chair.

Drawing meaning

We mean when we talk and gesture. We make meaning.

We also draw meaning. When you talk, when you gesture, I draw meaning.

We draw meaning from a dark cloud, from a girl's blushing, from a scent of water in the forest. But that's inference. Inference? There is no inferring but only knowing following hard on the sign.

How then do signs—a cloud, a blush, a scent—differ from our talking? It can't be the intention, at least not generally, for we often do not intend to mean; we just mean.

What is the difference then? We talk, we gesture, we mean by using a learned, shared system of acts that we agree are symbolic. We draw meaning from the clouds, but the clouds do not learn to mean. We draw meaning from the young girl's blushing, but she has not learned to blush to convey more than the act itself; the blushing is not symbolic. It is more or less standardized use in a shared system that distinguishes our talking from signs.

We mean because we have the habit of drawing meaning. We believe that the other—person, dog, even cat—can draw meaning from our talking and gesturing.

We mean because we draw meaning.

Language shapes thought?
I agree with this, but I suspect I understand it very differently from you.

Our previous discussion leads me to conceive of thought in this saying as something quite broad, including not just language—for saying that language shapes language is trivial—but also mental imagery, and how we feel in connection with our actions, and our actions and reactions.

By "language" in this saying I understand not just or even primarily our vocabulary. Rather, it is the more fundamental part of our language, our grammar, that shapes how we see the world. Our grammar, which is transparent to most of us almost all the time, shapes how we think of the world. It shapes how we act, react, have emotions, conjure up images, conjure up words to describe our experiences. Indeed, our language shapes what we consider to be an experience. It gives us ready-made categories, categories that are reinforced by being shared in talking with others.

For example, the grammar of Indo-European languages focuses strongly on the thing-aspect of the world. We experience ourselves as acting on and being acted upon by things; we experience ourselves as moving through things in space; we experience ourselves as wishing for or wanting things. The grammar of other languages, such as Nootka or Chinese, focuses more on the process/mass aspect of the world. It leads speakers of those languages to conceive of what they have done or are doing quite differently. But that's not right: they don't conceive of anything. They and we are just in the world, and we have experiences, and what those experiences are we try to describe with our languages. Much of our mental imagery is shaped by the grammar of our language, too. Mystics try to lead us to experiences beyond our language. We sometimes do have such experiences, and they stand out in our memory. We can be led to such experiences by learning another language. Even the vocabulary of another language can shape our experience.

Compare: In English we like things. In Spanish "to like" is reflexive, as if it were somehow passive. I say "I like dogs" and that is supposed to describe my experience. My friend says "Me gustan los perros", which literally translated is "me (indirect object) like (present tense, third person plural) the dogs", and to assume that we have the same experience is unfounded in any evidence. Yes, the experiences are similar, sufficiently similar that we can expect somewhat similar actions and reactions by me and my friend relating to dogs. If that were all there were to meaning, we could say they mean the same. But there is much more.

Language, principally but not only through grammar, shapes what counts as an experience, shapes how we process sensory inputs into perceptions. In that sense, language shapes thought. But recalling the discussion so far, it hardly seems that all of our experience, all of our thinking is shaped by language. We can and do make new categories.

"Yes," I say as someone shows me a picture with a label in a book, "I see now that the creature I couldn't identify and saw only fleetingly last week in the forest was a javelina." Memory is certainly dependent on our being able to categorize our experience, but it is not entirely so. Calling up a memory is re-living the experience, but only as much of it as we paid attention to when we lived it the first time. Or rather, not as much of it as, but no more than we first paid attention to.

But that is not right. We often do not choose to pay attention to only part of our experience. And we can recall much more than what we were thinking or consciously paying attention to. A clock striking four o'clock may not register as four to us; but if asked to recall, often we can say, "One, two, three, four. Yes, it struck four times."

Thinking, meaning, and our bodies

To say that we think with our brains is our new way of conceiving our bodies, the modern version of the old conceit that we think with our stomach or that the seat of our mind is the liver.

Even today, we say that someone thinks with his stomach or thinks with her heart. These are true, though not exclusively true.

I think with all of my body. Meaning is in all of my body. I think "hammer" and I have a sensation in my hand of grasping my old hammer that lies on my workbench and my hand twitches ever so slightly. I think "cat" and I sense a nasty, cloying smell. I think "orange juice" and I have a taste in my mouth. I think siren and I can hear faintly an American-style siren sounding. Faintly. Not in the fullest extent of those previous experiences but enough that I know my thinking is in all of my body, the "meaning of those words" is in all of my body.

We think with all of our bodies. Our thoughts are not disembodied, most certainly not abstract. They do not sit in our brains any more than they used to sit in our stomachs. Our thoughts are instantiated in our bodies—though that way of talking makes them sound as if they have an abstract existence that precedes their instantiation. Rather, they are certain states of our bodies, as our bodies act and react.

I think, therefore I have a body.

Meaning and life

What is the meaning of one's life? This is to think of meaning as purpose, and then it's begging the question, assuming that whatever exists has a purpose.

But meaning in the sense of the meaning of words, of sentences, of grammatical constructions is embedded in one's life, one's very skin and muscle.

That is why taking someone's life is so awful: it destroys a whole fabric of meaning, a way to "see" the world, that can never be duplicated.

That is why a language going extinct is so awful: it destroys what people have come together to share as a way to see the world that can never be duplicated.

Our stories

We form our experience, we face the world with the stories we make. "Why is it that stories only happen to people who can tell them?" But we all make stories, all day long. He walked away when I was talking, then started talking to that girl, so he's more interested in her than me. My mother toilet-trained me when I was only one-year old so I'm constipated a lot now. The sun rises in the east every day, even though I didn't see it today.

Art is not imitation but creation, and all of our life is art as we create our stories. We create form in the world; we do not find it in the world.

Beginnings and endings, these, too, are of our categorizing. There is no beginning or ending of this table, of this rock, of this discussion, of this foot race except as we mark them. Beginnings and endings are not "in nature" but in our marking off our experiences so we can remember them and talk about them, for all is flow and continuing.

We make up stories. We connect the small pieces of our experience.

We see a ball thrown from one person passing behind another and landing on the ground. We say it continued in flight. We didn't see that: it was behind the other person. We didn't infer it. We just know it. That's the story we make up from the pieces of our experience.

This is why memory is so unreliable and malleable. We convert the bits. Others say we make inferences, but we have no awareness of doing that. Then someone gives us a better story, so we believe that's what happened. "It makes sense."

We correct our "mistaken impressions" by reasoning, conscious attempts to justify and correct our beliefs. But always that reasoning and justifying is relative to our most fundamental beliefs: things persist in time, they do not go out of existence then come back into existence, like the ball that is thrown.

Knowing
I hear a sound. It's a dog barking. A deep, bass sound, rounded volume. I know it's a big dog.

I hear yapping, high pitched, rapid, light, and I know it's a very small dog.

I never consciously learned to make these discriminations. I make no inference. I just know.

How is this different from what the mountain lions around my ranch do? They stay away from the sheep because my big sheep dog barks to keep them away; the sound is enough. If a Chihuahua were barking, they would come and eat it. They know in a way that I cannot distinguish from my knowing.

Of course I may be wrong. I could be wrong about everything I know. So? We test our knowledge with reasoning.

Logic and meaning and knowing
More and more I think of meaning as the whole of what we understand

with a word, phrase, or sentence—all of the web. The restricted sense of "meaning" that logicians use is an abstraction from that or even quite different in some way. It ignores all about the word except what it "officially" "denotes", that is, the shared meaning. It ignores all about a sentence except what "makes it true": the "truth-conditions", the way the world would have to be for it to be an accurate description (though not a complete description). That "denotes" is not just reference in the logician's usual approach but is very wide. "Beauty" denotes in this broader sense: the common, shared (at least shared enough) idea. There is also the problem that some words and sentences may have no common part of "meaning" shared by most people: overlapping but not transitive relating of ways to understand it. Yet we can often abstract from our own meanings, from our roughly similar actions and reactions, to stipulate sufficiently clearly a part of our meanings of a word or sentence for us to be able to reason together.

Then for a richer logical analysis, the logician can factor in more of what we share about a sentence, for example, the ways we conceive of how we could come to know whether the sentence is true, or the subject matter of the sentence, or the referential content of the sentence. To the extent that we can come to some agreement that at least some sentences have this as part of the web of their meaning, and to the extent that we can give some structural analysis of how those additional factors of meaning of sentences relate to one another, we can develop a formal analysis of meaning. And with that we can trace some of the web of meaning of this or that word or sentence or collection of sentences through their inferential relations. Meaning is not alone, a single instance, but a web of meaning, modeled in a formal logic by the inferential relations that are said to hold.

With the valid inferences we track the web of meanings imposed by our grammar. We then track the meanings of particular words and sentences by stipulating meaning-axioms. We have the predicate "— is a dog", and we relate that to "— is a mammal" by requiring that the formal version of "If anything is a dog, then it's a mammal" be counted as true.

Reasoning together, we can investigate our beliefs. I saw ripples on the water and then thought that the water is not frozen. I can justify that with an informal inference: "There are ripples on the surface of the water; they move; frozen water is solid; the surface of what is solid does not move; therefore, the water is not frozen." Explicit inferences can help us see whether we are justified in this or that belief. This explicit inference I use to examine my belief that the water is not frozen is not what I thought at the time. Nor do I have reason to think that Chocolate reasoned to the conclusion that he should not try to jump over the barbed wire.

Unless our conception of human cognition takes account of the continuity of animal and human thinking, it will fall into a deep mistake. We have good reason to believe that animals "cognize" as we do: their actions if they were done by humans we would certainly call thinking, planning, intending, categorizing. Yet if we focus solely on human cognition, we assume no continuity. Then we parse our cognition, our thoughts in terms of what is "most human": our language. So thought has the structure of our language. And then we begin to model our conception of human cognition on our best logical analyses, which are based fundamentally on our language.

We have no such assumption for animals. They have no language. Have they a logic?

This misconstrues the role of logic. It takes logic to be the laws of thought. Rather, logic is a model of how we consciously reason using language. Some do take logic to be the structure of thought. But if it is, it's only of conscious linguistic thought in our kind of language. Beyond that there is no empirical evidence—and even that misconstrues evidence. We do not reason according to those laws—we should reason according to those laws. The laws of logic are prescriptive— relative to the way we see the world, the language we use. Or perhaps they are relative to how we must see the world. But we have no evidence other than linguistic that we must see the world as made up of things, and much evidence from other languages that we need not see the world that way. Language does not shape all of our thought, but it certainly shapes our methods of reasoning.

In the end
Lying in bed, together, afterward. Two souls, united. At one. We couldn't be closer. So close, no communication could be closer. Only I am thinking . . . and she is thinking . . . . I am thinking . . . and he is thinking . . . . Not a clue what the other is thinking. So we talk, and we seem to be farther from each other, but only because we realize we

were never so close as we imagined. We talk, we negotiate, we try to be closer, as close as our emotions were.

She didn't understand me . . .
He didn't understand me . . .

No? What an illusion to think she would understand you fully. What an illusion to think that he would understand you fully. We have to work every day to negotiate meaning and understanding.

Let us negotiate meaning so we can be good to each other.

Dedicated to Andrea Hosang

Why Event-Talk Is a Problem

We talk about events all the time. Don't we? Actually, we don't. "What event was it last week before lunch at Suzy's house?" is so odd as to be bizarre. We want to say there was no event, just Suzy was playing with her cat Puff. An event is something big, like a circus or a fair.

Event-talk is what linguists and philosophers do. Something happened last week at Suzy's house, and they want to say that it was an event. They talk of events because they want to say that *what made* "Suzy was playing with Puff" *true* is a thing. And they do that because as English speakers we try to turn (almost) all our talk into talk of things.

But there is no *thing* that made "Suzy was playing with Puff" true. There's just the world and that proposition.

But don't we all talk about *what happened*? Yes. "What happened yesterday at Suzy's house before lunch?" "Suzy was playing with Puff." "What happened?" "Spot was barking." "What happened?" "Dick yelled." We answer with a sentence that if true describes the world at a time and place (actually, at a time will usually do in English). There is no need to interpose another set of *things* between (a) us and our use of language and (b) the world. Or at least between us with our use of language and our experience of the world.

It's not just that events are superfluous. Events are supposed to be things, part of the world. But as Benson Mates pointed out to me, if "The cat is on the mat" is supposed to be made true by or describe an event, what is included in that event? The cat is touching the mat? The cat is upon the mat? The earth, because up and down can only be determined relative to that? Where do we stop? Probably only at the entire universe. But simply, the event is that the cat is on the mat. We use "that" to restate the claim. And what is included or involved in the event is what we pick out with our language: we parse the world with the grammar of that proposition. A Chinese translation leads to parsing the event quite differently: there is no "being on" and the characters for what most closely translate "cat" and "mat" have not only different scope but are mass words.[1] Yet surely there is the same event there, just described differently. To say that is to ascribe to "the event" a reality independent of language, and we have arrived at the event as

---

[1] See A. C. Graham, "Conceptual Schemes and Linguistic Relativism in Relation to Chinese", p. 198.

a "thing in itself". How is that to help us understand how language connects to the world (of our experience)? What we take to be an event is the outcome of our parsing the world according to a proposition. As Benjamin Lee Whorf says in "Science and Linguistics":

> It will be found that an "event" to us means "what our language classes as a verb" or something analogized therefrom. And it will be found that it is not possible to define event, thing, object, relationship, and so on, from nature, but that to define them always involves a circuitous return to the grammatical categories of the definer's language. p. *196*

In mass-process languages there is no coherent way to talk of events because events are meant to be things. In those languages there is no way to interpose a level between talk and the world. Chad Hansen has pointed this out for pre-Han Chinese in *Language and Logic in Ancient China* to explain why many of the issues of philosophy in the West simply do not arise in ancient Chinese philosophy and reflection on language. To talk of events in analyzing a mass-process language is to impose our English-speaking focus on things onto a language that has at best a secondary notion of thing.

But there is a bigger problem with event-talk even in English. We can't reason about events as things because we have no criteria for what counts as two distinct events. Do the following describe the same event?

the stabbing of Caesar by Brutus
the stabbing of Caesar by Brutus with a knife
the stabbing of Caesar by Brutus with a knife in the Forum

With just language and the world, there are three propositions:

Caesar was stabbed by Brutus.
Caesar was stabbed by Brutus with a knife.
Caesar was stabbed by Brutus with a knife in the Forum.

If we say that each describes "the same event" successively in a more detailed manner, what is that event? When did it start? With Brutus conceiving of the action? With Brutus lifting his hand? With Brutus pushing the knife into Caesar? If the last, how far into Caesar did the knife go in that event? We have no answers to these questions because we never thought about them. To decide whether they describe the same event is to decide whether these are equivalent propositions — where that is understood as equivalent for our purposes at hand.

In logic, those purposes are determined by what we choose to pay attention to in the formal syntax and semantics. In daily talk it's the same, just not so clearly decided: they are equivalent according to what we are paying attention to. Compare: "Suzy was playing with Puff" and "Harold's niece was playing with her cat". If Suzy is Harold's niece, and Puff is her cat, do we count these two as equivalent? It depends on what we are paying attention to.

My doctor told me when starting a new medication, "You will either lose weight, or gain weight, or stay the same." And she was right! That is exactly what happened. What event was that which she described? If you say that she predicted one of three events, then events must be described only by atomic sentences, and we know that what is atomic is relative to the particular way we phrase in our language.

I went outside this afternoon. I saw the tree waving in the strong wind. Is that the same event as the tree waving in the wind? Is it the same event as my being outside and watching the tree waving in the wind? I had no sense of an event when I was outside at that moment, only the tree and the wind and the waving and me and . . . whatever I was paying attention to. I did have a strong sense of time, of the now of my being out there, and of the passage of time from when I stepped outdoors until I went back into my office. But an event? There's nothing I could point to, physically or intellectually, objectively or subjectively. I am simply at a loss for what was the event.

To say that summer is an event, that Suzy's niece graduating high school was an event, surely misleads. We don't need to invoke events or do event-talk to analyze how some people talk of "what happened" in some kind of temporal order. All we need is that they talk using some words like "before" or "after" to relate propositions, as in "Spot barked before Dick yelled."[2] More than that doesn't get us anywhere and will surely fall apart on closer examination.

I think Juan Francisco Rizzo has it better when he commented on a draft of this essay:

> Perhaps "what we do" is closer to "water" or even "mud" . . . Maybe the sum of our actions is more like water drops merging into one big shapeless puddle and not like pebbles that we can put into a jar or spread across the floor to be counted and sorted by color, shape and

---

[2] I develop a logic of "before" and "after" as propositional connectives in *Time and Space in Formal Logic*.

size. Yet we need to "describe" at least some of our doings, even if
it is to sort out as (relatively) correct or incorrect uses of of a word.

REFERENCES

EPSTEIN, Richard L.
  2021   *Time and Space in Formal Logic*
          To appear, Advanced Reasoning Forum.
GRAHAM, A. C.
  1991   Conceptual Schemes and Linguistic Relativism in Relation
          to Chinese
          In *Culture and Modernity: East-West Philosophic Perspectives,*
          ed. Eliot Deutsch, University of Hawaii Press, 1991, pp. 193–212.
HANSEN, Chad
  1983   *Language and Logic in Ancient China*
          The University of Michigan Press.
          Reprinted Advanced Reasoning Forum, 2020.
WHORF, Benjamin Lee
  1940   Science and Linguistics
          Technology Review (Massachusetts Institute of Technology),
          vol. 42, no. 6 (April), pp. 229–231 , 247–248. Reprinted in this volume.

On the Genesis of the Concept
of Object in Children

The work of Jean Piaget in *The Construction of Reality in the Child*
illustrates how the strength of the conception of the world as made
up of things colors and distorts research.

On the first page of his text Piaget says:

> A world composed of permanent objects constitutes not only a spatial
> universe but also a world obeying the principles of causality in the
> form of relationships between things, and regulated in time, without
> continuous annihilations and resurrections. Hence, it is a universe
> both stable and external, relatively distinct from the internal world
> and one in which the subject places himself as one particular term
> among all other terms. A universe without objects, on the other hand,
> is a world in which space does not constitute a solid environment but
> is limited to structuring the subject's very acts; it is a world of
> pictures each one of which can be known and analyzed but which
> disappear and reappear capriciously. From the point of view of
> causality it is a world in which the connections between things are
> masked by the relations between the action and its desired results;
> hence the subject's activity is conceived as being the primary and
> almost sole motive power. p. 3

Piaget presents a false dichotomy. He seems to think that if we do
not parse the world as made up of things, experience is so fluid that all
boundaries dissolve. But that is not obvious. He does not recognize
that it is our language that leads us to conceive of the world as made
up of things and that some people view the world as processes, and that
"processes" are stable in the sense that mothering continues, without
thinking of mother as a thing. To conceive of a process as continuous
over time is not the same as to conceive of a thing. He does not see that
his view of annihilations and resurrections and pictures appearing and
disappearing capriciously already assumes that the world is made up
of things. Moreover, there need be nothing capricious in conceiving of
the world as the flow of all, for we can discern causal relations without
talk of things, as I explain in the next essay in this volume, "The Thing-
Basis of Western Philosophy".

The real question isn't how the child constructs a reality of things
from his or her physical experiences. It is how we teach the child our

categories, our schemes of the world, so that he or she can use our language. What we are doing when the child is very young, I suspect, is conveying to it pre-linguistically how to operate in the world in such a way that he or she has the fundamental categories we have, in particular the notion of a thing.

In the description he gives of one experiment we can see how Piaget has built objects into his view, not recognized them in the child's view.

> Laurent, as early as the second day, seems to seek with his lips the breast which has escaped him. From the third day he gropes more systematically to find it. From [day 1] he searches in the same way for his thumb, which brushed his mouth or came out of it. Thus it seems that contact of the lips with the nipple and the thumb gives rise to a pursuit of those objects, once they have disappeared, a pursuit connected with reflex activity in the first case and with a nascent or acquired habit in the second case. p. 9

The categories of nipple and thumb are ones Piaget has in his language and mind; there is no reason to think that his description of them as objects is apt for the child's experience. Moreover, it is bizarre to say that the child's thumb has disappeared. It can't have disappeared from the child because it's part of him. Has it disappeared from view? But then why doesn't he say the child saw the thumb, rather than touched it with his mouth? Has it disappeared from his mouth? That is an odd way of talking.

This is very much like the anthropomorphisms we make when we interpret the actions of dogs. It is especially apparent in the following.

> I look at him through the hood of his bassinet and from time to time I appear at a more or less constant point; Laurent then watches that point when I am out of his sight and obviously expects to see me reappear. p. 9

There is less reason to believe that Laurent, in the scene described, expected to see Piaget reappear than there is reason to believe that my dog feels guilty when she has done something I disapprove of. We have even less reason still to believe that his description of the mental life of a 4-day-old child is accurate and not just a projection he makes from his own experiences:

> Then I withdraw; when [Lucienne] turns without finding me her expression is one of mingled disappointment and expectation. p. 11

Willard van Orman Quine in *Word & Object* made equally grand pronouncements about how children learn language. He did not show how children learn the concept of thing but simply assumed that they did and set out to explain it. He dismisses the work of Whorf, Sapir, and others in a short paragraph:

> One frequently hears it urged that deep differences of language carry with them ultimate differences in the way one thinks, or looks upon the world. I would urge that what is most generally involved is indeterminacy of correlation. There is less basis of comparison—less sense in saying what is good translation and what is bad—the farther we get away from sentences with visibly direct conditioning to non-verbal stimuli and the farther we get off home ground. pp. 77–78

Quine does not consider that what we consider a stimulus is determined in part by the language we use, so that the "home ground" of another language community might be quite different from the home ground he assumes.

Andrew Lock in "The Emergence of Language" provides another example of how the assumption that the world is made up of things colors analyses:

> I would suggest that at this stage in his development the child has *mastered* the fundamentals of language: but I would not wish to go as far as saying he now *possesses* language. While he can communicate his intentions in an unambiguous and structured manner, the messages he conveys are not objective in nature, nor are they propositional, and neither are they capable of being judged true or false. Language is still implicit in his activities, and will remain so until he becomes able to name objects. p. 8

But water is not an object, yet "water" is one of the earliest words children learn in English. Lock, like so many others, cannot see beyond the thing-focus of his own language, even when his own language has words and constructions that do not fit that focus.

This kind of criticism doesn't apply to Piaget's *The Child's Conception of Number*, for there he is examining how children learn to use a linguistic concept that we are teaching them. That is, he is doing what he should be doing in the examination of the concept of object: trying to find out how we teach the concept. That is exactly what Seymour Papert does:

For the infant, objects do not even exist; an initial structuration is needed to organize experience into *things*. Let us stress that the baby does not *discover* the existence of objects like an explorer discovers a mountain, but rather like someone discovers music: he has heard it for years, but before then it was only noise to his ears.

NOTE

A more general criticism of Piaget's work on language is made by John M. Ellis in *Language, Thought, and Logic*:

> Piaget conducted experiments to show that children learn to conceptualize only at the age of twelve years, and his results duly confirm this. And yet any reasonably sophisticated theory of language should have suggested at the outset that this would be an inherently nonsensical result: since all language use involves conceptualization—even learning to use the word *cat*, which must abstract from things that are of different size, shape, and color—the notion that human beings use language for ten years before they learn to conceptualize is not just highly improbable, it is simply impossible. To use a language is to conceptualize. . . . The fact that he was able to find results that confirmed this "hypothesis" is a tribute to the ability of the empirical researcher to find what he is looking for, even when his goal is an absurdity. Even granted his premises, however, one must also be completely unacquainted with children to imagine that they do not understand ideas such as "right" and "wrong," "illegal" and "democracy" long before they are twelve years old. Piaget also thought that intelligence antedates language, and that the contribution made by language to human reasoning is simply to make it "interpersonal"; these are extraordinarily primitive ideas for one who wishes to do research into language behavior. An empirical investigation of the development of language function that begins essentially by deciding that no important function will be found in language cannot be expected to produce anything worthwhile. p. 63

That researchers set up experiments with bias for finding what they want is also the subject of "A New Turing Test" in this volume.

REFERENCES

ELLIS, John M
    1993 *Language, Thought, and Logic*
        Northwestern University Press.

94   *Richard L. Epstein*

LOCK, Andrew J.
  1978   The Emergence of Language
         In *Action, Gesture and Symbol: The Emergence of Language*,
         ed. Andrew J. Lock, Academic Press, 1978, pp. 3–18.
PAPERT, Seymour
  1960   Problèmes épistémologiques et génétiques de la récurrence
         In *Ètudes de Épistemologie Génétique, Vol. II. Problèmes de la
         construction du nombre*, eds. P. Gréco, J.-B. Greize, S. Paper and
         J. Piaget, Presses Universitaires de France pp. 117–148. Translated
         by Stanislaus Dehaene in *The Number Sense*, Oxford University
         Press, 1997, revised 2011. The quotation is from p. 31 of that.
PIAGET, Jean
  1937   *La Construction du reel chez l'enfant*
         Delachaux & Niestlé. Translated by Margaret Cook as
         The Construction of Reality in the Child, Basic Books, 1954.
  1941   *La Genêse du Nombre chez l'Enfant*
         Delachaux & Niestlé. Translated by C. Gattegno and F. M.
         Hodgson as *The Child's Conception of Number*, Routledge
         & Kegan Paul, 1952.
QUINE, Willard van Orman
  1960   *Word and Object*
         The M.I.T. Press.

A New Turing Test

Alan Turing in 1950 proposed a test to answer the question "Can a machine think?" Roughly: There is one person who is the tester. In separate rooms there is another person and a machine. The only links are between the tester and the other person, and between the tester and the machine, and those links are via typed responses only. The tester puts questions to the other person and the machine, not knowing which is which. If in 5 minutes the tester cannot determine which is the machine, then, it's claimed, the machine can think.

Turing's test has been analyzed and criticized by many. But no one seems to have noticed that it can be used to test for the capacity of other subjects to think.

I have serious doubts about whether women think — they are so different! So I propose a test to answer the question "Can a woman think?" We'll have a man who is the tester, and in separate rooms another man and a woman. The only connections are between the other man and the tester, and between the woman and the tester, both via typed answers only. The tester puts questions to the other man and to the woman, not knowing which is which. If in 5 minutes the tester cannot determine which is the woman, then we can claim that the woman thinks.

Similar tests can be done to answer the questions: "Can African-Americans think?" "Can Native Americans think?" "Can Hispanics think?" "Can these people in a community near the Amazon in Brazil who speak a very different language think?"

We look for what we want to find, we set up psychological tests or simply evaluate other people or groups according to our standards. Do these people have this cognitive ability? Too often our tests have the answers already embedded in them.

I was motivated to write up this new test, which I first proposed more than 30 years ago, because of two works I recently read that show how important it is to involve a cultural context in evaluating cognition. Michael Cole and Jerome S. Bruner in "Cultural Differences and Inferences about Psychological Processes" show how "data collection" about cognitive abilities among minorities and impoverished people in the U. S. is terribly flawed by both the framing of the questions and the way that the data is collected. And Vera da Silva Sinha in

Linguistic and Cultural Conceptualisations of Time in Huni Kui,
Awety´, and Kamaiura Communities in Brazil shows how to avoid
imposing our answers on people who live and talk very differently,
while discussing the general problem of data collection about cognition.

Peter Adams, reading the interchange on a draft of this, got
frustrated and wrote: "Someone define thinking please." But that's
what Turing thought he could avoid with his test. Placed in the
movement of behaviorism at that time, he looked for behavior that
could characterize—not define—thinking. Objective data, subjective
conclusion. But as Fred Kroon, William S. Robinson, and I show
in "Subjective Claims" in *The Fundamentals of Argument Analysis*,
you can't get a subjective conclusion from only objective claims.
Some claim linking the objective claims (the "data") and the subjective
conclusion is needed as a premise, and any argument that lacks such a
subjective link and that concludes with "This person thinks" will either
be weak or beg the question. Still, in "Language-Thought-Meaning"
I make an attempt to show, if not define, how I understand thinking.

Kris Hardy in that same interchange raised another issue.

> From the tester's perspective, he is determining which player is
> "thinking" or "not thinking", a binary, exclusive assignment. If
> the desired result of the test is not to determine "is each player a
> person or computer (man or woman, etc.) thinking", but instead
> we presuppose that both players do think ("capable of replying to
> a communication"), we can change the question to one, admittedly,
> more difficult: "*How* does each player think?" Solving this question
> is one that I actually do every day in my software development and
> security research. What I am trying to determine is "what is the
> internal model that my subject is using in their communications
> with me?" The comparisons between levels of thinking then turns
> into a measure of complexity, entropy, predictability, broadness,
> and other such factors.

Walter Carnielli said that the new test I proposed could be used by
the woman to find out whether the tester, a man, thinks. But that's just
silly. We know that a man can think. After all, I do.

REFERENCES

COLE, Michael and Jerome S. BRUNER
  1971   Cultural Differences and Inferences about Psychological Processes
         American Psychologist, vol. 26, no. 10, 867–876.

EPSTEIN, Richard L., Fred KROON, William S. ROBINSON
   2013   Subjective Claims
           In Epstein, *The Fundamentals of Argument Analysis*,
           Advanced Reasoning Forum, pp. 95–130.

SINHA , Vera da SILVA
   2018   *Linguistic and Cultural Conceptualisations of Time in Huni*
           Kui, Awety´, and Kamaiura Communities in Brazil
           Ph.D. thesis, University of East Anglia.

TURING, Alan
   1950   Computing Machinery and Intelligence
           Mind, vol. 59, no. 236, pp. 433–460.

The Thing-Basis of Western Philosophy

Almost all philosophers in the Western tradition tie their work to the thing-view of the languages they speak. By contrasting such thing-based analyses with the metaphysics of the flow of all, we can gain a better understanding of issues in Western philosophy and the solutions that have been proposed.

Common sense in philosophy

Milton D. Hunnex in *Philosophies and Philosophers* describes G. E. Moore's "epistemological realism":

> The sensation of something, i.e., "knowing" something, is unique and irreducible. Also there are truths of common sense whose certainty is such that to doubt them would be to raise questions about our understanding of what it *means* to know anything at all, since knowing these common-sense truths is *paradigm*, i.e., the clear-cut example of *what it means to know anything*. Examples of "clear-cut" common-sense truths are:
>> (a) Things exist in space and time.
>> (b) We can only think and see and feel *where* our bodies are.
>> (c) Things exist when we are not conscious of them.　　p. 12

Here "doubt" is the wrong word. Yes, if one does not accept (a) and (c), then one would raise questions about what it means to know anything at all *in our language community*. But (a) and (c) are not basic, at best odd, in a mass-process language. Assumption (b) is also odd for a mass-process language culture in which speakers do not distinguish minds and bodies as things. Common-sense epistemology for speakers of such a language must be quite different.

Cause and effect

If a cause is a thing or a power in a thing, and an effect is what happens to some thing, how can we reason about cause and effect in a process-mass language?

The idea that causes are or are in things, that there is some kind of causal power in things, has been abandoned in science.[1] We often reason about cause and effect in English, too, without talk of things, as when we say "The drought caused the crops to fail".

---

[1] See my "Reasoning about Cause and Effect".

We don't need to think of causes as things or in things. Take, for example, the causal claim "Spot's barking caused Dick to wake up". We can describe the purported cause with the sentence "Spot barked" and the purported effect with "Dick woke up." Then to claim that there is cause and effect can be understood as claiming that the inference from "Spot barked" to "Dick woke up" satisfies conditions for a good causal inference, as set out in my "Reasoning about Cause and Effect". By describing purported causes and effects with sentences that are true or false of particular times, we can analyze causal claims in a mass-process language.

Consciousness
In *Individuals* P. F. Strawson says:

> . . . the other question we are considering — viz. "Why do we ascribe our states of consciousness to anything at all?" — is also a question which does not arise; for on this view it is only a linguistic illusion that one ascribes one's states of consciousness at all [*sic*], that there is any proper subject of these apparent ascriptions, that states of consciousness belong to, or are states of, anything. p. 94

Compare when we assert in the artificial mass-process language described in "The World as the Flow of All":

> Thinking, now, there.

There is thinking now; there in the flow of all: thinking. This is as true spoken of a room of students in a classroom as it is spoken of Suzy selecting a breakfast cereal at the supermarket. Without the demand for a subject for every verb, Descartes' inference "I think, therefore I am" is not only not convincing, it can't even be said.

The words "I", "you (singular)", "he", "she", "it", "we", "you (plural)", "they" are how we divide the mass of consciousness, as "here" and "there" divide up the mass of space.

The flow of all and the many-one problem
"Dog" as a base word in a mass-process language describes not one dog, not many dogs, not the class of dogs, not the process of being a dog, not the essence of being a dog, but all of those and somehow none of those. It is not dog as mass, not dog as process. Yet comparing "dog" in our new sense to how we use mass-words, such as "mud", and process words, such as "raining", is the only way I have to lead

you to this conception. Dorothy Lee suggested the terms "essence", "kind", or "genus" for what the base words "express" in some languages.[2] But those terms are tied to resolutions of an old and continuing issue in Western philosophy: What is it that is common or unifies many individuals as being of the same kind? What is common to all dogs that they are dogs, not coyotes or tables? Is it some essence —doggieness? Is it a universal of some sort that is more real than any individual dog? Or is it just how we use our language?

In a mass-process language, the "universal", the "essence" comes first; individuals are somehow picked out, if they are picked out at all, from that. There is no need or motive to worry about how different individuals share some common essence, any more than when I submerge a glass into a tub of water and lift it out do we worry how the water in the glass shares a common nature with the rest of the water in the tub.

Chad Hansen in *Language and Logic in Ancient China* contrasts the idea of universals meant to stand behind our learning languages with a mass-process view in Chinese:

> Baby Susie learns to utter "doggie" in the presence of Fido (the family dog—a collie) and the neighbor's German shepherd and a few other occasional mongrels as examples. However, the first time she sees Uncle Harry's Afghan hound, she promptly chirps, "Doggie!" How did she know? We tend to say she has learned to abstract from particular examples—learned abstract thinking. She has abstracted from all the particular dogs she had encountered the features common to all dogs. Seeing that the Afghan hound had these features, even though quite different in other respects, she correctly classifies it as a dog. This classification depends on her having learned an abstract idea.
>
> Baby Mei-Ling, on the other hand, has learned to use the word *kou* 'dog' for that stuff which she encounters at Uncle Jang's. But the story told does not involve any abstracting. Rather one says that she has acquired the ability to distinguish dog-stuff from non-dog-stuff.** The problem of learning for Mei-Ling is how she is able to reidentify the same stuff. But expressing the problem in that way makes us less likely to talk of abstracting properties from different objects.
>
> ** In fact, the puzzle about learning is identical in both stories. Our ability to acquire discriminatory skills adequate to learn a language is what needs to be explained. What is hard for us to acknowledge,

---

2 "Linguistic Reflection of Wintu Thought" and "Categories of the Generic and Particular in Wintu", reprinted in this volume.

given our commonsense commitment to mental abstract ideas, is
that the detour through ideas doesn't explain that ability at all. pp. 51–52

Some early Greek philosophers did have a vision of the world as
one-not-many, which they struggled to describe.[3] Aristotle in his
Physics, Book I, Sections 1 to 3, says:

> So some, like Lycophron, were led to omit 'is', others to change the
> mode of expression and say 'the man has been whitened' instead of
> 'is white', and 'walks' instead of 'is walking' for fear that if they
> added the word 'is' they should be making the one to *be* many . . . .

Aristotle's "refutation" of those who took the world to be one depended
on assuming, not showing, that there are individual things. But his work
was so influential that the idea of encountering the world as one-not-
many was relegated to mysticism in the Western tradition of philosophy.

Existence

For those of us who speak thing languages, questions of existence are
central not only to philosophy but to our daily lives. What exists? Is
there such a thing as a good cat? Does the apple exist after I've taken
a bite out of it? Existence and identity are intertwined in a great puzzle.[4]

But in a process-mass language such as the one I set out in "The
World as the Flow of All", we have simply:

Dog-ing (4:43 p.m. April 10, 2010; Dogshine)

To say that this is true is to say that dog-ing is going on at that time
and place. There's nothing more to say about existing. Similarly for
mud-ing and running. There are no assertions of existence but only
assertions of mass-process words for times and places.

"What exists?" isn't an intelligible question when we see the world
as the flow of all. We can't even say that "the world" exists, for there is
no contrast of what doesn't exist. There are no parts of the flow of all,
only parts as arise by our paying attention in certain ways. "Why is
there something rather than nothing?" is not a deep question leading us
to a conception of God but only ungrammatical nonsense in our process-
mass language.

---

[3] See *An Introduction to Early Greek Philosophy* by John Mansley Robinson.

[4] See "Naming, Pointing, and What There Is", Chapter IV.E of *Predicate
Logic*, revised slightly as Appendix 3 of *An Introduction to Formal Logic*,
Second edition.

Identity

When did the apple I was eating begin to exist? When did it end? To ask that is to view the apple as a thing in the world, real and distinct with distinguishable properties independent of us. Our work is to see it correctly. In a mass-process language we ask instead when it is correct to use the word "apple". We replace worries about the reality of what is "out there" with worries about how best to describe the world of our experience. The question of what is the thing-in-itself, pure of the properties we attribute to it, evaporates.

At a lecture I was asked whether I have criteria of identity for mass-process talk. What counts as "the same" when we say that the dog-ing here now is the same as the dog-ing then there? I have none. But the status of what counts as the same for things is still unsettled after 2,500 years of worry, though I hope to have clarified it some in my works.

Substance

Alfred North Whitehead, Nicholas Rescher, and others, take the contrast: process vs. substance.[5] Here I take the contrast: process vs. things. In contrasting process and substance, they rely heavily on the notion of thing, but now a substance-less thing. They talk of processes rather than just process. A big question for them is the status of things. There seem to be two choices. Things could be like Plato's forms, somehow real but abstract, placing form on the world of experience. Or they could be our attempt to impose order on our experience, our attempt to have stability and diversity in our experience. The latter can slip into subjective idealism, as it seems Whitehead sometimes does when he talks of processes as psychological.

Taking the contrast to be process vs. things, the issue of substance falls away. We don't have to ask what things are made of. There is just the flow of all, and we can, if we wish, impose some kind of thing-talk on that. But that's just our way of describing the flow of all at a particular time and place. There is no slipping into subjective idealism, though one could take that view. The flow of all can be quite real and not just our perception. What is subjective, or intersubjective through our language, is our describing the flow of all.

---

5 See Johanna Seibt, "Process Philosophy".

Abstracting

In my work in logic, I embrace the process of abstracting and reject the abstract. I had imagined that abstracting is something we all do, all the time. But Dorothy Lee suggests in "Symbolization and Value" that this may be a provincial view:

> This conception of the symbol as something distinct from and applicable to, can be held because of a mode of thinking according to which it is possible and desirable to abstract elements from a total situation, and to separate idea or form from substance. This conception is not a common one outside the province of Western civilization; and in many other cultures, it is inconceivable to make such a split. Here the symbol—the personal name, the picture, the emblem, the word—is an inextricable component of that which to Western thinking, it represents. And indeed there is a widely held theory to the effect that this conception is due to an inability to abstract, that it is the mark of a low stage in the development of the mind, apparently resting in the assumption that when human beings are able to abstract, they do so.   p. *158*

The external world

Of course there is an external world, separate from my thinking and your thinking. It is real, and it is what makes our assertions true or false. But we need not invoke all of the external world to justify that "Juney is a dog" is true. All we need is some part of it, some situation or state. Nor need we invoke all of the external world to justify that "Birta is running" is true; all we need is some part of it, the event.

Yet what is this external world? What is the event that makes "Birta is running" true? All we can say is that it's the part of the world described by "Birta is running". Events, states, situations are how we try to conceive of parts of the external world.[6] In doing so, we are conceiving of the external world as separate, a thing. Yet Dorothy Lee in "The Religious Dimension of Human Experience" describes how such a division of self and world does not arise for speakers of the mass-process language Wintu:

> Here we find people [the Wintu] who do not so much seek communion with environing nature as *find themselves* in communion with it. In many of these societies, not even mysticism is to be found, in our sense of the word. For us, mysticism presupposes a prior separation of man from nature; and communion is achieved through loss of self

---

[6] See "Why Event-Talk Is a Problem" in this volume.

and subsequent merging with that which is beyond; but for many other cultures, there is no distinct separation between self and other, which must be overcome. Here, man is *in* nature already, and we cannot speak of man *and* nature.[7]   p. 164

We, standing outside that community, can say that they are describing the "external world" differently. But what that world is, independent of our descriptions and their very different descriptions, we cannot say. It is as bloodless as the thing-in-itself, there only for us to have confidence in how we talk, idling except as a psychological prop.

But that psychological prop interferes with how we understand other people and their language and culture. A colleague of mine reasoned:

- My language sees the world right. I know because I speak it.
- There is only one world.
- So speakers of this other language must "see" that world more or less the same as I do with my language.
- So there has to be a good translation of their speaking into mine.

Yet how is my language right? I look out my window at a field and say to myself "It's spring, and already I can see the alfalfa rippling in the wind". Then I remark to myself that alfalfa is not a thing, the many growing plants, green there, is not a thing. Much closer to what I see and sense is to say "Alfalfa-ing + rippling + wind-ing".

What is common sense, what is obvious, what is clear, what we can assume in building a philosophy is tied to the (usually) unexpressed metaphysics of our common language. As Benjamin Lee Whorf says in "Languages and Logic":

> I can sympathize with those who say, "Put it into plain, simple English," especially when they protest against the empty formalism of loading discourse with pseudolearned words. But to restrict thinking to the patterns merely of English, and especially to those patterns which represent the acme of plainness in English, is to lose a power of thought which, once lost, can never be regained. It is the "plainest" English which contains the greatest number of unconscious assumptions about nature. p. *235*

Philosophers risk being provincial by ignoring the work of linguists and anthropologists.

---

[7] See also her discussion in "Responsibility among the Dakota".

NOTE

I am not the first to recognize how the thing-grammar of English, German, French and other European languages has shaped Western philosophy. The earliest I have found is by Friedrich Nietzsche in " 'Reason' in Philosophy" in 1888, reprinted here. An analysis of the significance for philosophy of the work of Whorf was made in 1986 by Benson Mates in *The Philosophy of Leibniz*, pp. 246–250, (reprinted here as "Metaphysics and Linguistic Relativity"). See also Friedrich Waismann "The Linguistic Technique", pp. 158–161.

REFERENCES

ARISTOTLE
  1991   *Physics*
          Translated by R. P. Hardie and R. K. Gaye in *The Complete Works
          of Aristotle*, Revised Oxford Translation, ed. J. Barnes, Vol. 1.
EPSTEIN, Richard L.
  1994   *Predicate Logic*
          Oxford University Press. Reprinted Advanced Reasoning Forum, 2012.
  2011   Reasoning about Cause and Effect
          In *Cause and Effect, Conditionals, Explanations*, Advanced
          Reasoning Forum, pp. 13–93.
  2020   *An Introduction to Formal Logic*, second edition
          Advanced Reasoning Forum.
  2022   *Reasoning and the World as the Flow of All*
          Typescript, available at www.AdvancedReasoningForum.org.
HANSEN, Chad
  1983   *Language and Logic in Ancient China*
          The University of Michigan Press. Reprinted Advanced Reasoning
          Forum, 2020.
HUNNEX, Milton D.
  1961   *Philosophies and Philosophers*
          Chandler Publishing Company.
LEE, Dorothy Demetracopoulou
  1952   The Religious Dimension of Human Experience
          In *Religious Perspectives in College Teaching*, ed. H. N. Fairchild,
          The Ronald Press Company. Reprinted in Lee, *Freedom and Culture*,
          Prentice-Hall, Inc., pp. 162–174.
  1954   Symbolization and Value
          In *Symbols and Values, an Initial Study*, Thirteenth Symposium of
          the Conference on Science, Philosophy, and Religion. Reprinted
          in Lee, *Freedom and Culture*, Prentice-Hall, Inc., pp. 78–88.
          Reprinted in this volume.

1959   Responsibility among the Dakota
        In Lee, *Freedom and Culture*, Prentice-Hall, Inc., pp. 59–69.
MATES, Benson
    1986   *The Philosophy of Leibniz: Metaphysics and Language*
            Oxford University Press.
ROBINSON, John Mansley
    1968   *An Introduction to Early Greek Philosophy*
            Houghton Mifflin. Reprinted Advanced Reasoning Forum, 2021.
SEIBT, Johanna
    2012   Process Philosophy
            Stanford Encyclopedia of Philosophy, https://plato.stanford.edu/
            entries/process-philosophy/ .
STRAWSON, P. F.
    1959   *Individuals: An Essay in Descriptive Metaphysics*
            Routledge.
WAISMANN, Friedrich
    1977   The Linguistic Technique
            Posthumous publication in Waismann, *Philosophical Papers*,
            ed. Brian McGuinness, D. Reidel Publishing Company.
WHORF, Benjamin Lee
    1941   Languages and Logic
            Technology Review (Massachusetts Institute of Technology), vol. 43
            (April), pp. 250–252, 266, 268, 272. Reprinted in this volume.

The Metaphysical Basis of Logic: Things and Masses

First comes metaphysics, then comes logic.

To develop predicate logic, to have any justification for the choice of syntax, we must make some assumption about the relation of our language and reasoning to the world. In *Predicate Logic* I make that explicit.

> *Things, the World, and Propositions*
> The world is made up at least in part of things.
> The only propositions we will be interested in are
>   those that are about things.

From this we justify our choice of parsing propositions into words that (are meant to) refer to things and what is said about those things, predicates

We begin with some intuition that a thing is what is individual, specific, what we can pick out or refer to. But we became tongue-tied trying to be clearer. So we look to an analysis in terms of how we use the notion of thing in our reasoning, we consider how naming and the identity of things are principal in our conception of things, and then develop a formal syntax and semantics for predicate logic.[1] That logic can now serve as a standard for what we mean by "thing": what is a thing is what can be reasoned about in predicate logic.[2]

Equally, what is not a thing cannot be reasoned about in predicate logic, for that would be to violate the assumptions on which we base the syntax and semantics.

> *Predicate Logic Characterizes Things*
> What is a thing is what can be reasoned about in predicate logic.
> What is not a thing cannot be reasoned about in predicate logic.

To decide if some part of the world or our experience that we are

---

[1] See my *Predicate Logic* or *An Introduction to Formal Logic*, second edition. I'll consider only classical predicate logic here. For other predicate logics, such as intuitionistic or many-valued, different assumptions about the nature of things might be needed.

[2] W. V. O. Quine in "On What There Is" (p. 13) says: "To be assumed as an entity is, purely and simply, to be reckoned as the value of a variable." The variables he considers are those used in first-order predicate logic.

reasoning about is or can be treated as a thing, we ask whether informal inferences and propositions involving words that describe that part can be formalized in predicate logic. To do that, we need to adopt criteria of what counts as a good formalization, which I give in *Predicate Logic* and have revised in *An Introduction to Formal Logic*.[3]

Some say that considering only propositions about things is no restriction. All there is in the world are things, collections of things, and relations among those. Implicitly or explicitly they adopt a stronger assumption.

Only Things, the World, and Propositions
The world is made up of individual things only.
All propositions are about individual things only.

Things, the World, and Propositions is a methodological assumption that can be understood as a choice about how we will analyze reasoning based on our use of language. We do not need to assume that there are things in the world, only that we view the world that way in our language. In contrast, *Only Things, the World, and Propositions* is not a methodological assumption but an assertion about the nature of the world.[4] According to it, predicate logic along with extensions of it to allow for quantifying over collections has the widest possible scope for a formal analysis of reasoning.

But some examples from ordinary reasoning make this last claim doubtful. Consider the following inference:

(1) (a) Snow is white.
     (b) All that's white is not black.
     Therefore,
     (c) Snow is not black.

We recognize this is valid. Can we formalize it in predicate logic?

---

[3] That analysis is extended to a fuller investigation of the notion of thing in *The Internal Structure of Predicates and Names* and *Time and Space in Formal Logic*. The latter is especially important because classical predicate logic allows for only atemporal reasoning about things.

[4] Henry Laycock in "Theories of Matter" gives a survey of works in which this stronger assumption is made. The most explicit formulation I know is in "The Fundamental Ideas of Pansomatism" by Tadeusz Kotarbin´ski:

Since every object is a thing, and since, therefore, only things exist . . . p. 489

The whole of reality consists entirely of bodies. p. 495

In (1a) and (1c) we seem to be using "Snow" as a name. But what thing does it name? What individual is there that is snow? Snow is physical, but it is not in one place. Yes, snow is distinct from all else in the world, but we cannot point to it, even in theory, and say that is snow. We can only use it to describe lots of masses or things that are made of snow. I can point and say "That snowman is made of snow." I can point to a tree when walking on the mountain and say, "The stuff on that tree is snow." But I can't point to snow complete, all snow.

Don't we have the same problem with "Dogs"? Consider:

(2) (a) Dogs bark.
   (b) All that barks is not a cat.
   Therefore,
   (c) Dogs are not cats.

We recognize this is valid, and "Dogs" is used as a subject much like a name. But we can't point to dogs complete at one time. I can point to this dog or that dog, but not all dogs even in theory. Rather, "Dogs" describes lots of things, individual things that we call "dogs". So we reformulate "Dogs" as a predicate and formalize (2) as:

(3) (a) $\forall x\,(\,(-\text{ is a dog})\,(x) \rightarrow (-\text{ barks})\,(x)\,)$
   (b) $\forall x\,(\,(-\text{ barks})\,(x) \rightarrow \neg\,(-\text{ is a cat})\,(x)\,)$
   Therefore,
   (c) $\forall x\,(\,(-\text{ is a dog})\,(x) \rightarrow \neg\,(-\text{ is a cat})\,(x)\,)$

This is valid. And in any model with a universe that contains all dogs and cats and in which "dog", "cat", and "barks" are given their usual interpretation, the meanings of the semi-formal propositions in (3) reflect what we intended in (2).

Why can't we do the same with snow? We might try formalizing (1) as:

   (a) $\forall x\,(\,(-\text{ is snow})\,(x) \rightarrow (-\text{ is white})\,(x)\,)$
   (b) $\forall x\,(\,(-\text{ is white})\,(x) \rightarrow \neg\,(-\text{ is black})\,(x)\,)$
   Therefore,
   (c) $\forall x\,(\,(-\text{ is snow})\,(x) \rightarrow \neg\,(-\text{ is black})\,(x)\,)$

But what in a model of predicate logic could be used as a reference to make "$(-\text{ is snow})\,(x)$" true? What could we put into the universe that is all snow? We would have to include all quantities of snow, whether shaped like a snowball or a snowman or lying on the branches

of a tree. But we would also have to include all parts of those, for
every part of snow is snow. I can pick up a handful of snow and there
are innumerable "quantities" of snow in it, as there are innumerable
"quantities" of water in a glass of water: the water up to one-third of
the way from the bottom of the glass, the water up to .01726825623 of
the way from the bottom of the glass, ... Only with a description
picking out a particular quantity of snow can we specify a thing that
is snow because snow, unlike dogs, does not come in identifiable
quantities, it does not come in distinct parts each of which is snow.
Snow is a mass, not a collection of things. We have no conception
of how we could pick out in a general way just any item that "snow"
describes. So we don't say "All snow is white" but "Snow is white".

What holds for "snow" holds equally for other words we use to
describe masses: "gold", "mud", "water", ... *Every part of a mass
is a mass of the same kind.* Every part of the water in my bathtub
is water. There is no smallest location for which we can say "There,
that's water, the least part of water" that would justify us in treating
water as a collection of things. In contrast, *no part of a thing is a
thing of the same kind.* No part of my dog Birta is a dog. Yes, the
right front paw of Birta is a thing; yes, the tail of Birta is a thing.
A thing may be composed of other things, but those other things are
not the same kind of thing.

That there is no smallest location at which there is, for example,
mud is not a sorites paradox or the fallacy of drawing the line. Simply,
in our conception of mud there is no smallest part; there is only, at
small enough places, some water, straw, and earth but not mud. Nor
in the glass of water on my table is there any smallest location at which
there is water.

Willard van Orman Quine in *Word and Object* disagrees. He
believes that talk of masses can be reduced to or simply is talk of
collections of things:

> In general a mass term in predicative position may be viewed as a
> general term which is true of each portion of the stuff in question,
> excluding only the parts too small to count. Thus "water" and "sugar",
> in the role of general terms, are true of each part of the world's water
> or sugar, down to single molecules but not to atoms; and "furniture",
> in the role of general term, is true of each part of the world's furniture
> down to single chairs but not to legs and spindles.   pp. 97–98.

So if talk about mud can't be reduced to talk about collections of things, then "mud" is too vague to use in our reasoning.

But if every quantity of water is a collection of H_2O molecules, and every collection of H_2O molecules is a quantity of water, most of what we know about water is false: water is a liquid, water freezes, water gives rise to a sensation of wetness. None of those are true about a single molecule, not even 17 molecules. No one would ever have drunk water, for any liquid we encounter, even in a laboratory, is not a collection of just H_2O molecules. We can have dirty water, salt water, and hard water, just as we have brown dogs, fat dogs, and gentle dogs. To say that water is H_2O is to confuse an abstraction that scientists use to make predictions about the world with a "truth" about the nature of the world. It gives us no guide for how to reason with "water".[5]

We cannot formalize (1) in predicate logic. We can't formalize in predicate logic any reasoning about masses because masses are not things or collections of things.[6] Nor has any method of extending predicate logic to incorporate words for masses gained general acceptance.[7]

At best, we can formalize reasoning with words for masses by using predicates like "— is made of snow", "— is a piece of ice", "— is a glass of beer". These would be true of what we do accept as things: snowballs, ice cubes, glasses of beer; and they would be false of other things such as my dogs or the pen on my desk. We don't put snow or ice or beer in the universe of a model, nor do we put bits of

---

5 See my "Models and Theories" for a fuller discussion.

6 Harry C. Bunt in *Mass Terms and Model Theoretic Semantics* agrees, giving the example:

> If we take some ice cubes from the refrigerator, crush them, and put them into a glass of coke, we may say:
>
>> The ice in the coke is the same ice that was in the refrigerator before.
>
> [This example] would be a true sentence about some ice, yet there is no individuating standard in terms of which we can express this, since the identity stated by the sentence is not an identity of any of the pieces of ice involved, but an identity of the totalities of ice made up of whatever pieces are involved. p. 36

7 For a survey of analyses see Francis Jeffrey Pelletier and Lenhart K. Schubert, "Mass Expressions". Jean van Heijenoort "Subject and Predicate in Western Logic" has a good discussion of mass terms and masses.

snow, bits of ice, or bits of beer in the universe of a model but only identifiable parts of snow, ice, and beer—parts that we can pick out and name. The universe of a model has things in it that we can use these predicates to describe.

*   *   *   *   *   *

Is the difference between masses and things a difference in the world or only a difference in how we conceive of the world through our language?

I am at a loss to know what it means for either of those alternatives to be true. I know of no standard of what there is in the world independent of our perceptions and language. And our language shapes our perceptions most certainly, as the papers in this volume show. But we can consider how we make this distinction in our ordinary language and how or whether other languages allow for making this distinction.

In English and in many other languages we have two kinds of nouns. A *count noun* is a noun to which we normally attach counting words or articles: a dog, three fires, the idea. A *non-count noun* is a noun to which we normally attach quantity words: some water, a lot of rice, much meat. Not all nouns are count or non-count. We can't have three sakes nor much sake; we can't have forty-seven proximities nor a lot of proximity.

Our conception of thing comes from or is reflected in our use of count nouns. "Dog", "table", "rock" are words for things, what comes in individual quantities that we can pick out for reference, what can be counted. But we have doubts about whether some count nouns describe things: "number", "mood", "idea", "fire". We start with count nouns that we agree describe things, like "dog", "table", and "rock", and develop a clearer notion of thing in setting up predicate logic. Then we can use predicate logic to test whether those other words describe things in the world according to that clearer conception.

Our conception of mass comes from or is reflected in our use of non-count nouns. "Water", "mud", "gold", "snow" are words for masses. But not all non-count nouns are *mass terms*, that is, describe masses. For example, "rice" describes all grains of rice just as "dog" describes all individual dogs. We start with non-count nouns that we agree describe masses and, as in the analysis we saw above, we can come to a clearer conception of mass: it is what does not come in individual quantities, what we cannot pick out for reference to use in predicate logic, what has no smallest part, for every part of a mass is the same kind of mass.

Do "wisdom", "pride", "thought", "fire" describe masses or things? It seems that "wisdom" and "pride" describe masses: we talk of some wisdom and a lot of pride, and we don't think of wisdom or pride as coming in smallest parts. But we can replace uses of those words with either a predicate or predicate modifier, "— is wise" or "wise" and "— is proud" or "proud", and formalize reasoning about wisdom and pride in predicate logic.[8] What about thoughts? Our language treats them as things, but I suggest in "Language-Thought-Meaning" in this volume that we have no way to pick out thoughts except in retrospect with linguistic descriptions, much as we pick out particular quantities of water using descriptions. Thoughts are more like mass or process. What about "fire"? We use a count noun for it, which directs us to think of a fire as a thing, yet our experience of fire is as a mass-process, for every part of a fire is fire: there is no smallest part of a fire that is fire. We have sharpened our conception of mass and of thing enough to begin to investigate better how our language connects to "the world" or our experience.

In English we sometimes use count nouns as mass terms. Compare:

(5) Kim put an apple into the salad.
(6) Kim put apple into the salad.

In (5) "apple" is used as a count noun; in (6) it is used as a mass term. Does this reflect a blurring of the distinction between thing and mass?

We can think of apple as a mass and treat it that way: every part of apple is apple. We can do that with any count noun: it merely indicates that we're not concerned with how many or the provenance of the parts that make up the quantity. We say "some lamb" when we are talking about eating lamb meat and are not concerned with whether it came from one or many lambs, nor whether it is a leg or a neck, and every part of lamb meat is lamb meat. Conversely, we can talk of three waters, indicating that the water we are talking about is divided into three distinguishable parts. These and other examples don't show that there is no conceptual difference between things and masses. They show only that in some contexts we are interested in counting and in others we are not. The interest or direction of interest is given first by

---

8 See my *The Internal Structure of Predicates and Names*.

our language. For example, the French use the count noun "meuble" in place of our non-count noun "furniture" and the count noun "pellicule" in place of our non-count noun "dandruff"; Brazilians use the non-count noun "feijão" in place of our count noun "bean".

It is very hard to give rules of interpretation for the use of non-count nouns and count nouns in English, or French, or Portuguese, in part because of historical accident in what has led to some of the classifications. But the broad division corresponds to a distinction in how we conceive of the world or how the world is: masses vs. things.

G. B. Alice ter Meulen in *Substances, Quantities, and Individuals* describes the division as in the world:

> In some respects quantities of stuff are quite like individuals. Individuals are objects in space-time, and so are all quantities of stuff. They are in this sense part of the same physical reality. . . . But quantities of substances are in many other respects to be distinguished from individuals. The first most striking difference between quantities and individuals is the fact that the quantities of any substance can be divided into smaller parts that are also quantities of the same substance. Similarly, the quantities of some substance can become part of a larger quantity of the same substance. . . . The fact that quantities can be divided into quantities of the same substance together with the fact that any number of quantities of some substance can become part of a new quantity of the same substance is a logical property characteristic of quantities only. This property of quantities, called the *property of homogeneous reference*, has widely been recognized as distinctive of the semantic interpretation of mass terms. A more precise formulation of this property is the following. Any parts of a quantity of x that are themselves quantities of x can become parts of another quantity of x.
>
> pp. 67–68

Others view a homogeneous reference principle as an observation about how we talk and not about the nature of the world.[9]

*   *   *   *   *   *

The conception of the world as made up, at least in part, of masses, the idea that what we call snow is not a thing nor a collection of things, is part of the conception of the world we inherit in our use of English. But it is quite secondary to the view embodied in our language that the world is made up of things. This suggests we are right in stressing the

---

[9] See, for example, Harry C. Bunt, *Mass Terms and Model Theoretic Semantics*, especially p. 46.

conception of thing in building predicate logic, leaving as a secondary issue how to reason about mass.

But it is not just mass. There are processes, like running or eating. Those seem to have a mass-like quality in our English-speaking conception. There can be a lot of running, or much eating, but not two runnings and three eatings, at least not in our usual speech. Predicate logic cannot be used to reason about process and change, as I've shown in *The Internal Structure of Predicates and Names* and in *Time and Space in Formal Logic*. This is a serious problem even for speakers of English who wish to become clearer about how to reason well.

Yet there are languages for which the notion of mass-process is primary, and the idea of thing is either absent or quite secondary, such as Navajo and Wintu, as described in the articles by Dorothy Lee and others in this volume. It is not that those languages talk of masses and processes but that the world is conceived as the flow of all, and the language can be used to describe without partitioning. In such a language, change is not part of desciptions, for the idea of change is tied to the idea of a thing or things changing. Rather there are descriptions of the world as the flow of all, and identity over time is quite different. Such metaphysics leads to a very different logic, one in which there is no notion of thing, which I have developed into a formal language and logic in *Reasoning about the World as the Flow of All*. It is incompatible with predicate logic in that there is no translation between the two logics, no clear way to speak of the thing-nature of the world in the mass-process logic, nor any clear way to speak of the world as process-mass in predicate logic.

First comes metaphysics, then comes logic.

REFERENCES

BUNT, Harry C.
  1985 *Mass Terms and Model Theoretic Semantics*
        Cambridge University Press.
EPSTEIN, Richard L.
  1994 *Predicate Logic*
        Oxford University Press, 1994. Advanced Reasoning Forum, 2012.
  2004 Models and Theories
        Bulletin of Advanced Reasoning and Knowledge, vol. 2, 2004,
        pp. 77–98. Revised in Epstein, *Reasoning in Science and
        Mathematics*, pp. 20–45, Advanced Reasoning Forum, 2012.

2016   *The Internal Structure of Predicates and Names*
        Advanced Reasoning Forum.

2020   *Reasoning and the World as the Flow of All*
        Typescript available at www.AdvancedReasoningForum.org.

2020   *An Introduction to Formal Logic*, Second Edition
        Advanced Reasoning Forum.

2021   *Time and Space in Formal Logic*
        To appear, Advanced Reasoning Forum.

KOTARBIN´SKI, Tadeusz

1955   The Fundamental Ideas of Pansomatism
        Mind, n.s. vol. 64, pp. 488–500.

LAYCOCK, Henry

1975   Theories of Matter
        Synthese, vol. 34, 1975, pp. 411–422. Reprinted in *Mass Terms*,
        ed. Francis Jeffrey Pelletier, D. Reidel, 1979, pp. 89–120.

PELLETIER, Francis Jeffrey and Lenhart K. SCHUBERT

1989   Mass Expressions
        Chapter IV.4 of *Handbook of Philosophical Logic*, *Volume 4*,
        eds. D. Gabbay and F. Guenthner, D. Reidel.

QUINE, Willard van Orman

1953   On What There Is
        In *From a Logical Point of View*, Harvard, 2nd ed., 1961, pp. 1–19.

1960   *Word and Object*
        The M.I.T. Press.

Ter MEULEN, G.B. Alice

1980   *Substances, Quantities, and Individuals*
        Ph.D. Dissertation, Stanford University.

Van HEIJENOORT, Jean

1974   Subject and Predicate in Western Logic
        Philosophy East and West, vol. 24, pp. 253–268. Reprinted in
        van Heijenoort, *Selected Essays*, Bibliopolis, 1985, pp. 17–34.

Languages and Logics

The diagram on the next page sets out how I see the relation of formal logics and languages.

Starting at the bottom left there are thing-languages, such as English, German, and French. In the 19th and early 20th centuries, speakers of those created mathematics as we know it now. They replaced talk of process and transformation with talk of things, usually abstract things. They ignored all talk of masses. Set theory was seen as the ultimate basis of such mathematics, and is the ultimate in a thing-only view of the world. Motivated by examples in those thing languages and examples from mathematics that could not be formalized in Aristotelian logic, speakers of those languages developed predicate logic. They based it on the syntax and semantics of things in those languages, principally the noun-verb, subject-predicate distinctions. They ignored, just as in the mathematics they used in devising the logic, all talk of mass, process, and change.

Only much later, beginning with my *Predicate Logic*, was the use of predicate logic to formalize propositions and inferences of ordinary language investigated to devise criteria of formalizing, illuminating the implicit metaphysics of things in English and other ordinary languages.[1] More examples of formalizing in extensions of predicate logic in my *The Internal Structure of Predicates and Names* and *Time and Space in Formal Logic* made it clear that the thing metaphysics on which predicate logic was based did not allow for formalizing reasoning about mass, process, or change.[2]

Systems for formalizing reasoning about masses have been proposed, beginning with Aristotelian logic and continuing with the work of Harry C. Bunt and others. But none of those seemed suitable for formalizing reasoning about change or process.

So I set out to devise a formal language and logic that would be suitable for reasoning about mass, process, and change, which I outline in "The World as the Flow of All" in this volume and which I develop in *Reasoning and the World as the Flow of All*. I then discovered that the formal language and logic reflect much of languages such as

---

[1] The criteria are revised in *An Introduction to Formal Logic*, second edition.

[2] See "The Metaphysical Basis of Logic: Things and Masses" in this volume.

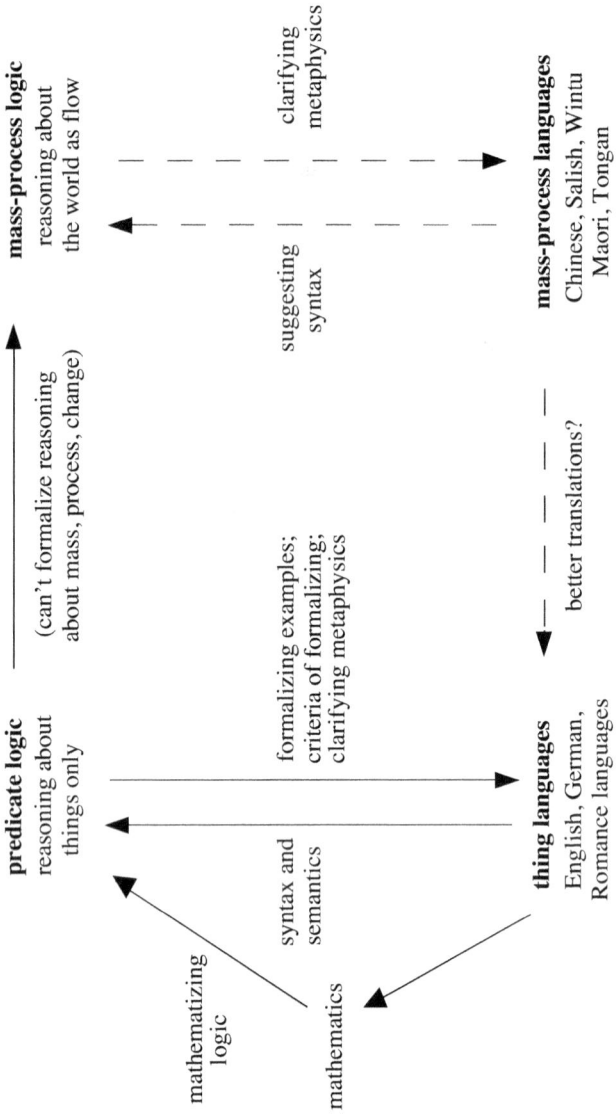

mass-process logic
reasoning about
the world as flow

clarifying
metaphysics

suggesting
syntax

mass-process languages
Chinese, Salish, Wintu
Maori, Tongan

(can't formalize reasoning
about mass, process, change)

formalizing examples;
criteria of formalizing;
clarifying metaphysics

better translations?

predicate logic
reasoning about
things only

thing languages
English, German,
Romance languages

syntax and
semantics

mathematizing
logic

mathematics

Chinese, Salishan, Maori, and Wintu.[3] We can now see how those languages are based on an implicit metaphysics that cannot be reconstructed in English or German or Romance languages but can only be pointed at, as I have tried in "The World as the Flow of All" and as Dorothy Lee and others do in their essays in this volume. Now we can draw from the syntax and conceptions of mass-process languages for the development of the formal mass-process logic. In the other direction, as people who speak mass-process languages begin to formalize propositions and inferences from those languages in the formal mass-process logic, we'll begin to understand better the implicit metaphysics of mass-process in those languages.

I am often asked how to formalize or say some sentence such as "I walked the dog yesterday, you didn't" in the artificial mass-process language I devised. Attempting to do so would be as much a mistake as trying to formalize "Snow is white" or "Running is harder than walking" in predicate logic. There is a metaphysical mismatch, trying to force one conception of the world into a grammar based on a very different one. Just as formalizing "Justice is a virtue" as "All things that are just are virtuous" is wrong, formalizing "My dog is bigger than your dog" in terms of mass-process would be wrong. The only reason to try to formalize English sentences in a mass-process logic would be to uncover how different the implicit metaphysics of English is from the metaphysics on which the mass-process logic is based.

Still, the issue of whether the logic and language of the world as process-mass reflects or tracks some ordinary language is separate from the issue of whether that language and logic give a way to talk about the world as process. I think that the flow of all vs. thing emphasis is a major division in languages, and that the language and logic I've devised helps us see that. I may be wrong. But regardless, the language and logic I have devised stand as a new way to encounter and reason about the world.

REFERENCES
BUNT, Harry C.
   1985 *Mass Terms and Model-Theoretic Semantics*
        Cambridge University Press.

---

[3] I later learned that Whorf in "Languages and Logic" (reprinted in this volume) urged the development of a logic to reflect reasoning in such languages.

EPSTEIN, Richard L.
   1994   *Predicate Logic*
          Oxford University Press. Reprinted Advanced Reasoning
          Forum, 2012.
   2016   *An Introduction to Formal Logic*
          Advanced Reasoning Forum. Second edition, 2020.
   2016   *The Internal Structure of Predicates and Names*
          Advanced Reasoning Forum.
   2020   *Reasoning and the World as the Flow of All*
          Typescript available at www.AdvancedReasoningForum.org.
   2021   *Time and Space in Formal Logic*
          To appear, AdvancedReasoningForum.

Essays Old

Dorothy Demetracopoulou Lee

Conceptual Implications of an Indian Language
(1938)

Categories of the Generic and the Particular
in Wintu" (1944)

Linguistic Reflections of Wintu Thought (1944)

Symbolization and Value (1954)

Dorothy Demetracopoulou Lee (1905–1975) was born in
Constantinople and attended the American School run by
missionaries there. She won a scholarship at Vassar
College, and later went to the University of California,
Berkeley where she studied cultural anthropology under
Alfred Kroeber. She did fieldwork with the Wintu Indians
and earned her Ph. D. from Berkeley in 1931. (For a full
biography by Jeffrey Ehrenreich see the epilogue to Lee's
book *Freedom and Culture,* Waveland Press, 1987. See
also *California Indian Languages* by Victor Golla, University of California Press, 2011 for a discussion of her
work and studies.)

Wintu is a language that was spoken by only a few
hundred people in northern California when Dorothy Lee
did her research. It is no longer spoken (but see Golla,
California Indian Languages). Lee relied on informants;
she did not make clear how much she could understand of
the spoken language.

Conceptual Implications
of an Indian Language

It has been said that a language will delineate and limit the logical
concepts of the individual who speaks it. Conversely, a language is
an organ for the expression of thought, of concepts and principles of
classification. True enough, the thought of the individual must run
along its grooves; but these grooves, themselves, are a heritage from
individuals who laid them down in an unconscious effort to express
their attitude toward the world. Grammar contains in crystallized form
the accumulated and accumulating experience, the Weltanschauung of
a people.

The study which I propose to present below, is an attempt to understand, through a study of grammar, the unformulated philosophy of the
Wintu tribe of California.

I

The Wintu speaker divides his predicative statements into
two categories: that of the subjective or experiential, and that of the
objective. He has two ablaut stems[1] to choose from, for every verb.
He uses one to express a state or action in bringing which about the
grammatical subject can or does participate, another for the state or
action that is irrespective of the agency of the subject. Correlatively,
the speaker himself participates in the event or state of the first category
(I), in so far as he perceives or apprehends it; but that of the second
category (II), is the object of his belief: in speaking of it, he asserts
a truth which is beyond experience.

Category I is the category of subjectivity, and expresses this
subjectivity through various mechanisms. The form of the stem
denotes experience on the part of the grammatical subject. A long
series of suffixes show cognizance of this experience on the part of
the speaker; and a small group of modal suffixes indicate the attitude
of the experiencing subject toward his experience, actual or projected.

The statements of this category, then, express only partial truth;
that is, truth as limited through the sensory and mental apparatus of

---

[1] For example, for the verb *to come* there is the pair of stems *wir-*
and *wer-*; *to swallow* has the stems *pira-, peru-*; *to wash*: *yuqa-, yoqu*;
to chop: *kup-, kop-*.

the knowing subject. So patent is this limitation, that the language provides suffixes expressive of the exact channel through which this particle of truth has become known. Each of these denotes, not only person, time and aspect, but also the manner in which the speaker himself has come by his information. The speaker can use the stem alone, without suffix, thus stating generally known fact. But if he tries to particularize this, to delimit it as to time or subject, he is forced to quote, in the same breath, that particular experience of his which is his authority for the statement. He cannot say simply, *the salmon is good.* That part of *is good* which implies the tense (now) and the person (it), further has to contain one of the following implications: (the salmon is good) I see, I taste (or know through some other sense than sight), I infer, I judge, I am told.

If the information given depends on hearsay, the suffix *-ke,*[2] expressive of all three persons, is attached to the stem. It is the suffix which is used exclusively in the narration of myths; also, in gossip, in descriptions of places which the speaker has not visited, etc. It is really the suffix of the third person, as there are seldom any occasions when it can be used in describing an event pertaining to the first or second persons. If the occasion calls for it, however, it is used in reference to these persons also. The following two sentences illustrate such use:

tsoyila*ke* ni: I *am* drunk, (*I hear*); they tell me
    I am drunk.
kilepma kuyabi*ke* mi: frightfully sick you *are,*
    (*I hear*); you are supposed to be very sick.

Visual evidence is expressed by means of *-da, -besken, -be* for the first, second and third persons respectively. The visual is the only evidence which is distinguished by means of a separate suffix. Primarily, this suffix seems to indicate unquestioned evidence. It is used in purely exclamatory, non-informative phrases. Apparently, it comes to refer to visual evidence only incidentally, only because through the eyes alone comes evidence which can be used as data without question. As a rule, then, this suffix indicates supremely reliable evidence; it usually denotes visual evidence only when emphasizing the contrast to evidence derived from other senses. This is especially true of the first person, since in this case the speaker is one with the directly

---

[2] The phonetics have been simplified throughout, in conformity with the non-technical nature of this paper.

experiencing grammatical subject. *harada, muteda, wineda, hureibida*: I am walking, I hear, I see, I am sewing, tell their own story. The following phrases illustrate the use of the suffixes for the second and third persons: mi yo tchala*be*: that *is* a beautiful tree (*I see*); kenpana saniha*be*: get up, it *is* morning (*I see*); tchepkala*besken*: *you are* in a bad state (*I see*); *you look* rotten. In this last, the suffix indicates specifically visual evidence; otherwise, say the Wintu, the statement is worthless, since it tells nothing which the addressee does not know.

When a statement is based on sensory evidence other than that of vision, the suffixes *-ntida, -nteresken, -nte* are used for the first, second and third persons respectively. hiren*te* qewel: the house *is* burning, says the blind man, who smells the smoke and feels the heat; tubelabin*te*: it *is* fragrant; pilamabin*te*: it *is* warm; pe nis iya*nteresken*: why, you *are* biting me! is said to an invisible insect; poyok kyubin*tida*: I *am* aching as to the head; I have a headache; una*nteresken*: you thus-ed (*to my hearing*); thus you said.

When a statement is based on inference, the suffix *-re* is used for all three persons. This suffix indicates that logic has been applied to circumstantial sensory evidence. Naturally, it refers chiefly to the third person, though it is occasionally used in statements about the first and second persons. ewin minelpukekir(*e*)kelesken: by means of this you almost died, (*I diagnose*), says the shaman, holding up an extracted spirit-arrow; nitchai yo hara*re* nor: my nephew *is* gone south (*I infer*); my nephew must have gone south, says Coyote. He sees Hummingbird's tracks ending suddenly, he sees that the valley to the south is covered with gay flowers, and infers that Hummingbird has flown south. The necessity here, which I render as *must,* lies in logic, not in nature. The Wintu does not confuse the two.

When his statement is based on conclusions derived from systematic thinking alone, or on judgement, the Wintu uses the suffix *-el*. Often the *-el* can be rendered into English only with the aid of *must*. As the preceding suffix, this refers to logical necessity. pite bera*el*, my father-in-law *is* hungry, is said by a man who knows that his father-in-law is bed-ridden and alone. When Coyote, who has decreed that there should be death in the world, loses his son, Fly says to him, tchala*el* mi man watchasuker: it *is* just (*I judge*) that you weep. har walel yowuna*el*: go, you two, he *is* homesick for you, says a father to his visiting daughters when he is sending them back to their husband. He has not seen the husband, nor has he heard news of him; but he

knows that the man loves his wives, and bases his statement on a
logical deduction from this known fact.

To summarize the functions of these five suffixes, I shall use
a paradigm. If I want to translate the sentence, "Harry is chopping
wood" into Wintu, I have a choice of the five following sentences,
according to my source of knowledge:

> Harry kupake, if I know this by hearsay.
> Harry kupabe, if I see or have seen Harry chopping.
> Harry kupante, if I hear him, or if a chip flies off and hits me.
> Harry kupare, if I have gone to his cabin to find him absent
> and his axe gone.
> Harry kupael, if I know that Harry has a job chopping
> wood everyday at this hour, that he is a dependable
> employee, and, perhaps, that he is not in his cabin.

These suffixes play an important part in the verbal structure of the
Wintu. With the aid of other affixes, they are used of past time, of the
subjective future, of the durative, the habitual, the responsive; in short,
with moods and tenses used in describing experience. Even questions
have to be couched in such a way as to elicit information derived
through a particular medium. For example, the interrogative *-bewi*
assumes that the questionee has been an eye witness. hestit ie*bwei*:
what sort of a person *is she,* contains the implication: you have seen
her. The *-nteri* shows the expectation of auditory evidence from the
questionee. watcha*nteri*: did *she* cry? (*did you hear her* cry?) The
interrogative correlative of the *-ke* of hearsay is *-boh.* My informant,
who could not keep pace with European politics, once asked me:
manapuribia*boh* popom: *are they* still fighting (*according to the
newspapers*)?

The distinctions made by the five suffixes so far given correspond
to subjective differences in the speaker, not the grammatical subject.
Other affixes, added to the stem and preceding any personal or
temporal suffixes there may be, indicate differences of attitude on
the part of the grammatical subject. These are: *-wira,* and *-puke.*
Both of these occur as independent stems, and, in their suffixed form,
may be said to be reminiscent of their meaning when independent.

-wira, when an independent stem, means *to come.* When a
suffix, it implies futurity which is dependent on the desire or intention
of the grammatical subject. Primarily, it is used to bind together two

events or states, whose mutual relationship is that of sequence, a
sequence brought, or to be brought about, through the agency of the
individual. Both of the two events may be in the past or in the future;
or one may be present and the other future. The suffix concerns itself,
not with their temporal relationship to the speaking subject, but with the
sequential relationship of each to the other. Thus it may be translated,
according to context, variously as: *to, so as to, before, with the expectation to, about to*; and, followed by the subjective suffixes described
above, it forms a future tense, which the Wintu render into English as
shall or *will*. But in every case, it is to be kept in mind that, implied
in the *-wira* itself as well as the subjective stem to which it is attached,
is the notion that succession of the two events has been or is being
brought about by the sentient, intending individual. To illustrate,
I quote a few sentences from texts:

> hina*wira*biar: being *about* to arrive.
> yuptcha*wira*kila: when they were *about to* shoot.
> hlaqal*wira* hinada: *so as to* play I have arrived;
>
> > I have *come to* play.
>
> ba*wira* we're: *to eat* come; come and eat.

Each of the last two sentences implied planned succession. In translation, either the planning or the succession is rendered, according
to which meaning seems to predominate. In a phrase such as the
following, it is difficult to make the choice: huntchiyekilake[3] nopum
ba*wira*: they invited him, it is said, *before* they ate the deer; or: they
invited him *to* eat the deer. The Wintu hearer is disturbed by no ambiguity in such a statement. The distinction which is of importance
to him—that of voluntarily determined succession versus necessary
sequence—has been made.

> winyupe*wira*ibe: they *will* assemble; they *plan to* assemble.
> hawa*wira*ibida: I *shall* go.

-puke, as an independent stem, means *to be not quite cooked;
to be partly raw.* As a suffix, it indicates approximation, not quite
realized experience, whether past, present, or future. In English, it
is necessarily rendered as *almost, like,* or with the aid of the irrealis
would. It must be noted here that *like* refers to different degrees

---

[3] the *-kilake* (hearsay knowledge of the distant past) is affixed to all verbal
phrases coming from the myths. In translating, I shall give only the past tense
and shall not add the implied, "it is said."

in the realization of the same state; it compares the almost realized to the completely realized.

hitchuna*puke*da semum: I *almost* cut my finger.
hara*puke*da: I *came near* going; I *almost* went.
qotisa*puke*besken: strong-*like*-you are (I see); you look
  as if you would prove to be strong.

I shall mention one more subjective suffix, which, however, is attached not to stem I, but to the nominal stem of the verb. Like -*wira*, it occurs either without accompanying suffixes, or with the subjective suffixes. As an independent stem, *kuya* means *to ache, to ail*. As a suffix, it means *to desire, to try*.[4] Like -*wira* and -*puke*, it does not express a temporal relation to the present in which the speaker makes his statement; even the temporality contained in its relation to other events is only incidental.

hiina*ku*(ya)da: I *want* to sleep; tlowmi*koyu* (ablaut form of
  -*kuya*): *try* to kill him

To summarize: In Category I the form of the stem implies that the grammatical subject participates or has participated as a free agent in the activity or state described by the verb. The grammatical subject may be the same as the speaker, as in the first person, or may be different, as in the second and third person. In either case, the speaker participates himself, insofar as he has become cognizant of the activity or state described. Further, we have the attitude of the grammatical subject toward a contemplated participation; his attitude may be that of intent or purpose, (-*wira*), of desire or effort, (-*kuya*), or merely a reflection on its feasibility without necessarily a determination to carry it out (-*puke*). Lastly, we have the position of the speaker toward his own statement, indicating the exact limitations in the validity of the known fact to which he gives expression.

II

The stem of Category II is essentially passive, though it is used for many forms which we do not recognize as passive in English. It is used in the formation of the passive and the mediopassive. It forms the

---

[4] This relationship between aching and desiring is present also in colloquial English. We say that we are "aching to do it"; we are "dying for a ride"; we "crave companionship."

imperative. It serves to pose questions whose answers do not depend on knowledge on the part of the speaker or hearer, and to make wishes of the day-dream type. The suffix of ignorance, used variously to express negation, interrogation, or wonder, is affixed to this stem. Furthermore, to this stem of Category II is attached a suffix whose underlying meaning seems to be that of natural necessity and which corresponds to the modal suffixes of Category I. This suffix is used to express, all in one, futurity, causality, potentiality, probability, necessity; to refer to an inevitable future which might, can and must be, in the face of which the individual is helpless. Category II has reference to a state of being in which the individual is not a free agent.

In the statements of this Category, attention is concentrated on the event and its ramifications, not on the actor. The verb is not particularized in terms of participation. There are rarely any personal suffixes, and the speaker never refers to himself. He is not an authority. He speaks of the unknown, and when he makes his assertion, he asserts truth which is subject neither to experience, doubt or proof.

For the formation of the imperative proper, that is, for the issuance of a command to the hearer, stem II is used alone. Allied closely to this, and felt to be merely the first person of the imperative, is the command one gives to oneself—exhortative. In the expression of this, we have the breakdown of the rigidity in the distinction between subjectivity and objectivity. Either *-wira* of intention or *-le* of necessity may be suffixed to stem II, apparently according to no principle, but rather according to momentary preference. However, the breakdown is only partial; the *-wira* itself appears in stem II, as *-we(r)*. There is some reason to believe that the *-le* in this connection is going generally out of use. It occurs in old songs, and in stylized conversation in one myth. Only in the inclusive plural is the *-le* commonly in use now; i.e., only when the speaker includes those spoken to with himself in his exhortation, an occasion where a strong element of command is necessarily present.

To express an idle wish, which he does nothing to further, the speaker uses stem II with the suffix *-di* or *-u*. I quote a few such wishes to illustrate:

witil sniha*di* po: *may it* soon be daylight!
ewin be*di* po: *would that* he were here!
olelas po ni be*di*: *would that* I were tall!

The *-u* may form either an optative or a question, and its specific function can be understood only by context.

tera di*lu*: (at his feet) gliding down may I fall!
hekenbom weri*lu* paqam: from where shall we bring
    manzanita wood?
heken pele pominilheme*u*: where shall we set him down?

The two latter sentences could have been translated as optatives, as *heken* also means *somewhere*; for instance: from somewhere may we bring manzanita wood!

Stem II is further used in the formation of negative statements. May we take this to mean that the Wintu feels that not-being cannot be known? The function of the *-mina*, which helps form the negative, seems to be to emphasize the ignorance involved in the use of stem II. It takes assertiveness from the verb, and makes the verbal phrase contain, in disjunction, both affirmative and negative meaning. It is only the auxiliary words used in the sentence which give it specific meaning. In the sentence, it comes to mean negation, interrogation, or merely a sense of wonder over the unknown.

elebe nis nop minelpaqas koyu*mina*: not-do[5] for me deer
    die-for-want-wantnot; deer do not want to die for me.
    (*-koyu* is stem II of the suffix *-kuya*: to want).
eleukilake peh tin*mina*: not-did anything say-saynot; he did
    not say anything.
hadi henulebo Harry were*mina*: unknown whether-shall
    (actually *some-alternative-shall*) Harry bring-
    bringnot; I wonder whether Harry will bring it.
hestam nurum weril*mina*: which-did-you (or: how-did-you)
    salmon bring-bringnot? did you bring the salmon?

As already mentioned, there is only one suffix, *-le,* corresponding to the three modal suffixes in group I. It denotes the sequential relationship between events, a relationship which is, apparently, inevitable. It is a contracted form of stem II of the independent verb *lila*. This verb, in stem I, means *to make, to become*; in stem II it might be said to carry the connotation: *to become perforce*.

The *-le* takes a suffix when it refers to what we would call future,

---

[5] I translate *eleu* as *to not-do* or *to not-be*; actually, it means: *to not*. It is not a negative statement, but rather, a positive assertion of negation.

that is, a condition which is future to the time in which the statement is made. The suffix is formed from the contracted forms of *buha; to be, to dwell,* and probably contains a durative element. It is differentiated according to the three persons. The futurity referred to is a necessary futurity. According to context, one or the other of these concepts—necessity and futurity—is uppermost, though the other is always present. I quote phrases from texts:

> mia man minel (*l*)*ebosken*: you too *shall* die.
> mi uniharakila qotisa*lebosken*: when you get to be as old
>   as I am *you are bound to* be strong.

> There is an instance where a bird is instructing two boys
>   how to kill a flying monster. "She comes flying in the
>   evening," says the bird, "and her wings make a terrific
>   noise. mu*lebosken* lel weret: *you shall* hear her come
>   (*you can't help it*)." There is no element of intention in
>   this stated future. I have recorded a short love-song which
>   illustrates this futurity. A man and a woman, lovers, are
>   about to part finally. They sing: pelen tosmaliton be*lebom*:
>   the sleeping-place which you and I hollowed out *shall*
>   remain. The Wintu explain that this really means: you
>   and I can put an end to our relations; but we cannot
>   obliterate the place on the hill where we have slept.
>   It is that -*lebom, it shall, despite ourselves,* which give
>   poignancy to the song.

In the examples given so far, the element of futurity was predominant in the -*le*. In the following illustrations the concept of necessity lies uppermost.

> har walel be*lebada*: go, you two, I must stay (says the
>   bedridden man).
> In one of the myths, when the hunter sends Grasshopper to
>   Coyote with a message giving him directions as to how
>   to procure food magically, Coyote is in bed, sick with
>   starvation, and knows nothing of the hunter's kind
>   intentions. The hunter says to the messenger: hon*lebom*
>   baleso: *he shall* get dry before he eats. This is equivalent
>   to saying: he must get dry before he eats. He shall because
>   he must; he is starving, he knows what the conditions for

securing food are, and he shall fulfill them. But he has no
intention of doing so, as he knows nothing of this yet.
Compare such a future, with the future expressed in
Coyote's petulant threat to Grasshopper, who is biting
him on the back by way of announcing his presence:
ba*wira*ibida mis: I shall eat you. Even English recognizes
the weakness of such a future and renders it idiomatically
as *I have a mind to eat you.*

Concepts of potentiality, obligation and probability are undifferentiated morphologically. They are expressed by means of *-les,* the
nominalized form of *-le.* In translation, only, they have to be distinguished because of the necessary use of distinct auxiliaries in English.
In the following examples, the person is given by separate personal
pronouns (ni, mi), or not at all.

nurpaq ni hawal(*l*)es: I *would* choke on a salmon bone
    (if, or when, I went to the McCloud).
naname*les* mi: you *must* tell the truth.
ha*les* mi: you *must* go.
minelkila tchalu*les*: if he died it *would* be good;
    or: when he dies, it *shall* be good.
henu*les* ni: how *can* I (I wonder).
ni kute man tipe*les*: I am *able to* send off few sparks.

In the negative phrase, the concept of capacity comes to be distinguished from that of obligation and probability. This separation is
possible because the negation can apply to the potential event itself, or
to the potentiality of the event. It is the difference between saying: the
next step is not-potential, and: the next step is-not potential. The first
then comes to be reserved for the expression, "I cannot because I must
not"; or: "I would not because I must not"; the second for "I cannot
because I lack the capacity."

To express negative obligation the *-les* is affixed to the negative
auxiliary *ele(u)* which means *to not (do), to not (be).*

ele*les* ni yoqumina: I *must* not wash; or: I *can*not wash
    (*because I am not allowed to*).
ele*les* mi harmina kilepmabinte: you can*not* go, it is frightful;
    i.e. you must not go.

To indicate lack of capacity *-pina, to lack* is affixed to *-les.*

kenpana*lespina*kilake kiye: Coyote *could not* get up;
   (he was very old).
baskenperu*lespina*da: I *cannot* swallow food; (it would
   stick in my throat; my parents just died).
qayu*lespina*da: I *cannot* travel.

Due to the generic meaning of *-les* there can be overlapping of
the functions of *eleles* and *–lespina*. The sharp division, however,
is to be found between the "cannot" which has to be accepted because
nothing can be done about it, and that which can be repaired. There
is no suffix to indicate inability due to some purely subjective and
reparable cause; but the verb *iwiya* is used, when incapacity is due
to ignorance.

hur*lespina*da: I *cannot* sew (*because I am blind*); but:
   hurus *iwiya*da: I *cannot* sew (*because I don't know how*).

Without a personal suffix, the *-le,* as rendered into English, is
necessarily indistinguishable from *-wira,* due to the limitations of
the English language. Like *-wira,* it is translated as: *before, so as to,
about to.* Actually, the *-wira* implies free agency and intention,
whereas the *-le* does not.

When the *-le* means *about to,* an auxiliary *nuya* is often used
in the sentence. When the *-le* means specifically *before,* it is sometimes followed by the suffix *-so.*

saniha*le* nuyakilake: it was (*perforce*) *about to* be morning.
kenwanu*le* nuyakilake: it was (*perforce*) *about to* be evening.
kiyetchepet minel(*l*)e nuyakilake: poor old Coyote was
   (*perforce*) *about to* die.
ha(r)*le* nuyada: I am (*perforce*) *about to* go: I *must* go.
1. [6]holebo ba*leso*: he shall get dry, being (*perforce*) *about
to* eat;
     i.e. he shall get dry *before* he eats. This excerpt from the
     texts was given earlier in connection with the future. It is
     clear that the eating is not intended by the grammatical
     subject as he knows nothing about it at the time this state-
     ment is made. The *perforce* in this case would have refer-
     ence to the fact that the future is coming despite Coyote,

---

[6] Some of the following examples have been numbered so as to facilitate
subsequent reference.

the eventual eater. tintinpurebuhakilake hiina*leso*: they
sat talking, being (*perforce*) *about to* sleep; in English
idiom: they sat talking *before* they went to bed. They
went to bed by force of custom, as a matter of course;
talking beforehand was a matter of momentary preference.

tschus tlitiq*leso*setlamahnabuhakilake: (*perforce*) *about to*
gather wood, he sat thinking; before he gathered wood he
sat thinking. Gathering wood was a daily duty.

2. yole yoqu*le* tchawuwen: (*perforce*) *about to* wash,
let me sing a while; let me sing a while before I wash.

3. yoruna*le* yole tlitiqmina sukeda: (*perforce*) *about to* work
for wages, I stand a while working on nothing; I am doing
nothing for a while *before* I go to my job. (I have to go to
my job, but I can do what I like before I go).

4. harebo hlosu*le*: *about to* launder (*perforce*), let us go;
or: let us go *so that I may* launder; or: let us go *before*
I launder. Actually, when my informant used this, she
meant *so that I may launder*.

The -*le* and -*leso* refer only to the first and third person. The
corresponding suffixes for the second person are -*men* and -*menso*.
There is no particular significance in this change of suffix. There is
reason to suppose that the introduction of the use of the second person
in the verbal phrase of the Wintu has come after the development of the
other two persons.

5. waiken har*menso* . . . yelwinit: *before you* go over
the brow of the hill . . . look back at me!

6. kenwawu tepu*men*: open your mouth wide *so that
you can* get across.

7. hul*men* boi ba: eat much *so as to* get fat.

hima har*men* lel pominpana: *before you* leave tomorrow
morning go to bed. This is the translation of my informant.
We would have said: go to bed *since you must* leave
tomorrow morning.

8. we'e war sechosuna*men*: come *to* seek luck!

When we look over the preceding examples, it becomes clear that
the necessity in the sequence may lie either in that the indicated event
is inevitable, or merely in the relation between the two events. In either
case, the phrase shows an interplay between free will and necessity.

Event B is fixed; there cannot be an AB sequence unless event A
occurs; but event A is in the power of the individual. Such, I take it,
is the meaning of examples 2, 3, 5. Apparently we can also have the
following situation: there is a sequence AB; neither A nor B need come
about; but if A comes, B must come; so, if you want B, you must bring
about A. If you want to get across without drowning, open your mouth
wide (says the wily old man to the pursuing bear). If you want to get
fat, you have to eat much. So in examples 4, 6, 7, 8, the necessity
seems to exist in the first event, though, actually, this need not take
place except at the wish of the individual. We should have called this
a causal sequence, if it were not that causality is simply one of the concepts read by English-speaking people into the broadly sequential *-le*.

To give a complete description of this latter function of *-le,* it
would be well to mention another suffix whose function is the reverse
of this. Like *-le,* this suffix points to an AB sequence, but contrary
to *-le,* it stresses the undesirability of the realization of B. It indicates
that a dreaded event hangs upon the fulfillment of a preceding event;
if event A does not come to pass, event B will be prevented from
coming; or, if event C is substituted for A, B will be avoided. Instead
of the implication of *-le*: do, so that you may, it has the meaning: do
not, so that you may not, or: do otherwise, so that you may not. Thus
it comes to be translated variously as *might,* or *don't.* I found it
impossible to understand it, till the meaning of *-le* and *-men* became
clear. The suffix is differentiated according to person: *-kida* for the
first, *-ken* for the second and *-kedi* for the third. Examples follow:

elewen dumtchaharmina; toptchuher*kida* tlaqun: let me
   not go to bathe; *I might* get stung by a rattlesnake;
   or: *let me not* get stung by a rattlesnake.

tchaluma ih tal*ken*: look out, *you might* fall! or: look out,
   don't fall!

tchaluma winebiar yuptchu; mana*ken*: look carefully when
   you shoot; *don't* miss.

pia ih*kedi*: he *might* do it himself; or: *don't* let him do it
   (do it yourself).

–kilili tchinu*kedi*: (if you were to let her come) she *might* get
   the bulbs; or: *don't* let her get the bulbs.

It is impossible to do justice to this suffix in translation, as my
informant complained.

The *-le,* then, with its variants, is used for referring not to events, but to the relationship between events. Stem II, itself, implies lack of knowledge. The suffixes of the imperative, optative, negative etc., necessarily do not refer to present actuality. In short, Category II refers either to helplessness in face of events, or to ignorance, or to a future which, from a stated point of vantage, has not been realized. In this sense, Category II does not correspond to Category I, as it does not refer to that which is, contemporaneously with the present of the speaker, or of the grammatical subject. Yet there is a way in which Category II can be used to make, circuitously, a statement about the present. It does not describe this, but, so to speak, points to the ineffable. To do this, the suffix *-les* is affixed to stem II of the verb of being (*u-*) and is followed by *uni,* which means *thus,* forming *ulesuni*: *to-be-thus.* The Wintu sometimes translate this as *almost,* thus making it indistinguishable from *-puke.* But, *-puke* refers to an approximation, a stage in the process of becoming, whereas *ulesuni* refers only to a similarity between two disparate situations. It might be said to indicate appearance only. More often, the Wintu translate it as *like,* and as *like* do I translate it, ungrammatically, in the illustrations given below. The *ulesuni* is then used in a verbal phrase where the verb is in Category I and with suffixes of experience. We take it that the speaker likens something unknown to something within his experience. The burden of proof is left, then, to the event itself, not to the speaker; or, the speaker gets out of all responsibility for the truth or falsity of his statement by implying that something has the appearance, only, of being such-and-such, so far as he knows.[7]

> pom oltikal*ulesuni*kilake: the land flashed-*like;*
> (a metaphor; the land was covered with bright flame-
> colored poppies).
> seponora*ulesuni*kilake: he was running about *like*;
> *it seemed as if* he was running about.
> tuteliqta*ulesuni*kilake: took him in (into her mouth) *as it
> were* with one lick.

---

[7] The connection between similarity and appearance is thoroughgoing in the Wintu language. The usual word for *like,* or a *similar one* -oqti means etymologically: surface-of-the-identical. It has been formed from *uqa, oq-*: identical, and *-ti*: side of, surface of, and it might be taken to mean: the appearance of the identical.

heken kaha*ulesuni*kilake: somewhere there-was-blowing-
   like; there was something like wind.
tlitiq*ulesuni*besken: you work-*like* (I see); you seem to
   be working.

III

To conclude: The Wintu has a small sphere wherein he can choose
and do, can feel and think and make decisions. Cutting through this
and circumscribing it, is the world of natural necessity wherein all
things that are potential and probable are also inevitable, wherein
existence is unknowable and ineffable. This world the Wintu does
not know, but he believes in it without question; such belief he does
not tender even to the supernatural, which is within experience and
can be referred to by means of -*nte* (I sense).

The Wintu are not conscious of their own distinctions, or of their
own Weltanschauung. But, obviously, their coherent morphological
system is no accident, and must have been created throughout the years
because of their unconscious attitude toward the world without and
within them. It is doubtful that the Wintu developed by themselves
the various mechanisms by which they express this Weltanschauung.
The verbal ablaut is found in related and unrelated languages among
surrounding tribes; but there its function is either not regular or is
entirely different from its function in Wintu. Suffixes giving the
source of information are found in unrelated languages of neighboring
tribes to the north. The Wintu may have borrowed the ablaut and
informational suffixes from their neighbors or may have contributed
them. They undoubtedly originated themselves the idea of combining
the concepts given above under the one suffix -*le*. But the question
of origins is non-essential. Whether they invented, or used material at
hand, they have integrated a number of discrete grammatical phenomena into one consistent morphological system, to express their fundamental categories: subjectivity versus objectivity, knowledge versus
belief, freedom versus natural necessity.

Pomona College
Claremont, California

Categories of the Generic
and the Particular in Wintuˑ

To the Wintuˑ, generic concepts are primary and the particular is
derivative. I use the term *generic* rather than *universal* advisedly.
To the Wintuˑ, the given is not a succession of particulars, to be
conceptualized and classified under universals. Rather, it is immediate
apprehension of qualitatively differentiated being. For the Wintuˑ
speaker, the phrase *there-is-fog,* with a separate word for the subject
and the predicate, is only a grammatical alternative for his other
expression, *it-fogs.* He prefers an expression such as *it-roes* to *roe
exists, it darks* to *it-is dark*; he will say *she-soups* instead of *she-
makes soup. Round* is derived from *to-be-round, thunder* from
to-thunder, nest from *to-build-a-nest.* Actor and result are one
with the act. Substance is one with existence; it cannot be said to
be particular, as it is conceived of in European thought. Substances,
as for example roe, fog, wood, deer, are originally differentiated but
since they are not delimited, the particular is a secondary concept.

When the noun is separated from the verb, its primary form is
generic. It refers to a genus, to a kind of being; not, like the universal,
to a class. The primacy of the generic over the particular is to be seen
in different aspects of Wintuˑ culture. It is evident in their myths
where Coyote, Bear, Dentalium come first and timelessly, whereas *a*
coyote, the many different specific coyotes, come afterward, delimited
as to time and circumstance. In the verbal phrase, the category of the
given, or the directly apprehended, is primary; morphologically, it is
expressed by the simple, unmodified form of the stem. To express
activity or being which is delimited according to time and specific
personal experience, a modified stem is used.[1] The same attitude
is to be seen in the noun. The generic aspect of any object is primary,
and is expressed by the simple stem; the particular is derivative. These
nominal categories of the generic and the particular form the subject of
this paper.

I should state at the outset that I am now referring to what, on
cursory acquaintance, appears to be a distinction between animate

[1] I have described the verbal phrase in my article on *Conceptual Implications of an Indian Language,* in *Philosophy of Science,* vol. 5, (1938),
pp. 89–102. [Reprinted in this volume.]

and inanimate.[2] Upon my first study of the Wintu·' noun, I found
the expected grouping into animate and inanimate; I also found that
a large number of nouns were assigned, apparently at will, to either of
the groups. This I accepted as natural to the "irrationality" of language.
But soon the very basis of the distinction seemed untenable. Why
should live deer, presumed to be on a mountainside, be considered
consistently inanimate? Why should game slung from a man's
shoulder be considered animate, and game carried in a woman's
back-basket be inanimate? When I discarded the animate-inanimate
grouping, I could see the distinction between genus and particularized
individual within a genus.

I

Morphologically, the category of the generic is the simpler. The
nominal stem, unmodified, is used for subject and object, for attributive
and partitive. A number of nouns have a final -n or -m in the stem,
which does not appear in the category of the particular. There are
reasons to suppose that this was an old formative suffix, which is being
lost, rather than a suffix of the generic category; it is probably dropped
in the particular because of the particular suffix -'. The generic has one
morphological suffix -in, or -n after -i, which indicates a space or,
rarely, a time relationship, and serves to form the instrumental. The
relationship which in English would have been expressed by means
of *of* or *belonging to* is here expressed as a spatial relationship. For
example:[3]

k̓ as: live acorns.
k̓ as duya·: (she) gave acorns.
k̓ astɫal: live acorn shell.

puyuq: mountain.
ʙuiᴅiʙa puyuqᴅo·n: east-crossed mountain-disjunctive;
    he crossed the ridge of the mountain eastward.

---

[2] I exclude the kinship terms from the class of nouns. Kinship terms belong
morphologically with relational terms in general, such as relative pronouns and
pronouns of participation. For a fuller description see my article on *Kinship
Terms in Wintu·' Speech* (AMERICAN ANTHROPOLOGIST, vol. 42, 1940), p. 605.
[3] In the examples given throughout the paper, the verb as a rule occurs in the
stem of subjectivity without the usual suffixes which indicate time of occurrence
and source of information. This is because the examples come from narratives,
where the *-kilakε·* denoting hearsay knowledge is given usually only once at
the beginning of the tale. I render such verbs in the past tense.

puyuqinsu·s: mountain-at-stander: beings of the mountain,
   mountain beings.
Dol∈, Dol∈m: leg.
Dol∈m xaDalahara·da: legs weaken-progress-I; my legs
   are growing weaker.

The category of the generic since it refers only to a quality of
being, is adjectival in force. There is no adjective as such in Wintu·'.
The generic noun, on the one hand, and the generic form of the
nominalized verb, on the other, function as attributives. Good is a
derivative of being-good, bad is a generic noun, attributively used.
For example, the generic form of wintu·', person, means *human*;
as in wintu·'n bo·s: human habitation. *Black* tculu·li, is derived
from tculu·la: *to-be-black*.

The category of the particular has suffixes to express different
syntactical relationships. A number of nouns are given a strong
aspiration at the end, when they serve as the subject of a sentence.
Verbal derivatives, and a number of pronouns which have the force of
nouns, are given the suffix -t when they have the function of subject in
the sentence. The suffix -un (-n) indicates a possession and denotes the
agent of an action, whether this is expressed through the passive or the
nominal form. The object affected is indicated though the suffixation
of -um (-m); the verb which such an object delimits is not always transitive. For example:

xilit mintcuna· ila·m: Fly died-in-reference-to-himself child:
   Fly's child died.
no·Bum tło·mab∈·: a deer (no·B plus -um) he killed.
no·p Banabir∈·: deer (no·B plus -') must be moving about.
no·Bun q'ayi: deer's travelling; tracks of a deer.
no·Btcir: deer meat.

It appears that the generic, lacking specification as it does, has no specific syntactical relationships; the particularized noun, on the other hand,
has particular relationships which are expressed by means of a suffix.

Now the process of particularization makes its distinction within
a genus, not between genera. The function of differentiation between
genera is carried by the disjunctive suffix -Do or -Do·n, for the generic,
and -Do·t for the particular. The disjunctive suffix alone may carry the
burden of particularization, or may be added to the particularized form
of the noun.

DumDЄ·di . . . χanuʙaq ʙЄ·l ya·ʙaiDu . . . una· ya·ʙaiDuDo·t . . .
wЄri·likilak : Red-face (a Wintu·ʻ) grabbed it, they
(he and) the White . . . So the White-disjunctive (i.e.,
not the Wintu·ʻ) carried it home.

ʙiDЄp'urum usaDo.t hina qЄwЄl. UD ʙi ЄlЄu hЄnmina k'ЄDЄt:
(of a number of brothers who go hunting one is killed)
they some-disjunctive (i.e. those in the other class, the
class of those not-killed; the rest) arrived home. And
he did not arrive, the one.

Furthermore, the category of the particular must not be confused with
the "definite" of our grammar books. I quote a sentence to illustrate
this point: k'astɬal kЄndilЄ ukin tɬo·lDo'nin . . . χa.ɬ p'o·qDa . . . niqa·
k'astɬal tɬo·lDo·nin ʙ Є·s : live-oak-acorn-shell fell there in-the-cradle
. . . another woman . . . found live-oak-acorn-shell in-the-cradle which-
was. Here the second k'astɬal is obviously definite, yet it is in the category of the generic. The distinction is entirely incommensurate with
that made through the use of the "definite" *the* and the "indefinite" *a*.
Terms such as *the good, the ant*, as in *the ant is an insect*, are generic;
on the other hand, *the ant*, as in *he stepped on the ant*, is particular. On
the whole, however, the distinction corresponds roughly to that which we
make when we use an article (particular) or leave an article out (generic).
For example: *they ate fish at noon*, and: *they ate a fish at noon*.

The distinction between the generic and the particular is so far-
going that it is to be found in all the words which modify the noun.
Pronouns and kinship terms have different suffixes according to
whether the owned object is considered generic or particular. Adjectival words, including such terms as demonstratives and numbers, are
morphologically in concord with the noun they modify. When the
subject of a sentence is generic, the verb of statement will have an
existential suffix; but when the subject is particular, posture and motion
in reference to the speaker must also be given by implication. The
existential suffix now will make clear that the particular subject is
standing, sitting, lying down, moving toward or moving away from the
speaker. The category of the object also may be reflected in the verb.
The transitivizing suffix is -i·l (-wil) for a particular object, -ma for a
generic one. These, and especially the -i·l, are added on often when
the verb is transitive already, either so as to emphasize the category of
the object, or, in the case of the -i·l, to indicate action with.

II

A large number of nouns are assigned, as a rule, to either one or the other of the categories. My informant, when I questioned her about specific nouns, said that some were never found with suffixes of particularization, while others were never to be found without. Among those which, according to Sadie Marsh, were never particularized, we find two kinds: those which we ourselves consider generic and those which need no particularization because they are unique. The latter are represented by words such as: BOˑm: *earth, land*; holol: *sunshine*; k'oltci: *sky*.

Verbal nouns are treated as generic when they refer to the act or state of being; they are particularized when they refer to the actor. Whether this is merely a mechanism for distinction, or whether the act is regarded as unique, it is impossible for me to say. I give examples:

min∈l∈s: (gen.) dying, death; (part.) one who has died,
    a dead one.
min∈l∈sum win∈: (the) dead one (he) saw.
min∈l∈s haihaina'unaˑnt∈r∈sk∈n: dying (death) you like,
    so you said.

Nouns representing the means or implement for the act are also treated as generic. From łul∈': to sing girls' puberty songs we derive łuluˑs: a bunch of sticks for keeping a rattling rhythm while singing such songs; from t'amaˑ: to wear footwear, we get t'amuˑs: footwear. My informant considered łuluˑs and t'amuˑs as immutably generic. Words for delimited substances, such as water, smoke, rain, fire, wood she also considered as always generic. And in this category she included all dead things.

To the category of the particular, Sadie Marsh assigned in theory all people and live animals.

III

So far I have not shown that we have here in fact a distinction between generic and particular. The reader will say that footwear and earth and wood, and rain are regarded as inanimate, and animals as animate. To this I reply that often the same noun will be found referred sometimes to one, sometimes to the other of the categories, according to a principle which has obviously nothing to do with animation. Nouns representing dead animals are to be found in both categories, and, less frequently, so are nouns referring to live animals. At times, particularization seems to depend entirely on the whim of the speaker; at least, it is impossible for me to find the basis on which it is made. But, quite often, the assignment to the category of the particular is evidently a device, deliberately used.

Particularizations may be used to create a new word, denoting a delimited form of something commonly regarded as generic. I give a list of such words to illustrate my meaning:

s∈m: (gen.) hand or hands, including the fingers.
s∈' or s∈t: finger.
boh∈m s∈m: big hand.
boh∈' s∈': thumb.

mai: (gen.) feet, foot, including the toes.
ma': toe.

tłal: (gen.) shells of acorns, nuts.
tłał: (part.) mussel.

tc´oDos: (gen.) acorn bread, bread.
tc´oDos: (part.) bread flour, nowadays a sack of flour.

q∈w∈l: (gen.) house.
q∈w∈l: (part.) woodrat's nest.

This is a tribal convention which is not followed rigidly. For example, when Syke Mitchell told the story of the girl who ate her little finger and then her whole hand, he particularized the s∈m: hand. However, *little finger* has a special name of its own, so the generic need not be used for the purpose of making a distinction. On the other hand, the narrator has to indicate that he is speaking of one hand only; instead of using the more common *half-hand,* tc'ans∈m, he particularizes the s∈m.

And so with other words which are generic according to tribal habit, we find that the speaker will particularize whenever the occasion demands this. *Wood* and *fire,* theoretically, are never particularized. Yet, in a myth, when a man goes fishing at night, and holds up a burning brand, the narrator says: "pohum Dowuna·: the fire (part.) he held in his own hand." Recently the particularized form of po'' is coming to be used for *match*; for example, pohum q'artcu means *strike a match!* In the Bear and Deer myth, Bear sends the two Deer boys up the hill to get fire-wood. She says: "har win∈u . . . paqatc'us: go get manzanita wood (gen.)." They go up the mountain and call down to ask what

manzanita wood she wants. The answer is: "mis waie˙labo˙m BuD
w∈ri˙l tcalim paqatc'usum: there further-uphill-being (part.) that (part.)
bring (part.) nice (part.) manzanita-wood (part.)."

The clearest indication that we are dealing here not with categories
of the animate and the inanimate, but with a distinction between generic
and particular, is to be seen, I think, in the treatment of animals. When
a hunter loses his luck and can get no deer, we are told: no˙Bmai
wi˙nt'an ∈l∈u no˙B wi˙nmina: deer-tracks though-he-saw did-not deer
(gen.) see-not: though he saw deer tracks he did not see any deer. The
first no˙B is attributive and perhaps may rightly be expected to be
"inanimate"; but what of the second no˙B which refers to the live deer?
Dead deer, as a rule, are treated as particular when they are whole,
maintaining so to speak their individuality; when they are cut up, they
are so much meat and are treated as generic. I give below a list of
examples referring to dead deer. It must be kept in mind that game
carried by men is slung whole from the shoulder; carried by women,
it is cut up in pieces in the back-basket. When it is being skinned it is
whole; when it is eaten, it is merely so much flesh-food. I have added
two examples referring to dead salmon. In every case, particularization
is indicated by the -um suffix, since all the occurrences of *deer* and
salmon are in the accusative; the absence of the suffix implies the
generic.

> hari˙l q∈w∈l no˙Bum tɬomit: (he) took to the house (a)
>   deer carrying-(it)-slung-from-his-shoulder.
> no˙B harm∈ abam∈s: deer take (along) carrying-in-your-back-basket.
> no˙Bum p'irtcak∈n∈hal∈˙s: we might have to skin (a) deer.
> no˙B ɬo˙ma humus: deer (she) boiled fat; (i.e. fat deer meat).
> boyum no˙Bum tɬomit . . . BuD no˙B tɬa˙ma: many deer
>   having-carried-slung-from-their-shoulders . . . to him deer
>   they-gave-as-gift.
> no˙B ba˙wida: deer we shall eat.
> ∈l∈u no˙Bum tɬomumina unir ∈l∈u no˙B ba˙mina: did-not (a)
>   deer kill, saying, (he)-did-not deer eat.
> nurum h∈ni˙lkila: salmon when-(the youths)-brought-home.
> nur tɬamtɬama'ikilak: salmon (he)-distributed.

Yet a piece of meat, too, may be particularized, when it is a special
piece of meat. In one of the myths, a number of brothers kill deer near
the earthlodge, and in the evening invite their elder brother to come and

eat of the venison. They say, "Come, we are about to eat venison (no·ʙ)."
The brother answers, "That offal-fed venison (no·ʙum) you better eat
yourselves." Again, two men pretending to be on their way to hunt, say
to a woman, "You shall eat good venison (no·ʙum), that carried home
slung on our shoulders."

I am tempted to conclude that originally the categories of generic
and the particular were used to indicate participation and otherness
respectively, and that only secondarily they are used to make other
distinctions. However that may be, in reference to the body the two
categories are actually used to make just this distinction:—identity
versus otherness.

Except where a particularization is used as a lectical device, as
in the examples which I quoted above, the body parts of an individual,
while they function as part of that individual, are referred to the generic
category. The impression given is that they are considered as attributes
of the individual; the individual acts, feels, exists as an integral whole.
I quote examples.

> k'∈D∈m q'∈d∈m w∈n∈mhara·: one arm he-went-in; one of
>   his arms went in.
> s∈mpoqpoquna·: hand-clapped-himself; he clapped his hands.
> tc'anq'∈d∈m xandiE s∈det: half-arms (he)-fell-off Coyote;
>   one of Coyote's arms fell off.
> poyoq ko·m D∈d∈·kit: head whole (he)-was-bloody; his
>   whole head was bloody.
> sono tcuba·da: nose I-drip; my nose is running.

When grammatical subject and object are different, that is, when one
man does something to the body of another man, particularization is
used. For example, when the little bird is fighting the monster, he hugs
him hard and "he bent his ribs (particular)." But when the narrator goes
on to say that the monster, "ribs he-went-bent," she uses the generic.
Again, when body parts are physically separate from the individual
they are assigned to the category of the particular. For example:

> pu·rum ʙaDiłE: he took out the heart (part.)
> luba· pu·rum: she strung the hearts.
> But:
> ʙuD pu·rusłom∈s łuDtca: him heart (gen.)-exactly-stabbed. Since
>   we are inclined to identify the heart with the individual, we
>   render this as Wintu·' do: he stabbed him exactly in the heart.

However, the categories do not always distinguish the identical from the other because, once body parts are separate from the body, the words referring to them are treated like any other noun. For example, when head hair is part of the body, it is always referred to as generic, whether it is a head of hair or merely so much hair. When it is not on the body, hair remains generic, but a head of hair, such as a scalp, is referred to the category of the particular. For example maDom∈n qomosun Domoyum tconi·lar niD∈i∈' ibi·da: we are dancing with the hair (part.) of your elder relatives.

In addition, there is a large number of cases where particularization is not used as an implement for making either a semantic or conceptual distinction. In these cases, it seems to reflect the interests of the speaker, or even his momentary mood. It is not easy for the linguist to uncover the reason for the choice of category when this is purely subjective. The texts, however, give some suggestions. To give an example, I quote two lists of implements. One was given by a woman, the other by a man. Both informants are telling the myth of the little bird who fought the monster, and describe him as he is getting ready to set out. Jenny Curl tells of his putting "all sorts of things" in a sack: "barbed-stick (gen.), club (gen.), arrow-straightener (gen.), curve-topped-stick (gen.)." Syke Mitchell says: "a-drill (part.), in-the-sack he-put-in; and a-horn-wedge (part.) he-put-in, a-club (part.) he-put-in." The man particularizes; the woman, to whom these are just man's affairs, refers to them in the generic. Again, there is the case of EDC Thomas, who liked to dramatize herself. When she talked to me about flowers one day, she said: "Beautiful (part.) flowers (part.) I-have-found (part.); let-us-two-make-a-chain-of (part.) wild-azalia-blossoms (part.). When I read this to Sadie Marsh, she remarked that EDC liked to put on airs. Yet EDC herself sang a dream song where all the references to flowers are generic.

The distinction, then, superficially parallels but is not identical with the common distinction between animate and inanimate. It sets out into two different groups nouns referring to that which is generic in experience, and nouns referring to that which is delimited. The generic may imply participation, yet it may also be used because of a lack of interest; and particularization may be used as a purely lectical device. In paticularizing, the speaker may be following tribal linguistic convention; but often he merely expresses free and temporary choice.

Vassar College, Poughkeepsie, New York

Linguistic Reflection of Wintu Thought

A basic tenet of the Wintu language, expressed in both nominal and verbal categories, is that reality—ultimate truth—exists irrespective of man. Man's experience actualizes this reality, but does not otherwise affect its being. Outside man's experience, this reality is unbounded, undifferentiated, timeless.

In fact, if "existence" and "being" are seen as referring to history, to the here and now, then this reality cannot be said to exist, and the Wintu certainly do not assert its existence or being. Yet I must apply these terms to it, since I have to use the English language. Man believes it but does not know it. He refers to it in his speech but does not assert it; he leaves it untouched by his senses, inviolate. Within his experience, the reality assumes temporality and limits. As it impinges upon his consciousness he imposes temporary shape upon it. Out of the undifferentiated qualities and essences of the given reality, he individuates and particularizes, impressing himself diffidently and transiently, performing acts of will with circumspection. Matter and relationships, essence, quality are all given. The Wintu actualizes a given design endowing it with temporality and form through his experience. But he neither creates nor changes; the design remains immutable.

The given as undifferentiated content is implicit in the nominal categories of the Wintu. Nouns—except for kinship terms, which are classified with pronouns—all make reference primarily to generic substance. To the Wintu, the given is not a series of particulars, to be classed into universals. The given is unpartitioned mass; a part of this the Wintu delimits into a particular individual. The particular then exists, not in nature, but in the consciousness of the speaker. What to us is a class, a plurality of particulars, is to him a mass or a quality or an attribute. These concepts are one for the Wintu; the word *red*, for example, is the same as for *redness* or *red-mass*. Plurality, on the other hand, is not derived from the singular and is of slight interest to him. He has no nominal plural form, and when he does use a plural word, such as *men*, he uses a root which is completely different from the singular word; *man* is wita but *men* is gis.

To someone brought up in the Indo-European tradition, this is a position hard to understand. We know that the plural is derived from the singular. It is logical and natural for our grammars to start with the singular form of a noun or a verb, and then go to the plural. When we are faced with words like group or herd or flock, we call them, as a matter of course, collective plurals. Words like sheep or deer, which make no morphological distinction between the singular and plural, are explained on the basis of historical accident or the mechanics of enunciation. But to the Wintu, it is natural to speak of deer or salmon without distinction of number; to him a flock is a whole, not a collection of singular individuals. To us the distinction of number is so important that we cannot mention an object unless we simultaneously indicate whether it is singular or plural; and if we speak of it in the present tense, the verb we use much echo this number. And the Greek had to do more than this; if he had to make a statement such as *the third man who entered was old and blind*, the words *third*, *who entered*, *was*, *old* and *blind*, though referring to nonquantitative concepts, all had to reiterate the singularity of the man. The Wintu, on the other hand, indicates number only if he, the speaker, chooses to do so. In such a case he can qualify his noun with a word such as *many* or *one*; or he can express plurality of object or subject through special forms of the verb.

The care which we bestow on the distinction of number is lavished by the Wintu on the distinction between particular and generic. But here is a further difference. Whereas we find number already present in substance itself, the Wintu imposes particularity upon substance. We must use a plural when we are confronted by plural objects; the Wintu *chooses* to use a particularizing form. It is true that for certain nouns, such as those referring to live people and animals, the Wintu uses a particularizing form almost always; that for substances which we also regard as generic, such as fire and sand and wood, he almost always uses a generic form. But these are merely habitual modes of speaking from which he can and does deviate.

His distinction, then, is subjective. He starts from *whiteness* or *white* (hayi) a quality, and derives from this, as an observer, the particular—the *white one* (hayit). With the use of derivative suffixes, he delimits a part of the mass. We take the word for *deer* for example. In the instances I give, I shall use only the objective case, nop for the generic, and the nopum for the particular. A hunter went out but saw no *deer*, nop; another killed a *deer*, nopum. A woman carried *deer*, nop, to her mother; a hunter brought home *deer*, nopum. Now the

woman's deer was cut in pieces and carried, a formless mass, in her
back-basket; but the man carried his two deer slung from his shoulder.
Some brothers were about to eat venison; they called, "Old man,
come and eat *venison*, (nop)." The old man replied, "You can eat
that stinking *venison*, (nopum) yourselves." The brothers saw it
just as deer meat; to the old man it was the flesh of a particular deer,
one which had been killed near human habitation, fed on human offal.

I have recorded two versions of the same tale, told respectively by
a man and a woman. The man refers to a man's weapons and implements in the particular; the woman mentions them all as generic. The
use of the word sem (se) is illuminating in this connection. As generic,
sem, it means *hand* or *both hands* of one person, the fingers merged
in one mass; spread out the hand, and now you have delimited parts of
the hand: semum, *fingers*.

For the Wintu, then, essence or quality is generic and found in
nature; it is permanent and remains unaffected by man. Form is
imposed by man, through act of will. But the impress man makes is
temporary. The deer stands out as individual only at the moment of
man's speech; as soon as he ceases speaking, the deer merges into
deerness.

The concept of the immutability of essence and the transiency of
form, of the fleeting significance of delimitation, is reflected in Wintu
mythology. Matter was always there; the creater, *He who is above*,
a vague being, was really a Former. People do not *come into being*
as I say in my faulty literal translation of the myths; they *grow out of
the ground*; they always existed. Dawn and daylight, fire and obsidian
have always been in existence, hoarded; they are finally stolen and
given a new role. In the myths, various characters *form* men out of
materials which are already present; Coyote, for example, changes
sticks into men. Throughout, form is shifting and relatively unimportant.

The characters, Coyote, Buzzard, Grizzly Bear, etc., are bewilder-
ingly men and animals in their attributes, never assuming stable form.
Even this semi-defined form may be changed with ease; Grosbeak is
steamed faultily, for example, and turns into a grasshopper. The Wintu
speak of these characters in English as *Coyote, Loon*, not *a coyote*.
We have assumed by this they mean a proper name. But it is probable
that they refer to something undelimited, as we, for example, distinguish between fire and a fire. These characters die and reappear in
another myth without explanation. They become eventually the

coyotes and grizzly bears we know, but not through a process of gen-
eration. They are a prototype, a genus, a quality which, however, is
not rigidly differentiated from other qualities.

The premise of primacy of the whole finds expression in the Wintu
concept of himself as originally one, not a sum of limbs or members.
When I asked for a word for the body I was given the term *the whole
person*. The Wintu does not say *my head aches*; he says *I head ache*.
He does not say *my hands are hot*; he says *I hands am hot*. He does
not say *my leg*, except extremely rarely and for good reason, such as
that his leg had been severed from his body. The clothes he wears are
part of this whole. A Wintu girl does not say *her dress was striped* but
she was dress striped. In dealing with the whole, the various aspects
referred to are generic; only when particularization is necessary as a
device to distinguish toes or fingers from feet and hands is it used. But
when the leg is not part of the whole, when the subject is cutting out the
heart of a victim, then particularization is used, since the activity is seen
from the point of view of the subject. And when a woman is ironing
her dress, which is not part of her body any more, she refers to it as
something separate: *my dress*.

In his verbal phrase, the Wintu shows himself again humble in the
face of immutable reality, but not paralyzed into inactivity. Here again
he is faced with being which is, irrespective of himself, and which he
must accept without question. A limited part of this comes within his
ken; his consciousness, cognition, and sensation act as a limiting and
formalizing element upon the formless reality. Of this delimited part
he speaks completely in terms of the bounds of his own person. He
uses a stem, derived from the primary root, which means *I know*, or
this is within experience.

The definitive suffixes (in parentheses below) which he uses with
this convey, in every case, the particular source of his information, the
particular aspect of himself through which he has become cognizant of
what he states. The material he presents has become known to him
through his eyes,—'the child is playing (-be) in the sand'; or through
his other senses—'this is sour (-nte) or 'he is yelling (-nte)'; or through
his logic—'he is hungry (-el; he must be hungry since he had no food
for two days)'; or through the action of logic upon the circumstantial
evidence of the senses—'a doe went by with two fawns (-re; I see their
tracks)'; or through his acceptance of hearsay evidence—'they fought
long (-ke; someone told me).' In this category of experience, the future

is stated in terms of intention or desire or attempt. This is a future
which depends on an act of will and is not stated with certainty. This is
the aspect of experience with which the unreflective among us concern
themselves exclusively; as one of my students asked: 'And what is left
outside?'

Outside is the reality which is beyond personal cognition, a reality
which is accepted in faith. For this, the Wintu uses the primary form of
the verb. Alone this stem forms a command; yoqu means *wash!* (*you
must wash,*) a reference to a given necessity. With the aid of different
suffixes, this stem may refer to a timeless state, as when setting given
conditions for a certain activity; or to what we call the passive, when
the individual does not participate as a free agent. In general, it refers
to the not-experienced and not-known. To this stem is appended the
non-assertive -mina, and the resulting verbal form contains, then,
potentially both positive and negative alternatives simultaneously.
With the proper auxiliaries, this may either be used to negate, or to
ask a question requiring a yes-or-no answer; or in phrases implying
ignorance; but it can never assert the known. And when a Wintu gives
a negative command, he uses this form again; he does not say 'don't
chop' but *may it remain* (bedi) *unactualized-chop* (kop-mina).

To this not-experienced, timeless, necessary reality, the Wintu
refers chiefly in terms of natural necessity; by means of one suffix,
-les, (a nominal form of -le) he refers to a future that must be realized,
to a probability which is at the same time potential, necessary and
inevitable. Words modified by this suffix, are translated by the Wintu
variously with the aid of *may*, or *might*, or *would*, or *must*, or *can*
or *shall*. Another reference to this reality is made with the aid of the
unmodified -le. This suffix can be used with personal suffixes, to
indicate a future of certainty, in the realization of which the subject
does not participate as a free agent. It is a future so certain, that this
form, also, is sometimes translated with *must*; for example, "You, too,
shall die." Without personal endings, the -le ties together two events
or states of being in inevitable sequence, with no reference to specific
time. The sequence may be translated by the Wintu with the aid of the
purposive *so as to*, or *to* or with *about to*, but there is no subjective
purpose involved; or the word *before* may be used in the translation.

Now the -le refers to a succession of events in nature, and to an
inevitable sequence. But here the Wintu can act of his own free will
and decide on one of the members of the sequence. He can interpolate

an act of choice and thus bring about a desired sequence. Or the subject can intercept an undesirable sequence, by changing the first unit. The same stem is used for this, but a different suffix -ken (second person), which the Wintu translates either as *so that you should not,* or *you might* or *don't*; that is, the suffix warns of the pending sequence, and implies: avoid it. For example, a man shouts to his daughter who is standing on a ladder, *Be careful, you might fall off* or *don't fall off* (talken). Someone instructs two boys: sight carefully when you shoot, *so as not to miss,* or *you might miss,* or *don't miss* (manaken). And a woman, who hears that a rattlesnake has been seen near the water, says, 'Let me not go swimming; I *might get stung* (toptcukida).' Pia ihkedi (*he might do it himself,* or *don't let him do it*), is, according to my informant, equivalent to saying, 'you'd better do it yourself.' So the role of the Wintu in the future is not creative but can be formative, *i.e.*, it is either negative, or takes the form of an interpolation between necessary events. Here, again the act of will exists, but appears limited to a choice between actualizing and refraining from actualizing.

It is impossible to tell to what extent the reluctance to penetrate beyond external form is active in the formation of words. If the Wintu offers me an English word in translation for a Wintu one, I rarely have any way of knowing what exactly the word means to him. When he says that watca is to *weep,* for example, is he, like me, thinking of the whole kinesthetic activity with all its emotional implications, or is he merely concerned with the sound of keening, as I think he is? Whenever I find a group of words derived from the same root, I can clearly see that they point to a preoccupation with form alone. I find in my glossary a word for *to shave the head* (poyoqteluna) for example. There is no reason to question the English rendering till I examine the root from which it is derived. I find other derivatives from this root. One means: to *pull off a scab*; another *to have a damp forehead.* If there is to be a common meaning the first is not concerned with the activity of prying off a scab, or with the sensation of the skin; it refers only to the glistening skin exposed. Neither is the second concerned with the sensation of dampness, but, again, merely with the appearance of the skin. So, though the Wintu uses *to shave the head* as the equivalent to poyoqteluna, I am concerned rather with the activity of cutting itself, with the feel of the scalp, the complete removal of hair, whereas the Wintu refers only to the way the end result appears to the observer; his word means *to make one's own scalp glisten.*

I have recorded a word which applies to the pounding of non-brittle objects. I have translated it as *to pound to a pulp*. I have passed judgment as to what happens to the consistency of the buckeye when I pound it. But the Wintu is merely making a statement as to the external form of the pounded mass; from this word tira, he derives his word for terus, *tick*.

The same insistence upon outward form alone has influenced the the naming of White traits. Where I say *he plays the piano*, the Wintu says *he makes a braying noise*. I name the automobile after its loco-motion, an essential aspect of its being. But the Wintu in his preoccu-pation with form alone, finds no incongruity in classifying the automo-bile with the turtle as: *that which looks like an inverted pot in motion*.

Especially illustrative of this attitude are the words tlitiq and -lila, which the Wintu uses in situations where we would have used *make, create, manufacture*; or more colloquially, *fix*. But these English equivalents are far from the meaning of the Wintu words; -lila, which I have often translated as *manufacture*, actually means *to turn into, to transform*; that is, to change from one form to another. And tlitiq does not mean *make*; it means *to work on*. Our *make* often implies creation, the tlitiq finds matter, assumes its presence. *Make* presup-poses an act of aggression, the imposition of self upon matter; tlitiq also involves an act of will but one which is restrained and spends itself on the surface.

This respect for the inviolability of the given finds further expression in the conception of the relationship between self and other. Two Wintu suffixes, which in English are rendered as coercive, reflect this attitude. One of these is -il or -wil, used to make a verb transitive, when the object is particular. For example, tipa means *to cross* (a river or ridge); tepuwil means *to take across* (a child, beads, weapons, etc.). But the -il may also mean *to do with*; so that tepuwil may mean *to go across with*. There is the term bewil which means *to possess something particular*; but it also means *to be with*. The initiative is with the subject in both cases; but there is no act of aggression; there is a coordinate relationship. The word sukil, applied to a chief, I have translated as *to rule*; but the word means *to stand with*. We would say, at best, that the suffix has the two meanings at the same time; but the Wintu makes no distinction between the two concepts, except when he has to use a language which reflects a habit of thought that regards this distinction as natural.

Another suffix which, like the -il, deals with the relationship of self and other, is -ma. This sometimes appears as a causative; for example, ba means *to eat* and bama means *to feed,* that is, *to give to eat, to make eat.* Pira means *to swallow*; peruma *to fish with bait.* But like the -il this too implies a coordinate relationship, and one of great intimacy between self and other; for example a chief tells his people: (*with the coming* of the Whites) *you shall hunger*—biralebosken, *your children shall hunger*—biramalebosken (literally *children you shall hunger in respect of*). The relatives of a pubescent girl -bahlas— are referred to as bahlmas (*they were pubescent in respect of*). A man says, koyumada ilam; kuya is *to be ill*; the man says in effect *I am ill with respect to my child.* I use *in respect to* for an other which is not entirely separated from the self, and with which the self is intimately concerned. What we express as an act of force, is here expressed in terms of continuity between self and other.

I have avoided advisedly the use of the term identification here. This term implies an original delimitation and separation. It is the nearest that our social scientists, starting from delimitation, can come to unity. But if the Wintu starts with an original oneness, we must speak, not of identification, but of a premise of continuity.

We find this premise underlying, not only linguistic categories, but his thought and behavior throughout. It is basic to the Wintu attitude toward society, for example. It explains why kinship terms are classified, not with the substantives, but with the pronouns such as *this*; why the special possessives used with them, such as the net, in nettan *my father*, are really pronouns of participation, to be used also with aspects of one's identity as, for example, my act, my intention, my future death. To us, in the words of Ralph Linton, 'society has as its foundation an aggregate of individuals.' For the Wintu, the individual is a delimited part of society; it is society that is basic, not a plurality of individuals. Again, this premise of the primacy of the unpartitioned whole gives a valid basis to beliefs such as that a man will lose his hunting luck if he goes on a hunt while his wife is menstruating. Where formal distinctions are derivative and transitory, a man is at one with his wife in a way which is difficult if not impossible for us to appreciate.

There is further the Wintu premise of a reality beyond his delimiting experience. His experience is that of a reality as shaped by his perception and conceptualization. Beyond it is the timeless design to which his experience has given temporality. He believes in it, and he taps it through his ritual acts and his magic, seeking "luck" to reinforce and validate his experiential skills and knowledge, to endow his acts with effectiveness. A hunter must have both skill and luck; but skill is the more limited. An unskilled hunter who has luck, can still hit a deer by rare chance, but a skilled hunter without luck can never do so. The myths contain examples of hunters who, having lost their luck, can never kill a deer again. Now knowledge and skill are phrased agentively and experientially; but luck is phrased passively or in terms of non-actualized reality. The hunter who has lost his luck does not say *I cannot kill deer anymore*, but *Deer don't want to die for me*.

The natural, reached through luck, is impersonal; it cannot be known or sensed, and it is never addressed; but not so the supernatural. It can be felt or seen; it is personal. It is within experience. Such experience can be questioned and proof of it is often offered; the doctoring shaman produces as evidence the fish he has extracted from a patient, the missile of some supernatural being. Klutchie, a shaman, offers his knowledge of a coast language as proof that, during a pro-tracted trance of which he has no memory, he was carried by a spirit to the West Coast. But natural necessity is beyond question, and demands no proof. It is only implied; there is no name for it. The supernatural is named and can be spoken of. Toward the supernatural the Wintu performs acts of will. The shaman, speaking to the spirit he controls, will command and demand. But the man who dives deep into a sacred pool to seek luck, will say *May it happen that I win at gambling*. His request is non-agentive and impersonal; he does not address nature, neither does he command.

Recurring through all this is the attitude of humility and respect toward reality, toward nature and society. I cannot find an adequate English term to apply to a habit of thought which is so alien to our culture. We are aggressive toward reality. We say, This is bread; we do not say like the Wintu, *I call this bread,* or *I feel* or *taste* or *see it to be bread*. The Wintu never says starkly *this is*; if he speaks of reality which is not within his own restricting experience, he does not affirm it, he only implies it. If he speaks of his experience, he does not express it as categorically true. Our attitude toward nature is colored by desire to control and exploit. The Wintu relationship with nature is one of intimacy and mutual courtesy. He kills a deer only when he needs it for his livelihood, and utilizes every part of it, hoofs and marrow and hide and sinew and flesh. Waste is abhorrent to him, not because he believes in the intrinsic virtue of thrift, but because the deer had died for him. A man too old to fend for himself prays:

> . . . I cannot go up to the mountains in the west to you, deer;
> I cannot kill you and bring you home . . .
> You, water, I can never dip you up and fetch you home again . . .
> You who are wood, you wood, I cannot carry you home on
>   my shoulder.

This is not the speech of one who has plucked the fruits of nature by brute force; it is the speech of a friend.

REFERENCES

Dubois, Cora. *Wintu Ethnography*. University of California Publications in Archaeology and Ethnology, 36, 1935.

Lee, Dorothy. "Some Indian Texts Dealing with the Supernatural." *The Review of Religion*, May, 1944.

[The reprint of this paper in *Freedom and Culture* directs the reader to a later paper in the collection for the following further references.

Lee, Dorothy. "Conceptual Implications of an Indian Language." *Philosophy of Science* 5: 89-102 (1938).

_____. "The Place of Kinship Terms in Wintu Speech." *American Anthropologist*, 42: 604–616 (1940).

_____. "The Linguistic Aspect of Wintu Acculturation." *American Anthropologist*, 45: 435–440 (1943).

_____. "Concepts of the Generic and Particular in Wintu." *American Anthropologist*, 46: 362–369 (1944).

_____. "Stylistic Use of the Negative in Wintu." *International Journal of American Linguistics*, 12: 79–81 (1946).]

Symbolization and Value

In Western thought, a symbol is usually something which "represents," which "fits." We "apply" such symbols, as for example, when we "apply" words to things or names to persons; and these symbols then "stand for" the things to which they have been "applied." We even speak of "inventing" symbols; and our social scientists, worried over this age which has lost its values, speak of the need to "create" new symbols, so as to impart value to a meaningless life. This conception of the symbol as something distinct from and applicable to, can be held because of a mode of thinking according to which it is possible and desirable to abstract elements from a total situation, and to separate idea or form from substance. This conception is not a common one outside the province of Western civilization; and in many other cultures, it is inconceivable to make such a split. Here the symbol—the personal name, the picture, the emblem, the word—is an inextricable component of that which to Western thinking, it represents. And indeed there is a widely held theory to the effect that this conception is due to an inability to abstract, that it is the mark of a low stage in the development of the mind, apparently resting in the assumption that when human beings are able to abstract, they do so. Yet the most recent scientific thought, the most highly "developed," rejects abstraction as impossible. According to the field theory, elements are considered as incapable of retaining their identity once removed from the field.

The thesis of this essay is that the symbol is in fact a part of a whole, a component of a field which also contains the so-called *thing*, as well as the process of symbolizing, and the apprehending individual. In this view, the concept of the symbol is close to the original meaning of the word in Greek. The *symbol*, the broken off part of the coin given to the parting friend, is not a separate element, but carries with it wherever it goes the whole coin in which it has participated, as well as the situation of hospitality during which the coin was broken in half; and when it is finally matched with the remaining half, the whole has value because the symbol has conveyed—not created or applied or evoked—this value. According to the view presented here, symbols are a part of the process whereby the experienced world, the world of perception and concept, is created out of the world of physical reality, the so-called given, the undifferentiated mass, or energy or set of relations.

The system of symbolization, by means of which the individual punctuates, categorizes, shapes this physical reality, transforming it into the world of sensory perception and concept, is implicit in a variety of behavioral patterns within a culture. Language may be called such a system of symbols or acts of symbolization. It is not a system of names for passively sensed objects and relations already existing in the outer world; but neither does it fit experience into predetermined molds. It is a creative process, in which the individual has an agentive function; it is part of a field, which contains, in addition, the world of physical reality, the sensing and thinking individual, and the experienced reality. In this way, each word, each grammatical formation, is not an empty label to be applied; it has meaning, not because meaning has been arbitrarily assigned to it, but because it contains the meaning of the concrete situations in which it participates and has participated, and which it has helped create. With participation in situations the meaning of the symbol increases; and when the situation contains value, the symbol itself contains and conveys value. We have societies which proceed on this assumption, and systematically increase the content of their symbols.

A discussion of language as a system through which the individual transforms physical reality into experienced reality will clarify what I mean. By language, I do not mean only oral or written expression, but the entire system of codification underlying all verbal expression.

According to the classical view, the word is not the *thing*. This object that I hold in my hand is independent of the label I give it. It *is* not a pencil; I only assign to it the name pencil. What *it is*, is assumed to be independent of what *I call it*. Pencil is only a sound-complex, a word for the reality, the *thing*. But the sound aspect of "pencil" is only one aspect of it. When I call this "pencil," I also classify it, as a substantive, a noun; I separate it as other than the fingers it elongates. Is it a *thing* before I call it a pencil?

If it is not, then I am not "applying" a name to an already existing thing. This physical reality, this formless mass or energy, or set of relations, is delimited, is given form and substance, becomes the *thing* pencil, only through my calling it a pencil. In naming it, I give it recognition and a status in the categories of experienced reality. Calling it a pencil is the symbolic process through which I have created it; so that its name, or rather its naming, is a necessary part of itself, without which it is not this *thing*. And, conversely, its name cannot be separated from it as a self-contained element, it has no independent existence as symbol to be applied to an already existing *thing*. A Maidu Indian, for example, would probably have given no recognition to, or would not have delimited this reality into, the pencil as object; instead, he would have perceived the specific act of the hand—in this case the act of pointing with a pencil—and would have expressed this by means of a suffix which, attached to the verb, "to point," means: to-point-with-a-long-thin-instrument (such as a pencil or a straight pipe, or a cigarette, or a stick). There is no reference to substance or to an object in this suffix. What is a pencil to me is a qualification or an attribute of an act for him, and belongs to a class with cigarettes and other objects of this shape only in so far as they elongate the hand making such an act possible. If this can be called a *thing*, then the symbolic process has at any rate helped create different *things* out of the physical reality.

I would say, therefore, that the classical *this* is not the *thing*, but the reality itself. At the point where it is a *thing*, it has already been made into a thing. The word and the thing are not discrete elements to be related by the speaker; they are interdependent, incapable of exis-tence apart from and without the act of the individual.

Again, where we teach our children the proper use of singular and plural, we assume that we are teaching them the proper verbal symbols for an already existing singularity and plurality. But in this respect also, we find a difference in other cultures. There is evidence that the Wintu Indians recognize or perceive first of all humanity, human-being-ness, and only secondarily the delimited person. They make no distinction between singular and plural, and a cardinal number is never used with this generic, primary form of the word. They individuate, however, making a particular out of the original generic form of the word; out of *nop*—deermeat or venison—they derive *nopum*— (a) deer; out of *se*—handness, hand—they derive *semum*—finger. Yet here also, unless the Wintu chooses to use a separate word meaning one or several or giving the definite number, there is nothing to show whether the word refers to a singular or plural; *nopum* may be one or many individual deer; *semum* may be one or several fingers. When the Wintu want to show that two or more individuals are involved in the same situation, they do not use the *and* to express connection. They will say, "Mary we gathered wood," not: "Mary and I . . ."; "Coyote they mutually-grandmothered dwelled," not: "Coyote and his grand mother dwelled." *We* and *they* are primary; the specific, the singular, is derivative, and seems to be used only by way or clarification. That this is the way they perceive, the *thing* they create, is suggested by the fact that when they are referring to individuals who do not participate in the same situation already, that is, when they bring two individuals together in their statement, they do use the *and*; for example, "Shell *and* Fly (unrelated and living in different villages) each had a son." I find no instance, however, when the *and* is used to connect relatives, or individuals who are intimately connected, to put it in our terms.

The Wintu share this characteristic with many other cultures. Raymond Firth reporting on the Tikopia of the South Pacific, has to explain certain occurrences and terms of speech which are totally unacceptable to Western minds. There was one such occasion during a ceremonial cycle, when he saw several women assembled in a house. He asked a friend what the women were doing there, and received the answer: "The Atua Fafine (the Chief Goddess) it is she." For all his efforts, it is impossible for him to make this sound logical and acceptable to people who know that ten women are plural; to people who learn from early childhood that the singular comes first, before the plural; who, when they decline and conjugate start from one and go on to many, who soon learn that one plus one equals two, and later to speak of the one and the many, implying the distinction and the hierarchy even when they are questioning it.

When we try to translate terms such as brother and sister into non-Indo-European languages, we become aware of the share which our linguistic categories have in creating the *thing*, the so-called referent of the word. Take the word for brother, for example. In English, its referent is a "male considered in his relation to another having the same parents." Is the individual to whom I apply this word the *thing*? If the word, "brother," merely "stands for" an already existing *thing*, then I should be able to translate this word successfully into other languages. Only the sound complex will vary; the referent will stay the same.

But when I try to translate this word into Wintu, I find that, in the perceived world of these people there is no such *thing*. I need three words for this one referent, and one of these words has in addition reference to something which I recognize as a different *thing*. I need to say *labei*—"Male consider in relation to a younger male having the same parents," or *leikut*—"male considered in relation to an older male . . ."; or I must say *soh*—"male or female considered in relation to an individual of opposite sex having the same parents." If my word, "brother," refers to a given, a thing existing irrespective of me and my naming, then the Wintu and the Turks and the Andamanese and a large number of other societies perceive falsely; but how can I prove that I am right and all these others are wrong?

There is further the question of relations; are these found in nature and does the relational word then merely refer to an already existing relation? According to Western thought, these objects are *on* the table; the word, "on," refers to the present relationship between objects and table. Yet a Wintu who saw this might very well say, "The table lumps severally." At any rate, he does say, "The hill lumps," when I would have said, "There is a house on the hill," or "a rock on the hill"; and he says, "The hill lumps-severally," when I would have said, "People have spread their blankets over the bushes to sun them." In the face of this it is difficult to maintain that the *thing*, the perceived, is the same in the two cases. In one case, through the process of symbolization, two disparate objects and a relation are created; in another, a continuity.

I do not mean to imply by all this that communication is impossible. Ethnographers in the field have found it possible and even easy to explain what they mean by the word, "brother," and to understand what their informants meant by their terms for individuals having the same parents. What this implies, however, is that, for true communication, we cannot assume as a matter of course that our classifications are the same for people of all cultures; that translation is merely the substitution of one sound-complex for another. Once we are aware that the basis of classification is not a universal one, we can find out whether our different words do name the same thing, and if they do not, we can qualify our word. With such qualification, the English term can be understood; but I doubt whether, without repeated usage in relevant situations, this word will convey immediately, for the new user, the same *thing* which it does for the English-speaking ethnographer.

Before I continue my discussion of the symbol, it should be clear that, to my mind, nothing of what I have said applies to the metaphor, in the literal sense of the word.

Only when the symbol is defined as something made to stand for something else can the two be thought of as similar. There is further the strong possibility that, whereas symbolization is a universal process, the existence of metaphors is limited to those cultures where the definition of the self is that of something discrete and other to everything else. In cultures where the self is not conceived of as entirely disparate from the other, the word which seems to us to be a metaphor is probably only a means of pointing out the participation of one thing in another.

I have tried to establish that the symbol is not a thing, but that it is rather a point in a creative process, that of symbolization, whereby the physical reality is transformed into the *thing*, the experienced reality; that the symbol conveys the meaning of the situation in which it participates, and has no existence and no meaning apart from this situation. When we study societies other than our own, we find that the cultural behavior can often be understood only on the assumption that here, in fact, symbols are regarded as being, rather than standing for, the *thing*. For example, according to Wilson, the priest in ancient Egypt, the symbol of the God, actually *was* God; so that when he was honored or insulted, the God was affected directly through the symbol, not indirectly through a representative. Wilson calls this principle of the participation of the symbol in the *thing*, the principle of consubstantiation. Because of this principle, he holds, it was possible to put small models of loaves of bread into a tomb and know that the dead was eating actual bread. Among primitive societies, we have the Trobrianders, among whom the garden magician performs a magical act in the village before every secular agricultural act on the part of the rest of the village group. He works on one standard plot, and only in one corner of this; yet, when he rubs the small corner with his handful of weeds, talking to it persuasively, he is treating the entire village garden. All the garden land has been persuaded to produce good yams.

The Tiv of Nigeria furnish a case where a large group of people perceive the *thing* in its symbol. The case is related by Akiga, a Tiv with a Western education, who was skeptical of the reports of magical killings of which he had heard. At one time he heard that his father had killed and flayed one of his (Akiga's) many sisters, and given her skin to her brother to wear on the occasion of a special ceremonial dance. Akiga went to the dance to see what would happen, and there he saw his brother dancing, holding a woman's filter and his father's pipe. The following day, the people who had gone to the dance were full of the story of how Hilehaan had danced in his sister's skin. They were not trying to deceive anyone; there were talking among themselves, discussing the important event they had witnessed. They had obviously perceived the skin-of-Hilehaan's-sister (in the filter) who-had-been-

flayed-by-her-father (in the father's pipe). Only the Western minded
Akiga saw just a filter and a pipe.

In Western civilization, the difference in the conception of the
symbol as representing or as participating, constitutes one of the main
differences of doctrine between the Catholic Church and most of the
Protestant sects. The question at issue is whether, at communion, the
bread *represents* the flesh of Christ, or *is* the flesh of Christ.

When "primitives" are said to be incapable of distinguishing the
word from the *thing*, or to confuse an object with its name, I suspect
that what we have is rather the recognition of this participation of the
symbol in the *thing*. When we reflect on our own use of words, we
find that with us also, words do more than designate; they have more
or less meaning, according to the situations in our personal lives in
which they have participated. For example, when I teach, I can use
terms for the function of evacuation and for sexual activity freely, so
long as I confine myself to Latin words. Otherwise there is discomfort
and emotional tension. This does not mean that the Latin terms do not
carry the situation in which they have participated. They do; but what
they convey is the passage in the textbook, or the paragraph in a dictionary; and these are eminently appropriate to the classroom. When
I use the word, "micturition," it carries with it, perhaps, a number of
defining words, but not the concrete act. Anglo-Saxon terms for sexual
activity would heighten the emotional atmosphere and be very disturbing in the classroom. But not so the Latin terms; they may have participated in love-making in the experience of Romans, but nobody makes
love in Latin nowadays.

This is true also of the words for death or dying. Those of us who
have experienced death tend to avoid the symbolizing word in speaking
of these situations, because the word conveys the unbearable situation.
The need for a term is filled then by a number of substitute terms, such
as "passed away" or by differently phrased sentences which avoid the
charged word. Yet none of us feels the urge to do this when speaking
of people we have not loved. Julius Caesar died; he did not pass away.

The symbol thus gets its meaning through participation in the
concrete situation; and it grows in meaning and even changes meaning,
with each participation. Before it functions in individual experience,
it holds no meaning. To the child who hears a word for the first time,
the word contains the meaning of the situation in which he hears it,
including the mother's tone of voice, her gestures and facial expression.

To someone learning the use of a word from a dictionary or from a classroom definition, the word holds only whatever value is present in this situation; probably none. But once the individual uses the newly learned word, once a concrete situation is experienced through the agency of the word, the word contains the value of this symbolized situation. So the symbol, in this case the word, is a thing in process, containing and conveying the value which has become embodied in it, and communicating it in so far as there is community of experience between speaker and hearer.

When I choose a name for my child, for example, I may only choose it because it sounds well with the surname. Perhaps the first time I use the name, I am actually only "applying" it to my newborn daughter. But from this time on, the name is not just a set of syllables, an empty designation. From now on it contains Anna-ness, it is a name not to be taken in vain. This is an attitude which we have officially about the name of God. Yet we do take God's name in vain, and in situations where we would not welcome his presence, apparently firm in our belief that the name does not convey the *thing*.

Those of us who are concerned with the meaningless of life of our industrial society speak of the need for introducing value through creating new symbols. But symbols in themselves have no value, and they cannot convey value to a situation. Only after they have participated in a situation can they have value, and then only in so far as the situation itself holds value.

In conclusion, I shall speak about the Bella Coola of British Columbia whose culture was based upon the definition of the symbol as I have presented it here, and who proceed deliberately and carefully to incorporate value in their symbols through having them participate in situations which they imbued with value for this purpose.

Among the Bella Coola, an individual was not complete without a name. He had no definition, no validity, no status without a name. He could not become a chief, or a hunter, or a carpenter without the necessary symbolic ingredient. The names were embodied in family myths, and carried with them certain prerogatives with which they become imbued at the special mythical occurrence during which they originated. Names did not "stand for." When they had become duly validated, when they belonged to a person as the symbolic component, they could be loaned over a period of time, or rented out, or given away as a gift; and the name was no more part of the man to whom it had

belonged up until that time. At death, a man's names died with him.
They were now in the burial ground, empty of value.

An infant lacked value as well as validity and social place at birth.
If he was the child of a slave, he had minus value, unless this had been
"washed away" in the womb through a special ceremonial gift-giving.
When a child was born, a family name was resurrected to be given to
the newborn. But the name at this time was "as nothing." It was weak;
and the prerogatives it contained could not be validly assumed. It was
necessary to give validity to the act of giving the name, and to infuse
value into the name.

For the Bella Coola, the process of validation of this introduction
of the symbolic component consisted of displaying the whole situation
—the name with the embodied prerogatives and the myth from which
they derived—in a structured public situation; and in this display, in
the singing of the song which the prerogative contains, in the recount-
ing of that portion of the myth in which it is embedded, the symbol
participated in the situation. But, for the symbol to acquire value, the
situation must have value; and the Bella Coola proceeded to imbue the
situation with value.

The creation of value consisted of giving a gift; and the value
created was exactly equal to the value of the gift. When a name was
given to a child, or assumed by an adult, and thereafter whenever any
of its ingredients were publicly displayed, gifts were given away. As
the gift was given, it was "emptied" of value; it became "nothing." Its
value flowed "away" into the name which was being publicly displayed. The gifts made the name "bright," "strong," "heavy," "firm,"
"clear," "upright"; and the strengthening of the name was the strengthening of the individual, so no clear distinction was made between the
two. Occasions for strengthening a name or for assuming a new name,
and particularly of those which carried with them the prerogative of a
special seat, required the accumulation of large amounts of property,
and often included a number of specific ceremonials—such as the
dance of the returned dead—and necessitate the invitation of widely
scattered guests, so that the display might be sufficiently public.

Eventually, as the occasions increased in extent, as a man's wife
"drags across" enough names—prerogatives properly validated—and as
enough other gifts had been given away to "shield him from the fire,"
to "make him strong and heavy as he moves about the earth," to "make
his seat soft," to "shore him up so he does not wobble," the occasions

became extensive enough to be potlatches. After giving four potlatches, a man has accumulated enough value inside himself to be considered a chief; now "he is so strong, he can go where he will." In all this, it is never clear whether reference is made to the symbolic component or to the whole individual, "the thing."[1]

The exercise of a craft or profession was the display of a prerogative, and must always be validated; and with each display, the value of the prerogative was increased. A man could have the physical skill of hunting, the knowledge and judgment necessary, but he could not be effective, he could not be a hunter without the duly validated symbolic component. On the other hand, as the prerogative was strengthened through repeated display, it might become eventually stronger than the rest of the man, than, for example, his (material) knowledge. This was particularly the case of the profession of warrior. Those who had the prerogative of being warriors, had to kill upon request—without fee, since this was the display of the prerogative. McIlwraith tells the story of one such warrior, who was sick of killing, yet could not stop, as his prerogative had become too strong for him through his repeated killings. In the end, he retired into a cave one winter, and his dead body was found there the following spring; this was the only way he could stop killing.

A precisely formulated case of creating value was found in the so-called coppers of the Bella Coola. These were thin pieces of copper of a special shape and size, which were displayed at public occasions, and eventually were destroyed to "make bone" for a returned dead relative. A copper, whose recognized value was known as three hundred dollars was broken in two, or thrown into the fire; its value flowed out of it and

---

[1] It should be made clear here that, for value to be accumulated in the name, no return gifts must be given. To do so would be a deliberate act of destruction. However, other gifts were in fact also given by the individual, increasing his prestige, his non-symbolic aspect. Such gifts did not "become nothing." The giving of such a gift diminished the recipient by as much as it increased the giver. If the gift was not returned, the recipient remained diminished in being; if an equal gift was returned, he recovered only his original stature. It was to his interest then, not only to return the gift, but to exceed the received gift as much as he could, even to double it. When he did so, the original giver became diminished, and proceeded to give a larger gift, as soon as he could do so. These were not validating gifts, and did not have to form a part of the potlatch, though they usually did so; and they were clearly distinguished from those gifts whose value "flows away" into the symbol.

into the dead. Now the copper, which a minute ago was full of value, became completely empty of value.

Presently the owner of the copper picked it up and gave it to a poor man, who cleaned and straightened and repaired it and sold it to a chief for perhaps twenty dollars which could be spent only for acquiring food to be given away publicly. That is, the twenty dollars were given away as a gift to infuse value into the copper, which now contained value to the degree of twenty dollars. The chief now proceeded to increase the value of the copper. Perhaps he gave it a name with the appropriate public display; and he gave away fifty dollars to validate the display. He next invited guests, displayed the copper, had it passed from hand to hand—had it fully participate in the event—and gave away gifts to the amount of eighty dollars. He did this gradually, for all growth was a matter of time. He could not merely assign a value to it; nor could he infuse value into it all at once. Eventually, when enough value had been imbued, so that the copper could function at a dance of the returned dead, the owner flung it into the fire, and again it was emptied of its value.

The white traders quickly spotted the importance of the coppers, and before long had flooded the market with them. They thought of them naturally as having value, or as representing value; perhaps as analogous to our paper money. But the coppers neither had nor lacked value in themselves. They were symbols only in the sense in which the symbol has been presented here; they acquired and conveyed only the value inherent in the situation in which they participated. No one wanted to buy a copper unless he was ready to go through the long and expensive procedure of infusing it with value. So the flood of coppers brought no inflation; the value of coppers neither could rise nor fall, through such manipulation. Being true symbols, they could acquire valid existence and value only through participation in meaningful situations.

REFERENCES

Akiga's Story, the Tiv Tribe as seen by one of its Members, translated and annotated by Rupert East, London: Oxford University Press, 1939.

Dixon, Roland B. "Maidu." *Handbook of American Indian Languages*, edited by Franz Boas, Bulletin 40, Part I, Washington, 1911.

Firth, Raymond. *The Work of the Gods in Tikopia*. London: Lund, Humphries & Co., Ltd., 1940.

Lee, Dorothy. "Linguistic Reflection of Wintu Thought." *International Journal of Linguistics,* 10: 181–187 (1944).

—. "Notes on the Conception of the Self Among the Wintu Indians." *Journal of Abnormal and Social Psychology,* 45: 538–543 (1950).

—. "Being and Value in a Primitive Culture." *Journal of Philosophy,* 46: 401–415 (1949).

McIlwraith, T. F. *The Bella Coola Indians.* Toronto: University of Toronto Press, 1948.

Malinowski, Bronislaw. *Coral Gardens and Their Magic.* New York: American Book Company, 1935.

Wilson, John A. "Egypt." In Frankfort, Henri and Henrietta A. *The Intellectual Adventure of Ancient Man.* Chicago: University of Chicago Press, 1946.

Comments on subjectivity and things

In "Conceptual Implications of an Indian Language" Lee shows that
assertions in Wintu must be marked for evidence: subjective experiential vs. objective. That these differences in grammar and meaning
enormously influence speakers of the language is obvious to anyone
who has struggled to get students to distinguish sources of evidence
when teaching critical thinking.

The evidence markers in Wintu grammar are used in descriptions
that we would call temporal. But the differences from our use of
tenses, particularly past, present, and future, are so great as to make
one wonder how any translation is possible, as we see Lee struggling
to that end.

In "Linguistic Reflection of Wintu Thought" Lee explores more
fully how the language and the world view of the Wintu are connected.
She directs us to seeing how language shapes thought not by examining
this or that behavior, but in terms of the whole culture, the world-view
—what I would call the metaphysics embodied in a language and
culture.

Her description of Wintu suggests that the partitioning of
"the world" in Wintu is, in our terms, subjective:

> His distinction, then, is subjective. He starts from *whiteness*
> or *white* (hayi) a quality, and derives from this, as an observer, the
> particular—the *white one* (hayit). With the use of derivative suffixes,
> he delimits a part of the mass. p. *149*

> Recurring through all this is the attitude of humility and respect
> toward reality, toward nature and society. I cannot find an adequate
> English term to apply to a habit of thought which is so alien to our
> culture. We are aggressive toward reality. We say, This is bread;
> we do not say like the Wintu, *I call this bread*, or *I feel* or *taste*
> or *see it to be bread*. The Wintu never says starkly *this is*; if he
> speaks of reality which is not within his own restricting experience,
> he does not affirm it, he only implies it. If he speaks of his exper-
> ience, he does not express it as categorically true. p. *156*

This conception of how to live in the world was offered by Sextus
Empiricus in *Outlines of Pyrrrhonism*.[1] It has been derided in the

---

[1] Translated by Benson Mates in *The Skeptic Way*, Oxford University
Press, 1996.

West as impossible to live, a fantasy of life without commitment.[2] To express it in English we preface all our claims with "It seems to me that", which is tedious and unnatural. Yet the Wintu do it naturally with the use of evidential markers.

In "Symbolization and Value" Lee explains how our notion of thing is ultimately subjective, too:

> I would say, therefore, that the classical *this* is not the *thing*, but the reality itself. At the point where it is a *thing*, it has already been made into a thing. The word and the thing are not discrete elements to be related by the speaker; they are interdependent, incapable of existence apart from and without the act of the individual. p. 160

> The thesis of this essay is that the symbol is in fact a part of the whole, a component of a field which also contains the so-called *thing*, as well as the process of symbolizing, and the apprehending individual. p. 158

This is very much like the view I came to in trying to understand reference in "Naming, Pointing, and What There Is"[3]:

   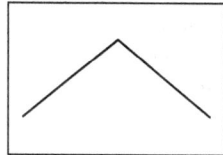

Sam   Louise

How many things are in the boxes? The intuitive response is, I believe:

In Sam: 1 (a line)
In Louise: 1 or 2 (2 segments? 1 line?)

Let's construe the diagrams not as representations of abstract lines but as actual physical parts. Now imagine my pointing rather than writing on the diagram, or better, imagine there's a clear plastic sheet with letters and dots on it that I can put over these boxes that makes them look like:

---

2 But see the rebuttal of this by Mates, op. cit., pp. 70ff.
3 pp. 77–84 of *Predicate Logic* (Oxford University Press, 1994, Advanced Reasoning Forum, 2012). See also the concluding chapter of *Propositional Logics* (Kluwer, 1990, 3rd edition Advanced Reasoning Forum, 2012).

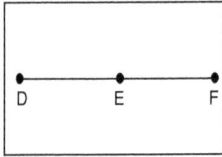

Sam

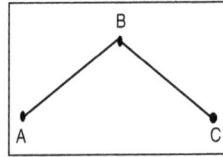

Louise

How many things are in Sam? It's still the same box.
    Or consider:

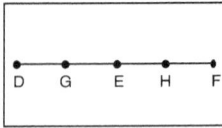

Sam

Now how many things are in Sam? Do we have more line segments?
Continue on—are there infinitely many line segments, infinitely
many points (real physical points)?

    What things we say are in Sam, what we classify as a thing,
seems to depend on what we pay attention to or what our attention
is drawn to, not simply on what kind of thing we are discussing,
though that, too, is important. Or perhaps only what kind of thing
is important: how many *labeled* line segments? But in Louise
no line segment was originally labeled. How many implicit line
segments?

    It's not what our attention is drawn to now but what we say
our attention can be drawn to: what pointing we accept, what ways
we accept for providing references for variables. Generally, saying
what kind of thing we are describing is enough. We rely on the
"obvious", our intuitions, clarified by specific agreements when
necessary, in determining what things there are and how we
distinguish them.

    It's what we pay attention to and what we choose to ignore that
is significant in reasoning. Even if you think there is one absolute,
overarching notion of individual thing, we don't (or can't?) use it.
Agreements on what things, perhaps what kind of things we are
discussing, and on what we shall count as pointing, are essential.

In this and elsewhere in my work I stress intersubjectivity,
coming to agreements, negotiating meaning, which Lee invokes
only implicitly.

Benjamin Lee Whorf

Grammatical Categories (1937/1945)

Science and Linguistics (1940)

The Relation of Habitual Thought and Behavior
to Language (1941)

Languages and Logic (1941)

Benjamin Lee Whorf (1897–1941)

[From the Editor's Foreword to the reprint of "The Relation
of Habitual Thought and Behavior to Language" in *ETC*.,
1944, p. 197.]

Born in 1897 in Winthrop, Mass., he was a graduate of M.I.T., and
served as a private in the engineering corps during World War I.
In 1919 he joined the Hartford Fire Insurance Company, and was
assistant secretary of the company at the time of his death, July 26,
1941. He began his study of Aztec and Mayan cultures, as a
hobby, in 1925. Within a few years he had become one of the
nation's leading Americanists. Many of his articles, the results of
field work in Mexico and the Southwest as well as of private study,
were published in *Technology Review*.

John B. Carroll has written a biography as the Introduction to the
volume of Whorf papers he edited, *Language, Thought, and Reality*
(M.I.T. Press, 1956).

Grammatical Categories

The very natural tendency to use terms derived from traditional grammar, like verb, noun, adjective, passive voice, in describing languages outside of Indo-European, is fraught with grave possibilities of misunderstanding. At the same time it is desirable to define these terms in such a way that we can avail ourselves of their great convenience and where possible apply them to exotic languages in a scientific and consistent way. To do this, we must re-examine the types of grammatical category that are found in languages, using a world-view of linguistic phenomena, frame concepts more or less new, and make needed additions to terminology. These observations apply pari passu to English, which hardly less than some American Indian languages is off the pattern of general European.[1]

In the reaction from conventional grammars of American languages based on classical models, there has been a tendency to restrict attention to the morphemes by which many grammatical forms are marked. This view loses sight of various word-classes that are marked not by morphemic tags but by types of patterning, e.g. by the systematic avoidance of certain morphemes, by lexical selection, by word-order that is also *class-order*; in general by association with definite linguistic configurations. At the beginning of investigation of a language, the 'functional' type of definition, e.g. that a word of a certain class, say a 'noun', is 'a word which does so-and-so', is to be avoided when this is the *only* test of distinction applied; for people's conceptions of what a given word 'does' in an unfamiliar language may be as diverse as their own native languages, linguistic educations, and philosophical predilections. The categories studied in grammar are those recognizable through facts of a configurational sort, and these facts are the same for all observers. Yet I do not share the complete distrust of all functional definitions which a few modern grammarians seem to show. After categories have been outlined according to configurative facts, it may be desirable to employ functional or operational symbolism as the investigation proceeds. Linked with configurative data, operational descriptions becomes valid as possible ways of stating *meaning* of

---

[1] The author wishes to acknowledge his indebtedness to his colleagues, Dr. George L. Trager and Dr. Morris Swadesh, with whom some of these questions of category have been discussed.

the forms, 'meaning' in such cases being a characterization which
succinctly accounts for all the semantic and configurational facts,
known or predictable.

We may first distinguish between *overt categories* and *covert
categories*.

An overt category is a category having a formal mark which is
present (with only infrequent exceptions) in every sentence containing
a member of the category. The mark need not be part of the same word
to which the category may be said to be attached in a paradigmatic
sense, i.e., it need not be a suffix, prefix, vowel-change, or other
'inflection', but may be a detached word or a certain patterning of
the whole sentence. Thus in English the plural of nouns is an overt
category, marked usually in the paradigm word (the noun in question)
by the suffix -*s* or a vowel change, but in the case of words like *fish,
sheep,* and certain gentilic plurals, marked by the form of the verb, the
manner of use of the articles, etc. In *fish appeared* the absence of any
article denotes plural, in *the fish will be plentiful* a pluralizing adjective
denotes it, in *the Chinese arrived* and *the Kwakiutl arrived,* the definite article coupled with lack of singular marker like *person, China-
man,* or *Indian* denotes plural. In all these cases plural is overtly
marked, and so with few exceptions are all noun plurals in English,
so that noun-plural is an overt category in English.[2] In Southern
Paiute the subject-person of a verb is marked by a sub-lexical element
(or 'bound morpheme') that cannot stand alone, like Eng. -*s*; but it
need not be attached to the verb, it may be attached to the first important word of the sentence. In English what may be called the potential
mode of the verb is an overt category marked by the morpheme *can* or
could, a word separate in the sentence from the verb but appearing in
every sentence containing the category. This category is as much a part
of the verb system of morphology as though it were denoted by a bound

---

[2] There is of course a minority group of possible or theoretically possible
sentences, e.g. *The fish appeared,* in which plural is not distinguished from
singular. But in actual speech such sentences are embedded in a larger context
which has already established the plurality or singularity of the thing discussed.
(Otherwise such a sentence is not likely to occur.) Such minority types are not
considered in the distinction between overt and covert, i.e. they do not prevent a
category from being classed as overt. In covert categories the unmarked forms
are relatively numerous, often in the majority, and are undistinguished even by
context.

element in a synthetic Algonkian or Sanskrit verb; its morpheme *can*
may replace coordinate elements in the same modal system, e.g. *may,
will,* but it may not, like a mere lexical item (e.g. *possibly*) be simply
added to them. In Hopi also there is a rigid system of mutually exclu-
sive 'modalities' denoted by detached words.

A covert category is marked, whether morphemically or by
sentence-pattern, only in certain types of sentences and not in every
sentence in which a word or element belonging to the category occurs.
The class-membership of the word is not apparent until there is a question of using it or referring to it in one of these special types of sentence, and then we find that this word belongs to a class requiring some
sort of distinctive treatment, which may even be the negative treatment
of excluding that type of sentence. This distinctive treatment we may
call the *reactance* of the category. In English, intransitive verbs form
a covert category marked by lack of the passive participle and the
passive and causative voices; we cannot substitute a verb of this class
(e.g. *go, lie, sit, rise, gleam, sleep, arrive, appear, rejoice*) into such
sentences as *It was cooked, It was being cooked, I had it cooked to
order.* An intransitive thus configuratively defined is quite a different
thing from the 'dummy' intransitive used in traditional English
grammar; it is a true grammatical class marked by these and other
constant grammatical features, such as non-occurrence of nouns or
pronouns after the verb; one does not say *I gleamed it, I appeared
the table.* Of course compound formations involving these same
lexemes may be transitive, e.g. *sleep (it) off, go (him) one better.*
In the American colloquial forms *go haywire, go South Sea Islander,*
etc., the word or phrase after the verb is a covert adjective, cf. *go
completely haywire.*

Another type of covert category is represented by English gender.
Each common noun and personal given name belongs to a certain
gender class, but a characteristic overt mark appears only when there
is occasion to refer to the noun by a personal pronoun in the singular
number—or in the case of the neuter it may be marked by the interrogative and relative pronouns *what, which.* The grammatical alignment
is no less strict than in an overt gender system like that of Latin, where
most nouns bear their gender mark. No doubt for many English
common nouns a knowledge of actual sex and of scientific biological
and physical classification of objects could serve a foreigner in lieu of
knowledge of the grammatical classes themselves, but such knowledge

would be of only limited use after all, for the greater part of the masculine and feminine classes consists of thousands of personal names, and a foreigner who knows nothing of the cultural background of Western European Christian names must simply learn, i.e. observe, that *Jane* belongs to the 'she' group and *John* to the 'he' group. There are plenty of names of overt similarity, but contrasted gender, e.g. *Alice: Ellis, Alison: Addison, Audrey: Aubrey, Winifred: Wilfred, Myra: Ira, Ester: Lester.*[3] Nor would knowledge of any 'natural' properties tell our observer that the names of biological classes themselves (e.g. *animal, bird, fish,* etc.) are 'it'; that smaller animals usually are 'it'; larger animals often 'he'; dogs, eagles, and turkeys usually 'he'; cats and wrens usually 'she'; body-parts and the whole botanical world 'it'; countries and states as fictive persons (but not as localities) 'she'; cities, societies, and corporations as fictive persons 'it'; the human body 'it'; a ghost 'it'; nature 'she'; watercraft with sail or power and named small craft 'she'; unnamed rowboats, canoes, rafts 'it', etc. The mistakes in English gender made by learners of the language, including those whose own languages are without gender, would alone show that we have here grammatical categories, and not reflections in speech of natural and non-cultural differences.

The classes of nouns based actually or ostensibly upon shape, in various American languages, may be either overt or covert. In Navaho they are covert. Some terms belong to the round (or roundish) class, others to the long-object class, others fall into classes not dependent on shape. No overt mark designates the class in every sentence. The class mark as in English gender is a reactance; not a pronoun, however, but a choice between certain verb stems that go definitely with one class and no other, although there are very many verb stems indifferent to this distinction. I doubt that such distinctions, at least in Navaho, are simply linguistic recognitions of non-linguistic, objective differences that would be the same for all observers, any more than the English genders are; they seem rather to be covert grammatical categories. Thus one must learn as a part of learning Navaho that 'sorrow' belongs in the 'round' class. One's first and 'common sense' impression of

[3] There are a very few names of indeterminate or double gender: *Frances* (*Francis*), *Jessie* (*Jesse*) or *Jess, Jean* (*Gene*), *Jocelyn, Sidney, Wynne,* and perhaps a few others. The number is increased if we include nicknames like *Bobby, Jerry,* etc.; but all in all such cases are relatively so few that they in no way disturb our alignment of facts.

covert categories like English gender and Navaho shape-class is that
they are simply distinctions between different kinds of experience or
knowledge; that we say *Jane went to her house* because we know that
Jane is a female. Actually we need not know anything about Jane, Jane
may be merely a name; yet having heard this name, perhaps over the
telephone, we say *What about her?*. Common-sense may then retreat
a step further and say that we know the name Jane to be given only to
females. But such experience is linguistic; it is learning English by
observation. Moreover it is easy to show that the pronoun agrees with
the name only, not with the experience. I can bestow the name *Jane*
on an automobile, a skeleton, or a cannon, and it will still require *she*
in pronominal references. I have two goldfish; I name one *Jane* and
one *Dick*. I can still say *Each goldfish likes its food*, but not *Jane
likes its food better than Dick*. I must say *Jane likes her food*. The
word *dog* belongs to a common gender class with a preference for *he*
or *it*, but the gender-classed given name of a dog determines its own
pronoun; we do not say *Tom came out if its kennel*, but *Tom came out
of his kennel*. 'Doggish' names like *Fido* are the 'he' class: *Towser
came out of his kennel*. We say *See the cat chase her tail*, but never
See Dick chase her tail. The words *child, baby, infant* belong to the
common class and can take *it*, but the given names of children take
either *he* or *she*. I can say *My baby enjoys its food*, but it would be
linguistically wrong to say *My baby's name is Helen—see how Helen
enjoys its food*. Nor can I say *My little daughter enjoys its food*, for
daughter, unlike *baby*, is grammatically in the feminine class.

   Likewise with various covert categories of exotic languages; where
they have been thought to be recognitions of objective differences, it
may rather be that they are grammatical categories that merely accord
up to a certain point with objective experience. They may represent
experience, it is true, but experience seen in terms of a definite linguistic scheme, not experience that is the same for all observers. On the
other hand, the distinctions between present and absent, visible and
invisible, made in many American languages, may well represent
experiential differences; and again we may have such experiential
differences engrafted upon purely grammatical classifications, yielding
mixed classes such as 'experiential-present plus grammatical-feminine'.

   A covert category may also be termed a *cryptotype*, a name which
calls attention to the rather hidden, cryptic nature of such word-groups,
especially when they are not strongly contrasted in idea, nor marked by

frequently-occurring reactances such as pronouns. They easily escape notice and may be hard to define, and yet may have profound influence on linguistic behavior. The English intransitive verbs as configuratively defined above are a cryptotype. A similar cryptotype comprises the verbs of 'copulative resolution' (*be, become, seem, stay, remain*, etc.), which also lack the passive and causative but may be followed by nouns, pronouns, and adjectives. Transitives (a cryptotype which includes *run, walk, return*, etc.—indeed most English verbs) possess the passive and causative and may be followed by nouns and pronouns but not by adjectives alone. Names of countries and cities in English form a cryptotype with the reactance that they are not referred to by personal pronouns as object of the prepositions *in, at, to, from*. We can say *I live in Boston* but not *That's Boston—I live in it*. A word of this cryptotype is referred to by *there* or *here* in place of *in it, at it, to it*, and by *from there (here)* in place of *from it*. In various American languages such place-names constitute a grammatical class; in Hopi they lack the nominative and objective cases, occurring only in locational cases; in Aztec they bear characteristic endings and exclude the use of certain prepositions.

English adjectives form two main cryptotypes with sub-classes. A group referring to 'inherent' qualities—including color, material, physical state (solid, liquid, porous, hard, etc.), provenience, breed, nationality, function, use—has the reactance of being placed nearer the noun than the other group, e.g., *large red house* (not *red large house*), *steep rocky hill, nice smooth floor*. The order may be reversed to make a balanced contrast, but only by changing the normal stress pattern, and the form is at once sensed as being reversed and peculiar. The normal pattern has primary stress either on the noun (*steep rocky hi´ll*) or on the inherent adjective (*pretty Fre´nch girl*). We cannot simply reverse the order of adjectives and say *French pre´tty girl*—the form suggests a contrasted *French plai´n girl* but the pattern of so contrasting adjectives is un-English; the proper contrast is *plai´n French girl*. We can however reverse the adjectives by altering the stress patter and say *Fre´nch pretty girl*, if in contrast with e.g. *Spa´nish pretty girl*, though such forms are clearly exceptional.

The contrasting *phenotype* may be applied to the overt category and, when no ambiguity results, to the mark which accompanies the overt category of the sentence.

The distinction between overt and covert categories, or *phenotypes*

and *cryptotypes*, is one of two distinctions of supreme importance
in the theory of grammatical categories. The other is the distinction
between what may be called *selective categories* and *modulus
categories*.

A selective category is a grammatical class with membership fixed,
and limited as compared with some larger class. A *primary* selective
category, or *lexemic* category, is one compared to which the next
larger class is the total lexicon of the language. Certain semantic and
grammatical properties are assured in the word by selecting it from
a certain class of fixed membership not coterminous with the whole
vocabulary. In order that a certain grammatical property may be 'in the
lexeme' it cannot be in all lexemes. The familiar 'parts of speech' of
most European languages, but not of English, are lexemic categories.
The situation in English is peculiar, and will be touched on later.
Lexemic categories may be either overt or covert. Hopi is an example
of a language in which they are covert. Possibly Maya may be another
such case, though we lack clear information on this point. In Hopi
there is no distinction in the simplex (bare stem) forms between nouns
and verbs, and sentences are possible in which there is no distinction
in the sentence. Thus *le·'na* or *pam le· 'na* means 'it is a flute'
And *pe·'na* means 'he writes it'. Hence nouns and verbs *may be*
alike in overt characteristics. But it is easily possible to make sentences
in which *le·'na* appears with case suffixes and in other forms quite
impossible for *pe·'na*, and vice versa. One has to learn, and cannot
always tell from the sentence, that *le· 'na* and *pe· 'na* belong to
different compartments of the lexicon.

It is probably more common to find lexemic classes that are overt,
as in Latin, French, Aztec, Tübatulabal, Taos, and Navaho. In French,
ange and *mange* belong to different compartments of the vocabulary
(noun and verb) and there is always a feature in the sentence that tells
which: one does not find such pairs as *il mange: il ange, c'est un
ange: c'est mange*. It may be possible to have *Ange!* versus *Mange!*,
but special and abbreviated types of sentence like these with their lack
of formal distinctions do not justify calling the categories covert. In
Latin, Aztec, Tübatulabal, and Taos, the distinction is marked not only
in the sentence, but usually in the paradigm word itself. Yet this overt
mark of the noun, verb, or other 'part of speech' cannot usually be
transferred to a lexeme outside of the proper group. The mark that
goes with a covert lexemic class need not stand for any other category

such as case, person, or tense, though it does e.g. in Latin, Greek, and Sanskrit. The 'absolutive suffixes' found attached to lexemic nouns in most Uto-Aztecan languages have basically no other character than that of class-marks, though in Aztec they are also tied up with number; and needless ingenuity has been wasted in trying to make them out to be 'articles' or the like. The absolutive suffixes in Taos go with the selective class of nouns but indicate gender and number also. In Latin the distinction between the nouns (including in this class the adjectives) and the verbs is selective and covert; compare *est gladius* and *est bonus*. As with all covert classes, the distinction is revealed upon forming the proper type of sentence; *est bona* occurs, but not *est gladia*.

Lexemic categories include not only nouns, verbs, adjectives, and other 'parts of speech', but also 'full' words and 'empty'[4] words or stems, as in Chinese and perhaps the Wakashan languages, and still other types of distinction; e.g. in Algonkian the lexemic classes include large groups of stems having different combinatory powers and different positions in the verbal complex.

A modulus category is a non-selective category, i.e. it is generally applicable and removable at will. Depending on its type it may be applied either to any 'major word' (any word excepting small and specialized classes, e.g. 'particles'), or, more often, to any word coming within a certain pre-requisite larger category, which may be either selective or another modulus category. The cases, tenses, aspects, modes, and voices of Indo-European and Azteco-Tanoan[5] languages are modulus categories, applicable at will to words belonging to the proper larger category — cases being moduli of the larger category of nouns; aspects, tenses, etc. moduli of the larger category of verbs. Hence the person versed only in Indo-European types of grammar poses to himself the distinction between selective and modulus classes (or between selectivity and modulation) as the distinction between 'parts of speech' on the one hand and 'grammatical forms' of the aspect, tense, and voice type on the other. But in widely

---

[4] An 'empty' word or stem is probably one that is highly specialized for grammatical or syntactic indication, perhaps in a way that does not admit of being assigned a concrete meaning. For example, such a form might have no other meaning than to serve as the reactance of some other category, or as the signature of a modulus category (see the next paragraph).

[5] B. L. Whorf and George Trager, The Relationship of Uto-Aztecan and Tanoan, American Anthropologist 39.609–24 (1937).

different types of speech these familiar types of meaning and function
cease to be associated with selectivity and modulation in the same way;
entirely different alignments there hold sway in the grammar, and until
this is recognized an adequate conception of the grammar cannot be
obtained. It is not necessary to have large categories, such as nouns
and verbs, in order to have modulus categories as aspect. In Nitinat[6]
(and presumably in the closely related Nootka and Kwakiutl) all major
words have aspects, such as durative, momentaneous, inceptive, etc.—
both the word for 'run' and the word for 'house' always bear some
element marking this aspect.

We may use the term modulus alone to denote the distinctive class
meaning and function of the category; thus the present-participle meaning is a modulus in English. We may also use modulus to mean the
grammatical operation of producing one such meaning, and hence,
when no ambiguity results, to mean the element or pattern that marks
the modulus. Thus we can say that in English the present-participle
modulus is the suffixing *-ing,* or for short that it is *-ing.* Where
greater preciseness is desirable, we may call the overt mark the (or a)
signature of the modulus. This distinction is ultimately important;
sometimes it is necessary to distinguish several signatures of the same
modulus. In illustrating overt categories we cited the English noun-
plural, which is a modulus category. The modulus, or plural type of
meaning, is one and the same thing throughout the examples; but the
signatures whereby this plural modulus may be applied to the word
fish are different from one example to another. To these signatures we
may add *-s* or *-es,* giving *fishes.* Since *sheep, deer, moose, caribou,*
etc. belong to a cryptotype that excludes *-s,* and 'fishermen's fish'
such as *trout, bass, salmon, mackerel, cod,* etc. (contrasted with 'low-
grade fish', e.g. *sharks, skates, eels, sculpins,* etc.) belong to another
cryptotype, we cannot use this last signature for them. As this example
shows, it is not necessary to have a one-to-one correspondence between
moduli and signatures. Where a high degree of such one-to-one correspondence obtains it has often been the custom to apply the graphic
but not very scientific catchword 'agglutinative' to the language.
Languages of the typical 'agglutinative' type, such as Turkish, have
been referred to as if they had such one-to-one correspondence, and
moreover as if they had no categories but modulus categories. The

---

[6] See Mary Haas Swadesh and Morris Swadesh, A Visit to the Other World:
a Nitinat Text, IJAL 7.3–4 (1933).

grammar of Yana (Hokan stock, California) consists largely of moduli, but has also a few selective categories, e.g. a class of stems which must first stand in the verbal complex and a class which must stand second.

A distinction of the same semantic type as that between verbs and nouns in selective categories may be handled by modulus categories instead. That is, the possible moduli include not only voice, aspect, etc., but also *verbation* and *stativation*.[7] Whenever, as e.g. in Yana, the mere application of certain distinctive suffixes or other signatures makes a 'verb' out of any stem, then we do not have a class of verbs in the same sense as in French, Latin, Greek, Hopi, Axtec [sic], Taos, and Navaho, i.e. a selective class. We have verbations instead of such verbs. The so-called verbs and nouns of Semitic are moduli, applicable to lexemes in general by signatures consisting largely of vowel-consonant sequence patterns, though there may be occasional gaps in the universality of lexical applicability. In Hebrew we have *e-e* as one of several signatures for statitivation and *ā-a* as one of several for verbation, e.g. *berek*[8] 'knee': *bārak* 'he kneeled', *derek* 'road': *dārak* 'he marched', *geber* 'man, as virile or strong': *gābar* 'he was strong', *hebel* 'cord': *hābal* 'he bound', *melek* 'king: *mālak* 'he reigned', *qedem* 'antecedence': *qādam* 'he was before', *regel* 'foot': *rāgal* 'he went on foot'. There are no doubt many Hebrew 'nouns' for which we do not know the verbation form in texts, but this seems to be largely because the textual Hebrew that we know does not represent the full resources of the ancient living language; Arabic shows better the general applicability of these moduli to the great majority of lexemes. But verbs and nouns which are modulus categories may be found nearer home than Semitic. The lexicon of English contains two major selective divisions. One division,

---

[7] Stativation is a term used to denote the modulus of forms which are contrasted with verbations in a way similar to that in which nouns, as a selective category, are contrasted with verbs in the languages that have such a contrast. It is used here instead of 'nomination' or 'nominalization' because these terms through past usage have come to suggest derivations rather than moduli, while 'stativation' helps us think of the form not as a noun derived from a verb, but simply as a lexeme which has been affected by a certain meaningful grammatical coloring as part of certain configurations.

[8] Since these Hebrew examples are used only to illustrate vowel-patterns, they are written in approximate morphophonemic orthography, which does not attempt to show the distinction between the stops *b, g, k*, etc. and the spirants which replace them after vowels under regular statable conditions.

consisting mostly of long words and words with certain endings, contains selective verbs like *reduce, survive, undertake, perplex, magnify, reciprocate,* and selective nouns like *instrument, elephant, longevity, altruism.* A limited number of short words belong also to the group of selective nouns and verbs, e.g. *heart, boy, street, road, town; sit, see, hear, think.* In this selective vocabulary, English is like French or Hopi. The other part of the lexicon, mostly the shorter words but some long ones, contains bare lexemes to which either verbation or stativation may be applied at will, e.g., *head, hand, stand, walk, exchange, sight, skin, weave, dog, surrender, massage,* etc.[9] This part of the vocabulary is like Arabic, though the signatures are of a quite different sort. Those for stativation include the articles, plural signatures, position after possessive pronouns and selective adjectives; those for verbation include position after a nominative pronoun, position before a pronoun, noun, or stativation, the tense forms, the verbal auxiliaries and modal particles, etc.

There may be wide variability in the semantic relations between verbations and stativations in the same language. When contrasted with corresponding stativations, verbations may seem to add in an inconstant manner such ideas as 'he engaged in' (*hunt, jump, dance*), 'behave like' (*mother, carpenter, dog*), 'be in' (*lodge, hive*), 'put in' (*place, seat, pocket, garage*), 'make, add, install' (*weave, plant, roof, pipe, tin*), 'take away' (*skin, peel, husk, bone*), 'get' (*fish, mouse*), 'use' (*spear, hammer, fiddle, bugle*); while on the other hand stativations seem to add inconstantly such ideas as 'result' (*weave, plant, form*), 'means' (*paint, trail*), 'action or place (*walk, slide, step, drop*), 'instrument' (*lift, cover, clasp, clip*), etc. This inconstancy, or better elasticity, in certain aspects of the meaning, seen in Semitic as well as English, is characteristic of the simple moduli of verbation and stativation, and it may be contrasted with the condition of having a number of different moduli, each a different specialized type of verbation or stativation, which appears to be the situation in Alaskan Eskimo. It merely means that in a language with simple primary types of moduli the meaning of the individual lexeme is more or less under the sway of the entire sentence, and at the mercy of the manifold possibilities of connotation and suggestion which thereby arise.

---

9 Adjectivation in English is another modulus which is applied both to bare lexemes and to selective nouns, but there are also selective adjectives, and these are not modulated into substantives.

Can there be languages not only without selective nouns and verbs, but even without stativations and verbations? Certainly. The power of making predications or declarative sentences and of taking on such moduli as voice, aspect, and tense, may be a property of every major word, without the addition of a preparatory modulus. This seems to be the case in Nitinat and the other Wakashan languages. An isolated word is a sentence; a sequence of such sentence words is like a compound sentence. We might ape such a compound sentence in English, e.g. 'There is one who is a man who is yonder who does running which traverses-it which is a street which elongates', though the exotic sentence consists simply of the predicative lexemes 'one', 'man', 'yonder', 'run', 'transverse', 'street', and 'long', and the proper translation is "A man yonder is running down the long street'. Such a structure might or might not be found in an isolating language; again it might or might not be found in a polysynthetic one like Nitinat. The polysynthetic language might or might not fuse some of the lexemes into long synthetic words, but it would doubtless have the power in any case of fusing in a great many aspectual, modal, and connective elements (signatures of moduli). Of such a polysynthetic tongue it is sometimes said that all words are verbs, or again that all words are nouns with verb-forming elements added. Actually, the terms verb and noun in such a language are meaningless. The situation therein is radically different from e.g. Hopi, for though in the latter *le´·na* 'it is a flute' and *pe´·na* 'he writes it' are both complete sentences, they are words which are not equally predicative in all positions of a sentence, and they also belong to selective covert classes of noun and verb that in general take different inflections, and look alike only in particular types of sentence. In Hopi the verb-noun distinction is important on a selective basis; in English it is important on a modulus basis; in Nitinat it seems not to exist.

So far we have dealt with categories which are distinct both con-figuratively and semantically, and these are typical formulations of grammar. But we also have word groups which are configuratively distinct yet have no difference in meaning; these we may call *isosemantic* or purely formal classes. They in turn are of two sorts corresponding to selective and modulus in the semantic categories, but here better styled *selective* and *alternative*. Selective isosemantic classes are typified by 'declensions' and 'conjugations', those very common features of languages the world over; richly developed in

Latin, Sanskrit, Hopi, and Maya, less developed in Semitic, English ('strong' and 'weak' verbs), and Aztec, and almost lacking in Southern Paiute. They also include gender-like classes without semantic difference, as in Bantu and in certain of the genders of Taos (all these might be called 'declensions' with pronominal agreement or the like); classes requiring different position in a sentence or complex without difference of type of meaning (stem position classes in Algonkian); and classes requiring different signatures for the same modulus without difference in type of meaning, e.g. in Hebrew the segholate (*e-e*) 'nouns' and parallel stativation-groups. Alternative isosemantic classes are what their name implies, e.g. the English group comprising *don't, won't, shan't, can't*, etc. and the group of *do not, will not, shall not, cannot*. In this case we could perhaps speak of a modulus of brevity, convenience, or colloquial attitude which is applied in the former group. Alternative classes sometimes show *stylistic* as opposed to grammatical difference. In other cases there seems to be no generalizable difference, as in English *electrical, cubical, cyclical, historical, geometrical* versus *electric, cubic, cyclic, historic, geometric*.

There remains another type of distinction: *specific categories* and *generic* ones. A specific category is an individual class existing in an individual language, e.g. English passive voice, Hopi segmentative aspect. A generic category, in the restricted sense of application to a particular language, is a hierarchy formed by grouping classes of similar or (and) complementary types, e.g. case in Latin, voice in Hopi. Here much depends on both the insight and the predilections of the systematizer or grammarian, for it may be easy to build up specific categories into very logical schemes, yet what is rather desired is that such generic categories should represent systems which the language itself contains. We do well to be skeptical of a grammarian's systematization when it is full of *enantiomorphism*, the pairing with every category of an opposite which is merely the lack of it. Specific categories of seemingly opposite meaning such as passive voice and active voice (when this term 'active' means merely 'non-passive') should be brought into one generic category ('voice') only when they are more than two, or when, if only two, taken together they contrast as a unit with some other system of forms.

Finally, in a still wider sense generic categories may be so formulated as to become equivalent to the concepts of a general science of grammar. Such categories are made by grouping what seem to us to be *similar specific categories in different languages.* Only in such a sense can we speak of a category of 'passive voice' which would embrace the forms called by that name in English, Latin, Aztec, and other tongues. Such categories or concepts we may call *taxonomic* categories, as opposed to *descriptive* categories. Taxonomic categories may be of the first degree, e.g. passive voice, objective case; or of the second degree, e.g. voice, case. Perhaps those of the second degree are the more important and ultimately the more valuable as linguistic concepts, as generalizations of the largest systemic formulations and outlines found in language when language is considered and described in terms of the whole human species.

Science and Linguistics

Every normal person in the world, past infancy in years, can and does talk. By virtue of that fact, every person—civilized or uncivilized— carries through life certain naive but deeply rooted ideas about talking and its relation to thinking. Because of their firm connection with speech habits that have become unconscious and automatic, these notions tend to be rather intolerant of opposition. They are by no means entirely personal and haphazard; their basis is definitely systematic, so that we are justified in calling them a system of natural logic —a term that seems preferable to the term common sense, often used for the same thing.

According to natural logic, the fact that every person has talked fluently since infancy makes every man his own authority on the process by which he formulates and communicates. He has merely to consult a substratum of logic or reason which he and everyone else are supposed to possess. Natural logic says that talking is merely an incidental process concerned strictly with communication, not with formulation of ideas. Talking, or the use of language, is supposed only to "express" what is essentially already formulated nonlinguistically. Formulation is an independent process, called thought or thinking, and is supposed to be largely indifferent to the nature of particular languages. Languages have grammars, which are assumed to be merely norms of conventional and social correctness, but the use of language is supposed to be guided not so much by them as by correct, rational, or intelligent *thinking*.

Thought, in this view, does not depend on grammar but on laws of logic or reason which are supposed to be the same for all observers of the universe—to represent a rationale in the universe that can be "found" independently by all intelligent observers, whether they speak Chinese or Choctaw. In our own culture, the formulations of mathematics and of formal logic have acquired the reputation of dealing with this order of things, i.e., with the realms and laws of pure thought. Natural logic holds that different languages are essentially parallel methods for expressing this one-and-the-same rationale of thought and, hence, differ really in but minor ways which may seem important only because they are seen at close range. It holds that mathematics, symbolic logic, philosophy, and so on are systems contrasted with language which deal directly with this realm of thought, not that they are themselves specialized extensions of language. The attitude of natural logic is well shown in an old quip about a German grammarian who devoted his whole life to the study of the dative case. From the point of view of natural logic, the dative case and grammar in general are an extremely minor issue. A different attitude is said to have been held by the ancient Arabians: Two princes, so the story goes, quarreled over the honor of putting on the shoes of the most learned grammarian of the realm; whereupon their father, the caliph, is said to have remarked that it was the glory of his kingdom that great grammarians were honored even above kings.

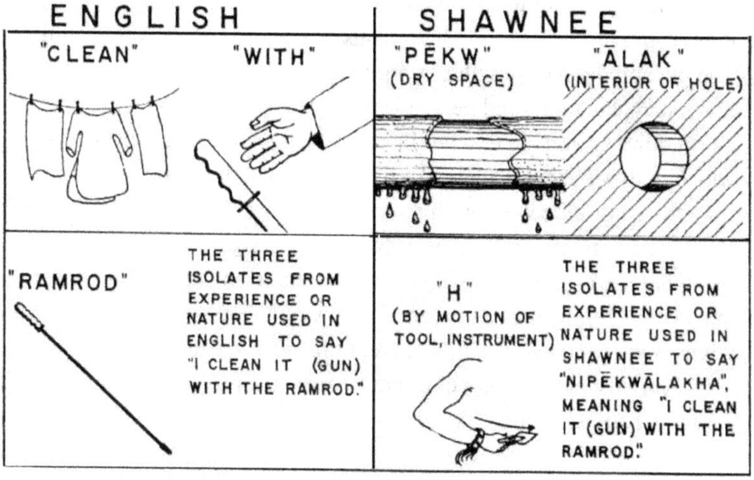

Figure 1. Languages dissect nature differently. The different isolates of meaning (thoughts) used by English and Shawnee in reporting the same experience, that of cleaning a gun by running the ramrod through it. The pronouns "I" and "it" are not shown by symbols, as they have the same meaning in each language. In Shawnee "ni-" equals "I"; "-a" equals "it."

The familiar saying that the exception proves the rule contains a great deal of wisdom, though from the standpoint of formal logic it became an absurdity as soon as "prove" no longer meant "put on trial." The old saw began to be profound psychology from the time it ceased to have standing in logic. What it might well suggest to us today is that if a rule has absolutely no exceptions, it is not recognized as a rule or as anything else; it is then part of the background of experience of which we tend to remain unconscious. Never having experienced anything in contrast to it, we cannot isolate it and formulate it as a rule until we so enlarge our experience and expand our base of reference that we encounter an interruption of its regularity. The situation is somewhat analogous to that of not missing the water till the well runs dry, or not realizing that we need air until we are choking.

For instance, if a race of people had the physiological defect of being able to see only the color blue, they would hardly be able to formulate the rule that they saw only blue. The term blue would convey no meaning to them, their language would lack color terms, and their words denoting their various sensations of blue would answer to, and translate, our words light, dark, white, black, and so on, not our word blue. In order to formulate the rule or norm of seeing only blue, they would need exceptional moments in which they saw other colors. The phenomenon of gravitation forms a rule without exceptions; needless to say, the untutored person is utterly unaware of any law of gravitation, for it would never enter his head to conceive of a universe in which bodies behaved otherwise than they do at the earth's surface. Like the color blue with our hypothetical race, the law of gravitation is part of the untutored individual's background, not something he isolates from that background. The law could not be formulated until bodies that always fell were seen in terms of a wider astronomical world in which bodies moved in orbits or went this way and that.

Similarly, whenever we turn our heads, the image of the scene passes across our retinas exactly as it would if the scene turned around us. But this effect is background, and we do not recognize it; we do not see a room turn around us but are conscious only of having turned our heads in a stationary room. If we observe critically while turning the head or eyes quickly, we shall see, no motion it is true, yet a blurring of the scene between two clear views. Normally we are quite unconscious of this continual blurring but seem to be looking about in an unblurred world. Whenever we walk past a tree or house, its image on the retina changes just as if the tree or house were turning on its axis; yet we do not see trees or houses turn as we travel about at ordinary speeds. Sometimes ill-fitting glasses will reveal queer movements in the scene as we look about, but normally we do not see the relative motion of the environment when we move; our psychic makeup is somehow adjusted to disregard whole realms of phenomena that are so all-pervasive as to be irrelevant to our daily lives and needs.

Figure 2. Languages classify items of experience differently. The class corresponding to one word and one thought in language A may be regarded by language B as two or more classes corresponding to two or more words and thoughts.

Natural logic contains two fallacies: First, it does not see that the phenomena of a language are to its own speakers largely of a background character and so are outside the critical consciousness and control of the speaker who is expounding natural logic. Hence, when anyone, as a natural logician, is talking about reason, logic, and the laws of correct thinking, he is apt to be simply marching in step with purely grammatical facts that have somewhat of a background character in his own language or family of languages but are by no means universal in all languages and in no sense a common substratum of reason. Second, natural logic confuses agreement about subject matter, attained through use of language, with knowledge of the linguistic process by which agreement is attained; i.e., with the province of the despised (and

to its notion superfluous) grammarian. Two fluent speakers, of English
let us say, quickly reach a point of assent about the subject matter of
their speech; they agree about what their language refers to. One of
them, A, can give directions that will be carried out by the other, B,
to A's complete satisfaction. Because they thus understand each other
so perfectly, A and B, as natural logicians, suppose they must of course
know how it is all done. They think, e.g., that it is simply a matter of
choosing words to express thoughts. If you ask A to explain how he
got B's agreement so readily, he will simply repeat to you, with more
or less elaboration or abbreviation, what he said to B. He has no notion
of the process involved. The amazingly complex system of linguistic
patterns and classifications, which A and B have in common before
they can adjust to each other at all, is all background to A and B.

   These background phenomena are the province of the grammarian
— or of the linguist, to give him his more modern name as a scientist.
The word linguist in common, and especially newspaper, parlance
means something entirely different, namely, a person who can quickly
attain agreement about subject matter with different people speaking a
number of different languages. Such a person is better termed a poly-
glot or a multilingual. Scientific linguists have long understood that
ability to speak a language fluently does not necessarily confer a linguistic knowledge of it, i.e., understanding of its background phenomena and its systematic processes and structure, any more than ability to
play a good game of billiards confers or requires any knowledge of the
laws of mechanics that operate upon the billiard table.

   The situation here is not unlike that in any other field of science.
All real scientists have their eyes primarily on background phenomena
that cut very little ice, as such, in our daily lives; and yet their studies
have a way of bringing out a close relation between these unsuspected
realms of fact and such decidedly foreground activities as transporting
goods, preparing food, treating the sick, or growing potatoes, which in
time may become very much modified, simply because of pure scientific investigation in no way concerned with these brute matters themselves. Linguistics is in quite similar case [sic]; the background
phenomena with which it deals are involved in all our foreground
activities of talking and of reaching agreement, in all reasoning and
arguing of cases, in all law, arbitration, conciliation, contracts, treaties,
public opinion, weighing of scientific theories, formulation of scientific
results. Whenever agreement or assent is arrived at in human affairs,

and whether or not mathematics or other specialized symbolisms are made part of the procedure, *this agreement is reached by linguistic processes, or else it is not reached.*

As we have seen, an overt knowledge of the linguistic processes by which agreement is attained is not necessary to reaching some sort of agreement, but it is certainly no bar thereto; the more complicated and difficult the matter, the more such knowledge is a distinct aid, till the point may be reached—I suspect that the modern world has about arrived at it—when the knowledge become not only an aid but a necessity. The situation may be likened to that of navigation. Every boat that sails is in the lap of planetary forces; yet a boy can pilot his small craft around a harbor without benefit of geography, astronomy, mathematics, or international politics. To the captain of an ocean liner, however, some knowledge of all these subjects is essential.

When linguists became able to examine critically and scientifically a large number of languages of widely different patterns, their base of reference was expanded; they experienced an interruption of phenomena hitherto held universal, and a whole new order of significances came into their ken. It was found that the background linguistic system (in other words, the grammar) of each language is not merely a reproducing instrument for voicing ideas but rather is itself the shaper of ideas, the program and guide for the individual's mental activity, for his analysis of impressions, for his synthesis of his mental stock in trade. Formulation of ideas is not an independent process, strictly rational in the old sense, but is part of a particular grammar, and differs, from slightly to greatly, between different grammars. We dissect nature along lines laid down by our native languages. The categories and types that we isolate from the world of phenomena we do not find there because they stare every observer in the face; on the contrary, the world is presented in a kaleidoscope flux of impressions which has to be organized by our minds—and this means largely by the linguistic systems in our minds. We cut nature up, organize it into concepts, and ascribe significances as we do, largely because we are parties to an agreement to organize it in this way—an agreement that holds throughout our speech community and is codified in the patterns of our language. The agreement is, of course, an implicit and unstated one, *but its terms are absolutely obligatory*; we cannot talk at all except by subscribing to the organization and classification of data which the agreement decrees.

OBJECTIVE FIELD	SPEAKER (SENDER)	HEARER (RECEIVER)	HANDLING OF TOPIC, RUNNING OF THIRD PERSON
SITUATION I a.			ENGLISH... "HE IS RUNNING"
			HOPI ... "WARI" (RUNNING. STATEMENT OF FACT)
SITUATION I b. OBJECTIVE FIELD BLANK DEVOID OF RUNNING			ENGLISH..."HE RAN" HOPI ... "WARI" (RUNNING, STATEMENT OF FACT)
SITUATION 2			ENGLISH..."HE IS RUNNING" HOPI ... "WARI" (RUNNING, STATEMENT OF FACT)
SITUATION 3 OBJECTIVE FIELD BLANK			ENGLISH..."HE RAN" HOPI ... "ERA WARI" (RUNNING. STATEMENT OF FACT FROM MEMORY)
SITUATION 4 OBJECTIVE FIELD BLANK			ENGLISH..."HE WILL RUN" HOPI ... "WARIKNI" (RUNNING, STATEMENT OF EXPECTATION)
SITUATION 5 OBJECTIVE FIELD BLANK			ENGLISH..."HE RUNS" (E.G. ON THE TRACK TEAM) HOPI ... "WARIKNGWE" (RUNNING. STATEMENT OF LAW)

Figure 3. Contrast between a "temporal" language (English), and a "timeless" language (Hopi). What are to English differences of time are to Hopi differences in the kind of validity.

This fact is very significant for modern science, for it means no individual is free to describe nature with absolute impartiality but is constrained to certain modes of interpretation even while he thinks himself most free. The person most free in such respects would be a linguist familiar with very many widely different linguistic systems. As yet no linguist even is in any such position. We are thus introduced to a new principle of relativity, which holds that all observers are not led by the same physical evidence to the same picture of the universe, unless their linguistic backgrounds are similar, or can in some way be calibrated.

This rather startling conclusion is not so apparent if we compare only our modern European languages, with perhaps Latin and Greek thrown in for good measure. Among these tongues there is a unanimity of major pattern which at first seems to bear out natural logic. But this unanimity exists only because these tongues are all Indo-European dialects cut to the same basic plan, being historically transmitted from what was long ago one speech community; because the modern dialects have long shared in building up a common culture; and because much of this culture, on the more intellectual side, is derived from the linguistic backgrounds of Latin and Greek. Thus this group of languages satisfies the special case of the clause beginning "unless" in the statement of the linguistic relativity principle at the end of the preceding paragraph. From this condition follows the unanimity of description of the world in the community of modern scientists. But it must be emphasized that "all modern Indo-European-speaking observers" is not the same thing as "all observers." That modern Chinese or Turkish scientists describe the world in the same terms as Western scientists means, of course, only that they have taken over bodily the entire Western system of rationalizations, not that they have corroborated that system from their native posts of observation.

When Semitic, Chinese, Tibetan, or African languages are contrasted with our own, the divergence in analysis of the world becomes more apparent; and when we bring in the native languages of the Americas, where speech communities for many millenniums have gone their ways independently of each other and of the Old World, the fact that languages dissect nature in many different ways becomes patent. The relativity of all conceptual systems, ours included, and their dependence upon language stand revealed. That American Indians speaking only their native tongues are never called upon to act as scientific observers is in no wise to the point. To exclude the evidence which their languages offer as to what the human mind can do is like expecting botanists to study nothing but food plants and hothouse roses and then tell us what the plant world is like!

Let us consider a few examples. In English we divide most of our words into two classes, which have different grammatical and logical properties. Class 1 we call nouns, e.g., "house," "man"; Class 2, verbs, e.g., "hit," "run." Many words of one class can act secondarily as of the other class, e.g., "a hit," "a run," or "to man" (the boat), but on the primary level, the division between the classes is absolute. Our language thus gives us a bipolar division of nature. But nature herself is not thus polarized. If it be said that strike, turn, run, are verbs because they denote temporary or short-lasting events, i.e., actions, why then is fist a noun? It is also a temporary event. Why are lightning, spark, wave, eddy, pulsation, flame, storm, phase, cycle, spasm, noise, emotion nouns? They are temporary events. If man and house are nouns because they are long-lasting and stable events, i.e., things, what then are keep, adhere, extend, project, continue, persist, grow, dwell, and so on doing among the verbs? If it be objected that possess, adhere are verbs because they are stable relationships rather than stable percepts, why then should equilibrium, pressure, current, peace, group, nation, society, tribe, sister, or any kinship term be among the nouns? It will be found that an "event" to us means "what our language classes as a verb" or something analogized therefrom. And it will be found that it is not possible to define event, thing, object, relationship, and so on, from nature, but that to define them always involves a circuitous return to the grammatical categories of the definer's language.

In the Hopi language, lightning, wave, flame, meteor, puff of smoke, pulsation are verbs—events of necessarily brief duration cannot be anything but verbs. Cloud and storm are at about the lower limit of duration for nouns. Hopi, you see, actually has a classification of events (or linguistic isolates) by duration type, something strange to our modes of thought. On the other hand, in Nootka, a language of Vancouver Island, all words seem to us to be verbs, but really there are no Classes 1 and 2; we have, as it were, a monistic view of nature that gives us only one class of word for all kinds of events. "A house occurs" or "it houses" is the way of saying "house," exactly like "a flame occurs" or "it burns." These terms seem to us like verbs because they are inflected for durational and temporal nuances, so that the suffixes of the word for house event make it mean long-lasting house, temporary house, future house, house that used to be, what started out as a house, and so on.

Hopi has one noun that covers every thing or being that flies, with the exception of birds, which class is denoted by another noun. The former noun may be said to denote the class (FC-B)—flying class minus bird. The Hopi actually call insect, airplane, and aviator all by the same word, and feel no difficulty about it. The situation, or course, decides any possible confusion among very disparate members of a broad linguistic class, such as this class (FC-B). This class seems to us too large and inclusive, but so would our class "snow" to an Eskimo. We have the same word for falling snow, snow on the ground, snow packed hard like ice, slushy snow, wind-driven flying snow—whatever the situation may be. To an Eskimo, this all-inclusive word would be almost unthinkable; he would say that falling snow, slushy snow, and so on, are sensuously and operationally different, different things to contend with; he uses different words for them and for other kinds of snow. The Aztecs go even farther than we in the opposite direction, with cold, ice, and snow all represented by the same basic word with different terminations: ice is the noun form; cold, the adjectival form; and for snow, "ice mist."

What surprises most is to find that various grand generalizations of the Western world, such as time, velocity, and matter, are not essential to the construction of a consistent picture of the universe. The psychic experiences that we class under these headings are, of course, not destroyed; rather, categories derived from other experiences take over the rulership of the cosmology and seem to function just as well. Hopi may be called a timeless language. It recognizes psychological time, which is much like Bergson's "duration," but this "time" is quite unlike the mathematical time, T, used by our physicists. Among the peculiar properties of Hopi time are that it varies with each observer, does not permit of simultaneity, and has zero dimensions; i.e., it cannot be given a number greater than one. The Hopi do not say, "I stayed five days," but "I left on the fifth day." A word referring to this kind of time, like the word day, can have no plural. The puzzle picture (Fig. 3) will give mental exercise to anyone who would like to figure out how the Hopi verb gets along without tenses. Actually, the only practical uses of our tenses, in one-verb sentences, is to distinguish among five typical situations, which are symbolized in the picture. The timeless Hopi verb does not distinguish between the present, past, and future of the event itself but must always indicate what type of validity the *speaker* intends the statement to have: (a) report of an event (situations 1, 2, 3 in the picture); (b) expectation of an event (situation 4); (c) generalization or law about events (situation 5). Situation 1, where the speaker and the listener are in contact with the same objective field, is divided by our language into two conditions, 1a and 1b, which it calls present and past, respectively. This division is unnecessary for a language which assures that the statement is a report.

Hopi grammar, by means of its forms called aspects and modes, also makes it easy to distinguish between momentary, continued, and repeated occurrences, and to indicate the actual sequence of reported events. Thus the universe can be described without recourse to a

concept of dimensional time. How would a physics constructed along
these lines work, with no *T* (time) in its equations? Perfectly, as far
as I can see, though of course it would require different ideology and
perhaps different mathematics. Of course *V* (velocity) would have
to go too. The Hopi language has no word really equivalent to our
"speed" or "rapid." What translates these terms is usually a word
meaning intense or very, accompanying any verb of motion. Here
is a clew to the nature of our new physics. We may have to introduce
a new term *I*, intensity. Every thing and event will have an *I*, whether
we regard the thing or event as moving or just enduring or being. Perhaps the *I* of an electric charge will turn out to be its voltage, or potential. We shall use clocks to measure some intensities, or, rather some
relative intensities, for the absolute intensity of anything will be
meaningless. Our old friend acceleration will still be there but
doubtless under a new name. We shall perhaps call it *V*, meaning
not velocity but variation. Perhaps all growths and accumulations
will be regarded as *V*'s. We should not have the concept of rate in the
temporal sense, since, like velocity, rate introduces a mathematical and
linguistic time. Of course we know that all measurements are ratios,
but the measurement of intensities made by comparison with the standard intensity of a clock or a planet we do not treat as ratios, any more
than we so treat a distance made by comparison with a yardstick.

A scientist from another culture that used time and velocity would
have great difficulty in getting us to understand these concepts. We
should talk about the intensity of a chemical reaction; he would speak
of its velocity or its rate, which words we should at first think were
simply words for intensity in his language. Likewise, he at first would
think that intensity was simply our own word for velocity. At first we
should agree, later we should begin to disagree, and it might dawn upon
both sides that different systems of rationalization were being used. He
would find it very hard to make us understand what he really meant by
velocity of a chemical reaction. We should have no words that would
fit. He would try to explain it by likening it to a running horse, to the
difference between a good horse and a lazy horse. We should try to
show him, with a superior laugh, that his analogy also was a matter
of different intensities, aside from which there was little similarity
between a horse and a chemical reaction in a beaker. We should
point out that a running horse is moving relative to the ground,
whereas the material in a beaker is at rest.

One significant contribution to science from the linguistic point of view may be the greater development of our sense of perspective. We shall no longer be able to see a few recent dialects of the Indo-European family, and the rationalizing techniques elaborated from their patterns, as the apex of the evolution of the human mind; nor their present wide spread as due to any survival from fitness or to anything but a few events of history—events that could be called fortunate only from the parochial point of view of the favored parties. They, and our own thought processes with them, can no longer be envisioned as spanning the gamut of reason and knowledge but only as one constellation in a galactic expanse. A fair realization of the incredible degree of diversity of linguistic system that ranges over the globe leaves one with an inescapable feeling that the human spirit is inconceivably old; that the few thousand years of history covered by our written records are no more than the thickness of a pencil mark on the scale that measures our past experience on this planet; that the events of these recent millenniums spell nothing in any evolutionary wise, that the race has taken no sudden spurt, achieved no commanding synthesis during recent millenniums, but has only played a little with a few of the linguistic formulations and views of nature bequeathed from an inexpressibly longer past. Yet neither this feeling nor the sense of precarious dependence of all we know upon linguistic tools which themselves are largely unknown need be discouraging to science but should, rather, foster that humility which accompanies the true scientific spirit, and thus forbid that arrogance of the mind which hinders real scientific curiosity and detachment.

The Relation of Habitual Thought
and Behavior to Language

There will probably be general assent to the proposition that an accepted pattern of using words is often prior to certain lines of thinking and forms of behavior, but he who assents often sees in such a statement nothing more than a platitudinous recognition of the hypnotic power of philosophical and learned terminology on the one hand or of catchwords, slogans, and rallying-cries on the other. To see only thus far is to miss the point of one of the important interconnections which Sapir saw between language, culture, and psychology, and succinctly expressed in the introductory quotation.* It is not so much in these special uses of language as in its constant ways of arranging data and its most ordinary every-day analysis of phenomena that we need to recognize the influence it has on other activities, cultural and personal.

THE NAME OF THE SITUATION AS AFFECTING BEHAVIOR

I came in touch with an aspect of this problem before I had studied with Dr. Sapir, and in a field usually considered remote from linguistics. It was in the course of my professional work for a fire insurance company, in which I undertook the task of analyzing many hundreds of reports of circumstances surrounding the start of fires, and in some

---

* [Here is the quotation by Edward Sapir that appears at the beginning of the section of the volume in which this paper appears.]

> Human beings do not live in the objective world alone, nor alone in the world of social activity as ordinarily understood, but are very much at the mercy of the particular language which has become the medium of expression for their society. It is quite an illusion to imagine that one adjusts to reality essentially without the use of language and that language is merely an incidental means of solving specific problems of communication or reflection. The fact of the matter is that the 'real world" is to a large extent unconsciously built up on the language habits of the group. ... We see and hear and otherwise experience very largely as we do because the language habits of our community predispose certain choices of interpretation.
> —The Status of Linguistics as a Science
> [From 'The Status of Linguistics as a Science", 1929, reprinted in Sapir, *Selected Writings in Language, Culture and Personality,* ed. David G. Mandelbaum, University of California Press, 1949, p. 162.]

cases, of explosions. My analysis was directed toward purely physical conditions, such as defective wiring, presence or absence of air spaces between metal flues and woodwork, etc., and the results were presented in these terms. Indeed, it was undertaken with no thought that any other significances would be or could be revealed. But in due course it became evident that not only a physical situation *qua* physics, but the meaning of that situation to people, was sometimes a factor, through the behavior of the people, in the start of the fire. And this factor of meaning was clearest when it was a *linguistic meaning*, residing in the name or the linguistic description commonly applied to the situation. Thus around a storage of what are called 'gasoline drums' behavior will tend to a certain type, that is, great care will be exercised; while around a storage of what are called 'empty gasoline drums' it will tend to be different—careless, with little repression of smoking or of tossing cigarette stubs about. Yet the 'empty' drums are perhaps the more dangerous, since they contain explosive vapor. Physically the situation is hazardous, but the linguistic analysis according to regular analogy must employ the word 'empty,' which inevitably suggests lack of hazard. The word 'empty' is used in two linguistic patterns: (1) as a virtual synonym for 'null and void, negative, inert,' (2) applied in analysis of physical situations without regard to, e.g., vapor, liquid vestiges, or stray rubbish, in the container. The situation is named in one pattern (2) and the name is then 'acted out' or 'lived up to' in another (1), this being a formula for the linguistic conditioning of behavior into hazardous forms.

In a wood distillation plant the metal stills were insulated with a composition prepared from limestone and called at the plant 'spun limestone.' Not attempt was made to protect this covering from excessive heat or the contact of flame. After a period of use, the fire below one of the stills spread to the 'limestone,' which to everyone's great surprise burned vigorously. Exposure to acetic acid fumes from the stills had converted part of the limestone (calcium carbonate) to calcium acetate. This when heated in a fire decomposes, forming inflammable acetone. Behavior that tolerated fire close to the covering was induced by use of the name 'limestone,' which because it ends in '-stone' implies non-combustibility.

A huge iron kettle of varnish was observed to be overheated, nearing the temperature at which it would ignite. The operator moved it off the fire and ran it on its wheels to a distance, but did not cover it. In a minute or so the varnish ignited. Here the linguistic influence is more complex; it is due to the metaphorical objectifying (of which more later) of 'cause' as contact or the spatial juxtaposition of 'things' — to analyzing the situation as 'on' versus 'off' the fire. In reality, the stage when the external fire was the main factor had passed; the over-heating was now an internal process of convection in the varnish from the intensely heated kettle, and still continued when 'off' the fire.

An electric glow heater on the wall was little used, and for one workman had the meaning of a convenient coathanger. At night a watchman entered and snapped a switch, which action he verbalized as 'turning on the light.' No light appeared, and this result he verbal-ized as 'light is burned out.' He could not see the glow of the heater because of the old coat hung on it. Soon the heater ignited the coat, which set fire to the building.

A tannery discharged waste water containing animal matter into an outdoor settling basin partly roofed with wood and partly open. This situation is one that ordinarily would be verbalized as 'pool of water.' A workman had occasion to light a blowtorch near by, and threw his match into the water. But the decomposing waste matter was evolving gas under the wood cover, so that the setup was the reverse of 'watery.' An instant flare of flame ignited the woodwork, and the fire quickly spread into the adjoining building.

A drying room for hides was arranged with a blower at one end to make a current of air along the room and thence outdoors through a vent at the other end. Fire started at a hot bearing on the blower, which blew the flames directly into the hides and fanned them along the room, destroying the entire stock. This hazardous setup followed naturally from the term 'blower' with its linguistic equivalence to 'that which blows,' implying that its function necessarily is to 'blow.' Also its function is verbalized as 'blowing air for drying,' overlooking that it can blow other things, e.g., flames and sparks. In reality, a blower sim-ply makes a current of air and can exhaust as well as blow. It should have been installed at the vent end to *draw* the air over the hides, then through the hazard (its own casing and bearings), and thence outdoors.

Beside a coal-fired melting pot for lead reclaiming was a pile of 'scrap lead' — a misleading verbalization, for it consisted of the lead sheets of old radio condensers, which still had paraffin paper between them. Soon the paraffin blazed up and fired the roof, half of which was burned off.

Such examples, which could be greatly multiplied, will suffice
to show how the cue to a certain line of behavior is often given by the
analogies of the linguistic formula in which the situation is spoken of,
and by which to some degree it is analyzed, classified, and allotted its
place in that world which is 'to a large extent unconsciously built up on
the language habits of the group.' And we shall always assume that the
linguistic analysis made by our group reflects reality better than it does.

GRAMMATICAL PATTERNS AS INTERPRETATIONS OF EXPERIENCE

The linguistic material in the above examples is limited to single
words, phrases, and patterns of limited range. One cannot study the
behavioral compulsiveness of such material without suspecting a much
more far-reaching compulsion from large-scale patterning of grammatical categories, such as plurality, gender and similar classifications (animate, inanimate, etc.), tenses, voices, and other verb forms, classifications of the type of 'parts of speech,' and the matter of whether a given
experience is denoted by a unit morpheme, an inflected word, or a syntactical combination. A category such as number (singular vs. plural) is
an attempted interpretation of a whole large order of experience, virtually of the world or of nature; it attempts to say how experience is to
be segmented, what experience is to be called 'one' and what 'several.'
But the difficulty of appraising such a far-reaching influence is great
because of its background character, because of the difficulty of standing
aside from our own language, which is a habit and a cultural *non est
disputandum*, and scrutinizing it objectively. And if we take a very
dissimilar language, this language becomes a part of nature, and we even
do to it what we have already done to nature. We tend to think in our
own language in order to examine the exotic language. Or we find the
task of unravelling the purely morphological intricacies so gigantic that
it seems to absorb all else. Yet the problem, though difficult, is feasible;
and the best approach is through an exotic language, for in its study we
are at long last pushed willy-nilly out of our ruts. Then we find that the
exotic language is a mirror held up to our own.

In my study of the Hopi language, what I now see as an opportunity
to work on this problem was first thrust upon me before I was clearly
aware of the problem. The seemingly endless task of describing the
morphology did finally end. Yet it was evident, especially in the light
of Sapir's lectures on Navaho, that the description of the *language* was
far from complete. I knew for example the morphological formation of

plurals, but not how to use plurals. It was evident that the category of plural in Hopi was not the same thing as in English, French, or German. Certain things that were plural in these languages were singular in Hopi. The phase of investigation which now began consumed nearly two more years.

The work began to assume the character of a comparison between Hopi and western European languages. It also became evident that even the grammar of Hopi bore a relation to Hopi culture, and the grammar of European tongues to our own 'western' or 'European' culture. And it appeared that the interrelation brought in those large subsummations of experience by language, such as our own terms 'time,' 'space,' 'substance,' and 'matter.' Since with respect to the traits compared, there is little difference between English, French, German, or other European languages with the *possible* (but doubtful) exception of Balto-Slavic and non-Indo European, I have lumped these languages into one group called SAE, or 'Standard Average European.'

That portion of the whole investigation here to be reported may be summed up in two questions: (1) Are our own concepts of 'time,' 'space,' and 'matter' given in substantially the same form by experience to all men, or are they in part conditioned by the structure of particular languages? (2) Are there traceable affinities between (a) cultural and behavioral norms and (b) large-scale linguistic patterns? I should be the last to pretend there is anything so definite as 'a correlation' between culture and language, and especially between ethnological rubrics such as 'agricultural,' 'hunting,' etc. and linguistic ones like 'inflected,' 'synthetic,' or 'isolating.'[1] When I began the study, the problem was by no means so clearly formulated, and I had little notion that the answers would turn out as they did.

PLURALITY AND NUMERATION IN SAE AND HOPI

In our language, that is SAE, plurality and cardinal numbers are applied in two ways: to real plurals and imaginary plurals. Or more exactly if less tersely: perceptible spatial aggregates and metaphorical aggregates. We say 'ten men' and also 'ten days.' Ten men either are

---

[1] We have plenty of evidence that this is not the case. Consider only the Hopi and the Ute, with languages that on the overt morphological and lexical level are as similar as, say, English and German. The idea of "correlation" between language and culture, in the generally accepted sense of correlation, is certainly a mistaken one.

or could be objectively perceived as ten, ten in one group perception[2]
—ten men on a street corner, for instance. But 'ten days' cannot be
objectively experienced. We experience only one day, today; the
other nine (or even all ten) are something conjured up from memory
or imagination. If 'ten days' be regarded as a group it must be as an
'imaginary,' mentally constructed group. Whence comes this mental
pattern? Just as in the case of the fire-causing errors, from the fact that
our language confuses the two different situations, has but one pattern
for both. When we speak of 'ten steps forward, ten strokes on a bell,
or any similarly described cyclic sequence, 'times' of any sort, we are
doing the same thing as with 'days.' *Cyclicity* brings the response
of imaginary plurals. But a likeness of cyclicity to aggregates is not
unmistakably given by experience prior to language, or it would be
found in all languages, and it is not.

Our *awareness* of time and cyclicity does contain something
immediate and subjective—the basic sense of 'becoming later and
later.' But, in the habitual thought of us SAE people this is covered
under something quite different, which though mental should not
be called subjective. I call it *objectified*, or imaginary, because it
is patterned on the *outer* world. It is this that reflects our linguistic
usage. Our tongue makes no distinction between numbers counted on
discrete entities and numbers that are simply counting itself. Habitual
thought then assumes that in the latter the numbers are just as much
counted on *something* as in the former. This is objectification. Concepts of time lose contact with the subjective experience of 'becoming
later' and are objectified as counted *quantities*, especially as lengths,
made up of units as a length can be visibly marked off into inches.
A 'length of time' is envisioned as a row of similar units, like a row
of bottles.

In Hopi there is a different linguistic situation. Plurals and cardi-
nals are used only for entities that form or can form an objective group.
There are no imaginary plurals, but instead ordinals used with singu-
lars. Such an expression as 'ten days' is not used. The equivalent
statement is an operational one that reaches one day by a suitable count.
'They stayed ten days' becomes 'they stayed until the eleventh day'
or 'they left after the tenth day.' 'Ten days is greater than nine days'

---

[2] As we say "ten at the *same time*," showing that in our language and
thought we restate the fact of group perception in terms of a concept "time,"
the large linguistic component of which will appear in the course of this paper.

becomes 'the tenth day is later than the ninth.' Our 'length of time'
is not regarded as a length but as a relation between two events in
laterness. Instead of our linguistically promoted objectification of the
datum of consciousness we call 'time,' the Hopi language has not laid
down any pattern that would cloak the subjective 'becoming later' that
is the essence of time.

NOUNS OF PHYSICAL QUANTITY IN SAE AND HOPI

We have two kinds of nouns denoting physical things: individual
nouns, and mass nouns, e.g., water, milk, wood, granite, sand, flour,
meat. Individual nouns denote bodies with definite outlines: a tree,
a stick, a man, a hill. Mass nouns denote homogeneous continua
without implied boundaries. The distinction is marked by linguistic
form; e.g., mass nouns lack plurals,[3] in English drop articles, and in
French take the partitive article *du, de la, des*. The distinction is more
widespread in language than in the observable appearance of things.
Rather few natural occurrences present themselves as unbounded
extents; air of course, and often water, rain, snow, sand, rock, dirt,
grass. We do not encounter butter, meat, cloth, iron, glass, or most
'materials' in such kind of manifestation, but in bodies small or large
with definite outlines. The distinction is somewhat forced upon our
description of events by an unavoidable pattern of language. It is
so inconvenient in a great many cases that we need some way of
individualizing the mass noun by further linguistic devices. This is
partly done by names of body-types: stick of wood, piece of cloth, pane
of glass, cake of soap; also, and even more, by introducing names of
containers though their contents be the real issue: glass of water, cup of
coffee, dish of food, bag of flour, bottle of beer. These very common
container formulas, in which 'of' has an obvious, visually perceptible
meaning ('contents'), influence our feeling about the less obvious type-
body formulas: stick of wood, lump of dough, etc. The formulas are
very similar: individual noun plus a similar relator (English 'of'). In
the obvious case this relator denotes contents. In the inobvious one

---

[3] It is no exception to this rule of lacking a plural that a mass noun may sometimes coincide in lexeme with an individual noun that of course has a plural; e.g.,
"stone" (no pl.) with "a stone" (pl. "stones"). The plural form denoting varieties,
e.g., "wines" is of course a different sort of thing from the true plural; it is a
curious outgrowth from the SAE mass nouns, leading to still another sort of
imaginary aggregates, which will have to be omitted from this paper.

it *suggests* contents. Hence, the lumps, chunks, blocks, pieces, etc., seem to contain something, a 'stuff,' 'substance,' or 'matter' that answers to water, coffee, or flour in the container formulas. So with SAE people the philosophic 'substance' and 'matter' are also the naïve idea; they are instantly acceptable, 'common sense.' It is so through linguistic habit. Our language patterns often require us to name a physical thing by a binomial that splits the reference into a formless item plus a form.

Hopi is again different. It has a formally distinguished class of nouns. But this class contains no formal subclass of mass nouns. All nouns have an individual sense and both singular and plural forms. Nouns translating most nearly our mass nouns still refer to vague bodies or vaguely bounded extents. They imply indefiniteness, but not lack, of outline and size. In specific statements, 'water' means one certain mass or quantity of water, not what we call 'the substance water.' Generality of statement is conveyed through the verb or predicator, not the noun. Since nouns are individual already, they are not individualized by either type-bodies or names of containers, if there is no special need to emphasize shape or container. The noun itself implies a suitable type-body or container. One says, not 'a glass of water' but kə·yi 'a water,' not 'a pool of water' but pa·hə,[4] not a 'dish of cornflour' but ŋəmni 'a (quantity) of cornflour,' not 'a piece of meat' but sikʷi 'a meat.' The language has neither a need for nor analogies on which to build the concept of existence as a duality of formless item and form. It deals with formlessness through other symbols than nouns.

PHASES OF CYCLES IN SAE AND HOPI

Such terms as summer, winter, September, morning, noon, sunset are with us nouns, and have little formal linguistic difference from other nouns. They can be subjects or objects, and we say 'at' sunset or 'in' winter just as we say at a corner or in an orchard.[5] They are

---

[4] Hopi has two words for water quantities: kə·yi and pa·hə. The difference is something like that between "stone" and "rock" in English, pa·hə implying greater size and "wildness'; flowing water, whether or not outdoors or in nature, is pa·hə; so is "moisture." But unlike "stone" and "rock," the difference is essential, not pertaining to a connotative margin, and the two can hardly ever be interchanged.

[5] To be sure, there are a few minor differences from other nouns, in English for instance in the use of the articles.

pluralized and numerated like nouns of physical objects, as we have seen. Our thought about the referents of such words hence becomes objectified. Without objectification, it would be a subjective experience of real time, i.e. of the consciousness of 'becoming later and later' — simply a cyclic phase in that ever-later-becoming duration. Only by imagination can such a cyclic phase be set beside another and another in the manner of a spatial (i.e. visually perceived) configuration. But such is the power of linguistic analogy that we do so objectify cyclic phasing. We do it even by saying 'a phase' and 'phases' instead of, e.g., 'phasing.' And the pattern of individual and mass nouns, with the resulting binomial formula of formless item plus form, is so general that it is implicit for all nouns, and hence our very generalized formless items like 'substance,' 'matter,' by which we can fill out the binomial for an enormously wide range of nouns. But even these are not quite generalized enough to take in our phase nouns. So for the phase nouns we have a formless item, 'time.' We have made it by using 'a time,' i.e. an occasion or a phase, in the pattern of a mass noun, just as from 'a summer' we make 'summer' in the pattern of a mass noun. Thus with our binomial formula we can say and think 'a moment of time,' 'a second of time,' 'a year of time.' Let me again point out that the pattern is simply that of 'a bottle of milk' or 'a piece of cheese.' Thus we are assisted to imagine that 'a summer' actually contains or consists of such-and-such a quantity of 'time.'

In Hopi however all phase terms, like summer, morning, etc., are not nouns but a kind of adverb, to use the nearest SAE analogy. They are a formal part of speech by themselves, distinct from nouns, verbs, and even other Hopi 'adverbs.' Such a word is not a case form or a locative pattern, like 'des Abends' or 'in the morning.' It contains no morpheme like one of 'in the house' or 'at the tree.'[6] It means 'when it is morning' or 'while morning-phase is occurring.' These 'temporals' are not used as subjects or objects, or at all like nouns. One does not say 'it's a hot summer' or 'summer is hot;' summer is not hot, summer is only *when* conditions are hot, *when* heat occurs. One does not say '*this* summer,' but 'summer now' or 'summer recently.' There is no objectification, as a region, an extent, a quantity,

---

[6] "Year" and certain combinations of "year" with name of season, rarely season names alone, can occur with a locative morpheme "at," but this is exceptional. It appears like historical detritus of an earlier, different patterning, or the effect of English analogy, or both.

of the subjective duration-feeling. Nothing is suggested about time except the perpetual 'getting later' of it. And so there is no basis here for a formless item answering to our 'time.'

TEMPORAL FORMS OF VERBS IN SAE AND HOPI

The three-tense system of SAE verbs colors all our thinking about time. This system is amalgamated with the larger scheme of objectification of the subjective experience of duration already noted in other patterns — in the binomial formula applicable to nouns in general, in temporal nouns, in plurality and numeration. This objectification enables us in imagination to 'stand time units in a row.' Imagination of time as like a row harmonizes with a system of *three* tenses; whereas a system of *two*, an earlier and a later, would seem to correspond better to the feeling of duration as it is experienced. For if we inspect consciousness we find no past, present, future, but a unity embracing complexity. *Everything* is in consciousness, and everything in consciousness *is*, and is together. There is in it a sensuous and a nonsensuous. We may call the sensuous — what we are seeing, hearing, touching — the 'present' while in the nonsensuous the vast image-world of memory is being labeled 'the past' and another realm of belief, intuition, and uncertainty 'the future;' yet sensation, memory, foresight, all are in consciousness together — one is not 'yet to be' nor another 'once but no more.' Where real time comes in is that all this in consciousness is 'getting later,' changing certain relations in an irreversible manner. In this 'latering' or 'durating' there seems to me to be a paramount contrast between the newest, latest, instant at the focus of attention and the rest — the earlier. Languages by the score get along well with two tense-like forms answering to this paramount relation of later to earlier. We can of course *construct and contemplate in thought* a system of past, present, future, in the objectified configuration of points on a line. This is what our general objectification tendency leads us to do and our tense system confirms it.

In English the present tense seems the one least in harmony with the paramount temporal relation. It is as if pressed into various and not wholly congruous duties. One duty is to stand as objectified middle term between objectified past and objectified future, in narration, discussion, argument, logic, philosophy. Another is to denote inclusion in the sensuous field: 'I *see* him.' Another is for nomic, i.e. customarily or generally valid, statements: 'We *see* with our eyes.' These varied uses introduce confusions of thought, of which for the most part we are unaware.

Hopi, as we might expect, is different here, too. Verbs have no 'tenses' like ours, but have validity-forms ('assertions'), aspects, and clause-linkage forms (modes), that yield even greater precision of speech. The validity-forms denote that the speaker (not the subject) reports the situation (answering to our past and present) or that he expects it (answering to our future)[7] or that he makes a nomic statement (answering to our nomic present). The aspects denote different degrees of duration and different kinds of tendency 'during duration.' As yet we have noted nothing to indicate whether an event is sooner or later than another when both are *reported*. But need for this does not arise until we have two verbs, i.e. two clauses. In that case the 'modes' denote relation between the clauses, including relations of later to earlier and of simultaneity. Then there are many detached words that express similar relations, supplementing the modes and aspects. The duties of our three-tense system and its tripartite linear objectified 'time' are distributed among various verb categories, all different from our tenses; and there is no more basis for an objectified time in Hopi verbs than in other Hopi patterns; although this does not in the least hinder the verb forms and other patterns from being closely adjusted to the pertinent realities of actual situations.

DURATION, INTENSITY, AND TENDENCY IN SAE AND HOPI

To fit discourse to manifold actual situations, all languages need to express durations, intensities, and tendencies. It is characteristic of SAE and perhaps of many other language types to express them metaphorically. The metaphors are those of spatial extension, i.e. of size, number (plurality), position, shape, and motion. We express duration by long, short, great, much, quick, slow, etc.; intensity by large, great, much, heavy, light, high, low, sharp, faint, etc.; tendency

---

[7] The expective and reportive assertions contrast according to the "paramount relation." The expective expresses anticipation existing *earlier* than objective fact, and coinciding with objective fact *later* than the status quo of the speaker, this status quo, including all the subsummation of the past therein, being expressed by the reportive. Our notion "future" seems to represent at once the earlier (anticipation), and the later (afterwards, what will be), as Hopi shows. This paradox may hint of how elusive the mystery of real time is, and how artificially it is expressed by a linear relation of past-present-future.

by more, increase, grow, turn, get, approach, go, come, rise, fall, stop, smooth, even, rapid, slow; and so on through an almost inexhaustible list of metaphors that we hardly recognize as such, since they are virtually the only linguistic media available. The nonmetaphorical terms in this field, like early, late, soon, lasting, intense, very, tending, are a mere handful, quite inadequate to the needs.

It is clear how this condition 'fits in.' It is part of our whole scheme of *objectifying*—imaginatively spatializing quantities and potentials that are quite non-spatial (so far as any spatially perceptive senses can tell us). Noun-meaning (with us) proceeds from physical bodies to referents of far other sort. Since physical bodies and their outlines in *perceived space* are denoted by size and shape terms and reckoned by cardinal numbers and plurals, these patterns of denotation and reckoning extend to the symbols of non-spatial meanings, and so suggest an *imaginary space*. Physical shapes move, stop, rise, sink, approach, etc., in perceived space; why not these other referents in their imaginary space? This has gone so far that we can hardly refer to the simplest non-spatial situation without constant resort to physical metaphors. I 'grasp' the 'thread' of another's arguments, but if its 'level' is 'over my head' my attention may 'wander' and 'lose touch' with the 'drift' of it, so that when he 'comes' to his 'point' we differ 'widely,' our 'views' being indeed so 'far apart' that the 'things' he says 'appear' much too arbitrary, or even 'a lot' of nonsense!

The absence of such metaphor from Hopi speech is striking. Use of space terms when there is no space involved is *not there*—as if on it had been laid the taboo teetotal! The reason is clear when we know that Hopi has abundant conjugational and lexical means of expressing duration, intensity, and tendency directly as such, and that major grammatical patterns do not, as with us, provide analogies for an imaginary space. The many verb 'aspects' express duration and tendency of manifestations, while some of the 'voices' express intensity, tendency, and duration of causes or forces producing manifestations. Then a special part of speech, the 'tensors,' a huge class of words, denotes only intensity, tendency, duration, and sequence. The function of the tensors is to express intensities, 'strengths,' and how they continue or vary, their rate-of-change; so that the broad concept of intensity, when considered as necessarily always varying and/or continuing, includes also tendency and duration. Tensors convey distinctions of degree, rate, constancy, repetition, increase and decrease of intensity, immediate sequence, interruption or sequence after an interval, etc., also *qualities* of strengths, such as we should express metaphorically as smooth, even, hard, rough. A striking feature is their lack of resemblance to the terms of real space and movement that to us 'mean the same.' There is not even more than a trace of apparent derivation from space terms.[8] So while Hopi in its nouns seems highly concrete, here in the tensors it becomes abstract beyond our power to follow.

HABITUAL THOUGHT IN SAE AND HOPI

The comparison now to be made between the habitual thought worlds of SAE and Hopi speakers is of course incomplete. It is possible only to touch upon certain dominant contrasts that appear to stem from the linguistic differences already noted. By 'habitual thought' and 'thought world' I mean more than simply language, i.e. than the linguistic patterns themselves. I include all the analogical and suggestive value of the patterns (e.g., our 'imaginary space' and its distant implications), and all the give-and-take between language and the culture as a whole, wherein is a vast amount that is not linguistic but yet shows the shaping influence of language. In brief, this 'thought world' is the microcosm that each man carries about within himself, by which he measures and understands what he can of the macrocosm.

The SAE microcosm has analyzed reality largely in terms of what it calls 'things' (bodies and quasibodies) plus modes of extensional but formless existence that it calls 'substances' or 'matter.' It tends to see existence through a binomial formula that expresses any existent as a spatial form plus a spatial formless continuum related to the form, as content is related to the outlines of its container. Non-spatial existents are imaginatively spatialized and charged with similar implications of form and continuum.

---

[8] One such trace is that the tensor "long in duration," while quite different from the adjective "long" of space, seems to contain the same root as the adjective "large" of space. Another is that "somewhere" of space used with certain tensors means "at some indefinite time." Possibly however this is not the case and it is only the tensor that gives the time element, so that "somewhere" still refers to space and that under these conditions indefinite space means simply general applicability regardless of either time or space. Another trace is that in the temporal (cycle word) "afternoon" the element meaning "after" is derived from the verb "to separate." There are other such traces, but they are few and exceptional, and obviously not like our own spatial meatphorizing.

The Hopi microcosm seems to have analyzed reality largely
in terms of *events* (or better 'eventing'), referred to in two ways,
objective and subjective. Objectively, and only if perceptible
physical experience, events are expressed mainly as outlines, colors,
movements, and other perceptive reports Subjectively, for both the
physical and non-physical, events are considered the expression of
invisible intensity factors, on which depend their stability and persistence, or their fugitiveness and proclivities. It implies that existents
do not 'become later and later' all in the same way; but some do by
growing like plants, some by diffusing and vanishing, some by a
procession of metamorphoses, some by enduring in one shape till
affected by violent forces. In the nature of each existent able to manifest as a definite whole is the power of its own mode of duration: its
growth, decline, stability, cyclicity, or creativeness. Everything is thus
already 'prepared' for the way it now manifests by earlier phases, and
what it will be later, partly has been, and partly is in the act of being
so 'prepared.' An emphasis and importance rests on this preparing or
being prepared aspect of the world that may to the Hopi correspond
to that 'quality and reality' that 'matter' or 'stuff' has for us.

HABITUAL BEHAVIOR FEATURES OF HOPI CULTURE

Our behavior, and that of Hopi, can be seen to be coordinated in
many ways to the linguistically-conditioned microcosm. As in my fire
case-book, people act about situations in ways which are like the ways
they talk about them. A characteristic of Hopi behavior is the emphasis
on preparation. This includes announcing and getting ready for events
well beforehand, elaborate precautions to insure persistence of desired
conditions, and stress on good will as the preparer of right results.
Consider the analogies of the day-counting pattern above. Time is
mainly reckoned 'by day' (taLk, -tala) or 'by night' (tok), which words
are not nouns but tensors, the first formed on a root 'light, day,' the
second on a root 'sleep.' The count is by *ordinals*. This is not the
pattern of counting a number of different men or things, even though
they appear successively, for even then, they *could* gather into an
assemblage. It is the pattern of counting successive reappearances
of the *same* man or thing, incapable of forming an assemblage.
The analogy is not to behave about day-cyclicity as to several men
('several days'), which is what we tend to do, but to behave as to the
successive visits of the *same man*. One does not alter several men by

working on just one, but one can prepare and so alter the later visits of the same man by working to affect the visit he is making now. This is the way Hopi deal with the future—by working within a present situation which is expected to carry impresses, both obvious and occult, forward into the future event of interest. One might say that Hopi society understands our proverb 'Well begun is half done,' but not our 'Tomorrow is another day.' This may explain much in Hopi character.

This Hopi preparing behavior may be roughly divided into announcing, outer preparing, inner preparing, covert participation, and persistence. Announcing, or preparative publicity, is an important function in the hands of a special official, the Crier Chief. Outer preparing is preparation involving much visible activity, not all necessarily directly useful within our understanding. It includes ordinary practicing, rehearsing, getting ready, introductory formalities, preparing of special food, etc. (all of these to a degree may seem over-elaborate to us), intensive sustained muscular activity like running, racing, dancing, which is thought to increase the intensity of the development of events (such as growth of crops), mimetic and other magic, preparations based on esoteric theory involving perhaps occult instruments like prayer sticks, prayer feathers, and prayer meal, and finally the great cyclic ceremonies and dances, which have the significance of preparing rain and crops. From one of the verbs meaning 'prepare' is derived the noun for 'harvest' or 'crop': na'twani 'the prepared' or the 'in preparation.'[9]

Inner preparing is use of prayer and meditation, and at lesser intensity good wishes and good will, to further desired results. Hopi attitudes stress the power of desire and thought. With their 'microcosm' it is utterly natural that they should. Desire and thought are the earliest, and therefore the most important, most critical and crucial, stage of preparing. Moreover, to the Hopi, one's desires and thoughts influence not only his own actions, but all nature. This too is wholly natural. Consciousness itself is aware of work, of the feel of effort and energy, in desire and thinking. Experience more basic than language tells us that if energy is expended effects are produced. *We* tend to believe that our bodies can stop up this energy, prevent if from affecting other things until we will our *bodies* to overt action. But this may be so only

---

[9] The Hopi verbs of preparing naturally do not correspond neatly to our "prepare": so that na'twani could also be rendered "the practised upon," "the tried-for," and otherwise.

because we have our own linguistic basis for a theory that formless items like 'matter' are things in themselves, malleable only by similar things, by more matter, and hence insulated from the powers of life and thought. It is no more unnatural to think that thought contacts everything and pervades the universe than to think, as we all do, that light kindled outdoors does this. And it is not unnatural to suppose that thought, like any other force, leaves everywhere traces of effect. Now, when *we* think of a certain actual rose-bush, we do not suppose that our thought goes to that actual bush, and engages with it, like a searchlight turned upon it. What then do we suppose our consciousness is dealing with when we are thinking of that rose-bush? Probably we think it is dealing with a 'mental image' which is not the rose-bush but a mental surrogate of it. Buy why should it be *natural* to think that our thought deals with a surrogate and not with the real rose-bush? Quite possibly because we are dimly aware that we carry about with us a whole imaginary space, full of mental surrogates. To us, mental surrogates are old familiar fare. Along with images of imaginary space, which we perhaps secretly know to be only imaginary, we tuck the thought-of actually existing rose-bush, which may be quite another story, perhaps just because we have that very convenient 'place' for it. The Hopi thought-world has no imaginary space. The corollary to this is that it may not locate thought dealing with real space anywhere but in real space, nor insulate real space from the effects of thought. A Hopi would naturally suppose that his thought (or himself) traffics with the actual rose-bush—or more likely corn-plant—that he is thinking about. The thought then should leave some trace of itself with the plant in the field. If it is a good thought, one about health and growth, it is good for the plant; if a bad thought, the reverse.

The Hopi emphasize the intensity-factor of thought. Thought to be most effective should be vivid in consciousness, definite, steady, sustained, charged with strongly-felt good intentions. They render the idea in English as 'concentrating' 'holding it in your heart,' 'putting your mind on it,' 'earnestly hoping.' Thought power is the force behind ceremonies, prayer sticks, ritual smoking, etc. The prayer-pipe is regarded as an aid to 'concentrating' (so said my informant). Its name, na´twanpi, means 'instrument of preparing.'

Covert participation is mental collaboration from people who do not take part in the actual affair, be it a job of work, hunt, race, or ceremony, but direct their thought and good will toward the affair's success.

Announcements often seek to elicit the support of such mental helpers as well as of overt participants, and contain exhortations to the people to aid with their active good will.[10] A similarity to our concepts of a sympathetic audience or the cheering section at a football game should not obscure the fact that it is primarily the power of directed thought, and not merely sympathy or encouragement, that is expected of covert participants. In fact these latter get in their deadliest work before, not during, the game! A corollary to the power of thought is the power of wrong thought for evil; hence one purpose of covert participation is to obtain the mass force of many good wishers to offset the harmful thought of ill wishers. Such attitudes greatly favor cooperation and community spirit. Not that the Hopi community is not full of rivalries and colliding interests. Against the tendency to social disintegration in such a small, isolated group, the theory of 'preparing' by the power of thought, logically leading to the great power of the combined, intensified and harmonized thought of the whole community, must help vastly toward the rather remarkable degree of cooperation that in spite of much private bickering the Hopi village displays in all the important cultural activities.

Hopi 'preparing' activities again show a result of their linguistic thought background in an emphasis on persistence and constant insistent repetition. A sense of the cumulative value of innumerable small momenta is dulled by an objectified, spatialized view of time like ours, enhanced by a way of thinking close to the subjective awareness of duration, of the ceaseless 'latering' of events. To us, for whom time is a motion on a space, unvarying repetition seems to scatter its force along a row of units of that space, and be wasted. To the Hopi, for whom time is not a motion but a 'getting later' of everything that has ever been done, unvarying repetition is not wasted but accumulated. It is storing up an invisible change that holds over into later events.[11]

[10] See, e.g., Earnest Beaglehole, *Note on Hopi Economic Life* (Yale University Publications in Anthropology, no. 15, 1937), especially the reference to the announcement of a rabbit hunt, and on p. 30, description of the activities in connection with the cleaning of Toreva Spring—announcing, various preparing activities, and finally, preparing the continuity of the good results already obtained and the continued flow of the spring.

[11] This notion of storing up power, which seems implied by much Hopi behavior, has an analog in physics: acceleration. It might be said that the linguistic background of Hopi thought equips it to recognize naturally that force manifests not as motion or velocity, but as cumulation or acceleration.

As we have seen, it is as if the return of the day were felt as the return of the same person, a little older but with all the impresses of yesterday, not as 'another day,' i.e. like an entirely different person. This principle joined with that of thought-power and with traits of general Pueblo culture is expressed in the theory of the Hopi ceremonial dance for furthering rain and crops, as well as in its short piston-like tread, repeated thousands of times, hour after hour.

SOME IMPRESSES OF LINGUISTIC HABIT IN WESTERN CIVILIZATION

It is harder to do justice in a few words to the linguistically conditioned features of our own culture than in the case of the Hopi, because of both vast scope and difficulty of objectivity—because of our ingrained familiarity with the attitudes to be analyzed. I wish merely to sketch certain characteristics adjusted to our linguistic binomialism of form plus formless item or 'substance,' to our metaphoricalness, our imaginary space, and our objectified time. These, as we have seen, are linguistic.

From the form-plus-substance dichotomy the philosophical views most traditionally characteristic of the 'Western world' have derived huge support. Here belong materialism, psychophysical parallelism, physics—at least in its traditional Newtonian form—and dualistic views of the universe in general. Indeed here belongs almost everything that is 'hard, practical, common sense.' Monistic, holistic, and relativistic views of reality appeal to philosophers and some scientists, but they are badly handicapped in appealing to the 'common sense' of the Western average man. This is not because nature herself refutes them (if she did, philosophers could have discovered this much), but because they must be talked about in what amounts to a new language. 'Common sense,' as its name shows, and 'practicality' as its name does not show, are largely matters of talking so that one is readily understood. It is sometimes stated that Newtonian space, time, and matter are sensed by everyone intuitively, whereupon relativity is cited as showing how mathematical analysis can prove intuition wrong. This,

---

Our linguistic background tends to hinder in us this same recognition, for having legitimately conceived force to be that which produces change, we then think of change by our linguistic *metaphorical analog*, motion, instead of by a pure motionless changingness concept, i.e. accumulation or acceleration. Hence it comes to our naïve feeling as a shock to find from physical experiments that it is not possible to define force by motion, that motion and speed, as also "being at rest," are wholly relative, and that force can be measured only by acceleration.

besides being unfair to intuition, is an attempt to answer offhand question (1) put at the outset of this paper [p. 201], to answer which this research was undertaken. Presentation of the findings now nears its end, and I think the answer is clear. The offhand answer, laying the blame upon intuition for our slowness in discovering the mysteries of the cosmos, such as relativity, is the wrong one. The right answer is: Newtonian space, time, and matter are no intuitions. They are recepts from culture and language. That is where Newton got them.

Our objectified view of time is however favorable to historicity and to everything connected with the keeping of records, while the Hopi view is unfavorable thereto. The latter is too subtle, complex, and ever-developing, supplying no ready-made answer to the question of when 'one' event ends and 'another' begins. When it is implicit that everything that ever happened still is, but is in a necessarily different form from what memory or record reports, there is less incentive to study the past. As for the present, the incentive would be not to record it but to treat it as 'preparing.' But *our* objectified time puts before imagination something like a ribbon or scroll marked off into equal blank spaces, suggesting that each be filled with an entry. Writing has no doubt helped toward our linguistic treatment of time, even as the linguistic treatment has guided the uses of writing. Through this give-and-take between language and the whole culture we get, for instance:

1. Records, diaries, bookkeeping, accounting, mathematics stimulated by accounting;
2. Interest in exact sequence, dating, calendars, chronology, clocks, time wages, time graphs, time used in physics;
3. Annals, histories, the historical attitude, interest in the past, archaeology, attitudes of introjection toward past periods, e.g. classicism, romanticism.

Just as we conceive our objectified time as extending in the future like the way that it extends in the past, so we set down our estimates of the future in the same shape as our records of the past, producing programs, schedules, budgets. The formal equality of the space-like units by which we measure and conceive time leads us to consider the 'formless item' or 'substance' of time to be homogeneous and in ratio to the number of units. Hence our prorata allocation of value to time, lending itself to the building of a commercial structure based on time-prorata values: time wages (time work constantly supersedes piece work), rent, credit, interest, depreciation charges, and insurance premiums. No doubt this vast system, once built, would continue to run under any sort of linguistic treatment of time; but that it should have been built at all, reaching the magnitude and particular form it has in the Western world, is a fact decidedly in consonance with the patterns of the SAE languages. Whether such a civilization as ours would be possible with widely different linguistic handling of time is a large question—in our civilization, our linguistic patterns and the fitting of our behavior to the temporal order are what they are, and they are in accord. We are of course stimulated to use calendars, clocks, and watches, and to try to measure time ever more precisely; this aids science, and science, in turn, following these well-worn cultural grooves, gives back to culture an ever-growing store of applications, habits, and values with which culture again directs science. But what lies outside this spiral? Science is beginning to find that there is something in the cosmos that is not in accord with the concepts we have formed in mounting the spiral. It is trying to frame a *new language* by which to adjust itself to a wider universe.

It is clear how the emphasis on 'saving time' which goes with all the above and is very obvious objectification of time, leads to a high valuation on 'speed,' which shows itself a great deal of behavior.

Still another behavioral effect is that the character of monotony and regularity possessed by our image of time as an evenly scaled limitless tape measure persuades us to behave as if that monotony were more true of events than it really is. That is, it helps to routinize us. We tend to select and favor whatever bears out this view, to 'play up to' the routine aspects of existence. One phase of this is behavior evincing a false sense of security or an assumption that all will always go smooth- ly, and a lack in foreseeing and protecting ourselves against hazards. Our technique of harnessing energy does well in routine performance, and it is along routine lines that we chiefly strive to improve it—we are, for example, relatively uninterested in stopping the energy from caus- ing accidents, fires, and explosions, which it is doing constantly and on a wide scale. Such indifference to the unexpectedness of life would be disastrous to a society as small, isolated, and precariously poised as the Hopi society is, or rather once was.

Thus our linguistically determined thought world not only collab- orates with our cultural idols and ideals, but engages even our uncon- scious personal reactions in its patterns and gives them certain typical characters. One such character, as we have seen, is *carelessness*,

as in reckless driving or throwing cigarette stubs into waste paper.
Another of different sort is *gesturing* when we talk. Very many
of the gestures made by English-speaking people at least, and probably
by all SAE speakers, serve to illustrate by a movement in space not a
real spatial reference but one of the non-spatial references that our
language handles by metaphors of imaginary space. That is, we are
more apt to make a grasping gesture when we speak of grasping an
elusive idea than when we speak of grasping a doorknob. The gesture
seeks to make a metaphorical and hence somewhat unclear reference
more clear. But, if a language refers to non-spatials without implying
a spatial analogy, the reference is not made any clearer by gesture.
The Hopi gesture very little, perhaps not at all in the sense we understand as gesture.

It would seem as if kinesthesia, or the sensing of muscular movement, though arising prior to language, should be made more highly
conscious by linguistic use of imaginary space and metaphorical images
of motion. Kinesthesia is marked by two facets of European culture:
art and sport. European sculpture, an art in which Europe excels, is
strongly kinesthetic, conveying great sense of the body's motions;
European painting likewise. The dance in our culture expresses delight
in motion rather than symbolism or ceremonial, and our music is greatly influenced by our dance forms. Our sports are strongly imbued with
this element of the 'poetry in motion.' Hopi races and games seem to
emphasize rather the virtues of endurance and sustained intensity. Hopi
dancing is highly symbolic and is performed with great intensity and
earnestness, but has not much movement or swing.

Synesthesia, or suggestion by certain sense receptions of characters
belonging to another sense, as of light and color by sounds and *vice
versa*, should be made more conscious by a linguistic metaphorical
system that refers to non-spatial experiences by terms for spatial ones,
though undoubtedly it arises from a deeper source. Probably in the
first instance metaphor arises from synesthesia and not the reverse; yet
metaphor need not become firmly rooted in linguistic pattern, as Hopi
shows. Non-spatial experience has one well-organized sense, *hearing*
—for smell and taste are but little organized. Non-spatial consciousness is a realm chiefly of thought, feeling, and *sound*. Spatial consciousness is a realm of light, color, sight, and touch, and presents
shapes and dimensions. Our metaphorical system, by naming non-
spatial experiences after spatial ones, imputes to sounds, smells, tastes,

emotions, and thoughts spatial qualities like the colors, luminosities, shapes, angles, textures, and motions of spatial experience. And to some extent the reverse transference occurs; for after much talking about tones as high, low, sharp, dull, heavy, brilliant, slow, the talker finds it easy to think of some factors in spatial experience as like factors of tone. Thus we speak of 'tones' of color, a gray 'monotone,' a 'loud' necktie, a 'taste' in dress: all spatial metaphors in reverse. Now European art is distinctive in the way it seeks directly to play with synesthesia. Music tries to suggest scenes, color, movement, geometric design; painting and sculpture are often consciously guided by the analogies of music's rhythm; colors are conjoined with feeling for the analogy to concords and discords. The European theater and opera seek a synthesis of many arts. It may be that in this way our metaphorical language that is in some sense a confusion of thought is producing, through art, a result of far-reaching value — a deeper esthetic sense leading toward a more direct apprehension of underlying unity behind the phenomena so variously reported by our sense channels.

HISTORICAL IMPLICATIONS

How does such a network of language, culture, and behavior come about historically? Which was first: the language patterns or the cultural norms? In main they have grown up together, constantly influencing each other. But in this partnership the nature of the language is the factor that limits the free plasticity and rigidifies channels of development in the more autocratic way. This is because a language is a system, not just an assemblage of norms. Large systematic outlines can change to something really new only very slowly, while many other cultural innovations are made with comparative quickness. Language thus represents the mass mind; it is affected by inventions and innovations, but affected little and slowly, whereas *to* inventors and innovators it legislates with the decree immediate.

The growth of the SAE language-culture complex dates from ancient times. Much of its metaphorical reference to the non-spatial by the spatial was already fixed in the ancient tongues, and more especially in Latin. It is indeed a marked trait of Latin. If we compare, say Hebrew, we find that, while Hebrew has some allusions to not-space as space, Latin has more. Latin terms for non-spatials, like *educo, religio, principia, comprehendo,* are usually metaphorized physical references: lead out, tying back, etc. This is not true of all

languages—it is quite untrue of Hopi. The fact that in Latin the
direction of development happened to be from spatial to non-spatial
(partly because of secondary stimulation to abstract thinking when
the intellectually crude Romans encountered Greek culture) and that
later tongues were strongly stimulated to mimic Latin, seems a likely
reason for a belief which still lingers on among linguists that this is
the natural direction of semantic change in all languages, and for the
persistent notion in Western learned circles (in strong contrast to
Eastern ones) that objective experience is prior to subjective. Philosophies make out a weighty case for the reverse, and certainly the
direction of development is sometimes the reverse. Thus the Hopi
word for 'heart' can be shown to be a late formation within Hopi from
a root meaning think or remember. Or consider what has happened to
the word 'radio' in such a sentence as 'he bought a new radio,' as
compared to its prior meaning 'science of wireless telephony.'

   In the middle ages the patterns already formed in Latin began to
interweave with the increased mechanical invention, industry, trade,
and scholastic and scientific thought. The need for measurement in
industry and trade, the stores and bulks of 'stuffs' in various containers,
the type-bodies in which various goods were handled, standardizing
of measure and weight units, invention of clocks and measurement of
'time,' keeping of records, accounts, chronicles, histories, growth of
mathematics and the partnership of mathematics and science, all
cooperated to bring our thought and language into its present form.

   In Hopi history, could we read it, we should find a different type
of language and a different set of cultural and environmental influences
working together. A peaceful agricultural society isolated by geographic
features and nomad enemies in a land of scanty rainfall, arid agriculture
that could be made successful only by the utmost perseverance (hence
the value of persistence and repetition), necessity for collaboration
(hence emphasis on the psychology of teamwork and on mental factors
in general), corn and rain as primary criteria of value, need of extensive
preparations and precautions to assure crops in the poor soil and precarious climate, keen realization of dependence upon nature favoring
prayer and a religious attitude toward the forces of nature, especially
prayer and religion directed toward the ever-needed blessing, rain—
these things interacted with Hopi linguistic patterns to mold them,
to be molded again by them, and so little by little to shape the Hopi
world-outlook.

To sum up the matter, our first question asked in the beginning [p. 201] is answered thus: Concepts of 'time' and 'matter' are not given in substantially the same form by experience to all men but depend upon the nature of the language or languages through the use of which they have been developed. They do not depend so much upon *any one system* (e.g., tense, or nouns) within the grammar as upon the ways of analyzing and reporting experience which have become fixed in the language as integrated 'fashions of speaking' and which cut across the typical grammatical classifications, so that such a 'fashion' may include lexical, morphological, syntactic, and otherwise systemically diverse means coordinated in a certain frame of consistency. Our own 'time' differs markedly from Hopi 'duration.' It is conceived as like a space of strictly limited dimensions, or sometimes as like a motion upon such space, and employed as an intellectual tool accordingly. Hopi 'duration' seems to be inconceivable in terms of space or motion, being the mode in which life differs from form, and consciousness *in toto* from the spatial elements of consciousness. Certain ideas born of our own time-concept, such as that of absolute simultaneity, would be either very difficult to express or impossible and devoid of meaning under the Hopi conception, and would be replaced by operational concepts. Our 'matter' is the physical subtype of 'substance' or 'stuff,' which is conceived as the formless extensional item that must be joined with form before there can be real existence. In Hopi there seems to be nothing corresponding to it; there are no formless extensional items; existence may or may not have form, but what it also has, with or without form, is intensity and duration, these being non-extensional and at bottom the same.

But what about our concept of 'space,' which was also included in our first question? There is no such striking difference between Hopi and SAE about space as about time, and probably the apprehension of space is given in substantially the same form by experience irrespective of language. The experiments of the Gestalt psychologists with visual perception appear to establish this as a fact. But the *concept of space* will vary somewhat with language, because, as an intellectual tool,[12] it is so closely linked with the concomitant employment of other intellectual tools, of the order of 'time' and 'matter,' which are linguistically conditioned. We see things with our eyes in the same space forms as the Hopi, but our idea of space has also the property

---

[12] Here belong "Newtonian" and "Euclidean" space, etc.

of acting as a surrogate of non-spatial relationships like time, intensity, tendency, and as a void to be filled with imagined formless items, one of which may even be called 'space.' Space as sensed by the Hopi would not be connected mentally with such surrogates, but would be comparatively 'pure,' unmixed with extraneous notions.

As for our second question (p. [201]): There are connections but not correlations or diagnostic correspondences between cultural norms and linguistic patterns. Although it would be impossible to infer the existence of Crier Chiefs from the lack of tenses in Hopi, or vice versa, there is a relation between a language and the rest of the culture of the society which uses it. There are cases where the 'fashions of speaking' are closely integrated with the whole general culture, whether or not this be universally true, and there are connections within this integration, between the kind of linguistic analyses employed and various behavioral reactions and also the shapes taken by various cultural developments. Thus the importance of Crier Chiefs does have a connection, not with tenselessness itself, but with a system of thought in which categories different from our tenses are natural. These connections are to be found not so much by focusing attention on the typical rubrics of linguistic, ethnographic, or sociological description as by examining the culture and language (always and only when the two have been together historically for a considerable time) as a whole in which concatenations that run across these departmental lines may be expected to exist, and, if they do exist, eventually to be discoverable by study.

Languages and Logic

Chemical compound or mechanical mixture, a sentence hides
within its structure laws of thought profoundly important to
the advance of science.

In English the sentences "I pull the branch aside" and "I have an extra
toe on my foot" have little similarity. Leaving out the subject pronoun
and the sign of the present tense, which are common features from
requirements of English syntax, we may say that no similarity exists.
Common, and even scientific, parlance would say that the sentences
are unlike because they are talking about things which are intrinsically
unlike. So Mr. Everyman, the natural logician, would be inclined to
argue. Formal logic of an older type would perhaps agree with him.

If, moreover, we appeal to an impartial scientific English-speaking
observer, asking him to make direct observations upon cases of the two
phenomena to see if they may not have some element of similarity
which we have overlooked, he will be more than likely to confirm the
dicta of Mr. Everyman and the logician. The observer whom we have
asked to make the test may not see quite eye to eye with the old-school
logician and would not be disappointed to find him wrong. Still he is
compelled sadly to confess failure. "I wish I could oblige you," he
says, "but try as I may, I cannot detect any similarity between these
phenomena."

By this time our stubborn streak is aroused; we wonder if a being
from Mars would also see no resemblance. But now a linguist points
out that it is not necessary to go as far as Mars. We have not yet
scouted around this earth to see if its many languages all classify
these phenomena as disparately as our speech does. We find that
in Shawnee these two statements are respectively *ni-l'θawa-'ko-n-a*
and *ni-l'θawa-'ko-θite* (the θ here denotes *th* as in "thin" and the
apostrophe denotes a breath-catch). The sentences are closely similar;
in fact, they differ only at the tail end. In Shawnee, moreover, the
beginning of a construction is generally the most important and
emphatic part. Both sentences start with *ni-* ("I"), which is a mere
prefix. Then comes the really important key word, *l'θawa*, a common
Shawnee term denoting a forked outline, like Fig. 3, No. 1 (page [229]).
The next element, *-'ko*, we cannot be sure of, but it agrees in form with
a variant of the suffix *-a'kw* or *-a'ko*, denoting tree, bush, tree part,

branch, or anything of that general shape. In the first sentence, -*n*-
means "by hand action" and may be either a causation of the basic
condition (forked outline) manually, an increase of it, or both. The
final -*a* means that the subject ("I") does this action to an appropriate
object. Hence the first sentence means "I pull it (something like branch
of tree) more open or apart where it forks." In the other sentence, the
suffix -*θite* means "pertaining to the toes," and the absence of further
suffixes means that subject manifests the condition in his own person.
Therefore, the sentence can mean only "I have an extra toe forking out
like a branch from a normal toe."

Shawnee logicians and observers would class the two phenomena
as intrinsically similar. Our own observer, to whom we tell all this,
focuses his instruments again upon the two phenomena and to his joy
sees at once a manifest resemblance. Figure 1 illustrates a similar
situation: "I push his head back" and "I drop it in water and it floats,"
though very dissimilar sentences in English, are similar in Shawnee.

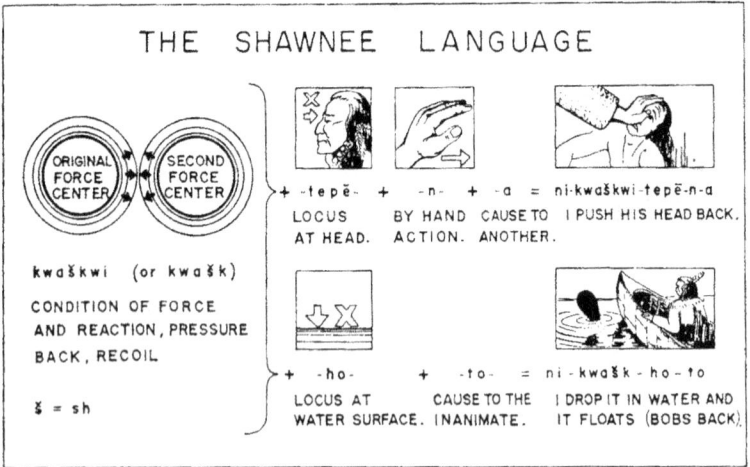

THE   SHAWNEE   LANGUAGE

ORIGINAL FORCE CENTER   SECOND FORCE CENTER

kwaškwi   (or kwašk)

CONDITION OF FORCE
AND REACTION, PRESSURE
BACK, RECOIL

š = sh

+ -tepĕ- + -n- + -a = ni-kwaškwi-tepĕ-n-a
LOCUS   BY HAND   CAUSE TO   I PUSH HIS HEAD BACK.
AT HEAD.   ACTION.   ANOTHER.

+ -ho-   + -to- = ni-kwašk-ho-to
LOCUS AT   CAUSE TO THE   I DROP IT IN WATER AND
WATER SURFACE.   INANIMATE.   IT FLOATS (BOBS BACK).

*Fig. 1. The English sentences "I push his head back" and "I drop it
in water and it floats" are unlike. But in Shawnee the corresponding
statements are closely similar, emphasizing the fact that analysis of
nature and classification of events as like or in the same category
(logic) are governed by grammar.*

The point of view of linguistic relativity changes Mr. Everyman's
dictum: Instead of saying, "Sentences are unlike because they tell about
unlike facts," he now reasons: "Facts are unlike to speakers whose
language background provides for unlike formulations of them."

Conversely, the English sentences, "The boat is grounded on the beach" and "The boat is manned by picked men," seem to us to be rather similar. Each is about a boat; each tells the relation of the boat to other objects — or that's *our* story. The linguist would point out the parallelism in grammatical pattern thus: "The boat is $x$ed preposition$y$." The logician might turn the linguist's analysis into: "A is in the state x in relation to y," and then perhaps into $fA = xRy$. Such symbolic methods lead to fruitful techniques of rational ordering, stimulate our thinking, and bring valuable insights. Yet we should realize that the similarities and contrasts in the original sentences, subsumed under the foregoing formula, are dependent on the choice of mother tongue and that the properties of the tongue are eventually reflected as peculiarities of structure in the fabric of logic or mathematics which we rear.

In the Nootka language of Vancouver Island, the first "boat" statement is *tlih-is-ma*; the second is, *lash-tskwiq-ista-ma*. The first is thus I-II-*ma*; the second, III-IV-V-*ma*; and they are quite unlike, for the final -*ma* is only the sign of the third person indicative. Neither sentence contains any unit of meaning akin to our word "boat" or even "canoe." Part I, in the first sentence, means "moving pointwise," or moving in a way like the suggestion of the outline in Fig. 3, No. 2; hence, "traveling in or as a canoe," or an event like one position of such motion. It is not a name for what we should call a "thing," but is more like a vector in physics. Part II means "on the beach"; hence I-II-*ma* means "it is on the beach pointwise as an event of canoe motion," and would normally refer to a boat that has come to land. In the other sentence, part III means "select, pick," and IV means "remainder, result," so that III-IV means "selected." Part V means "in a canoe (boat) as crew." The whole, III-IV-V-*ma*, means either "they are in the boat as a crew of picked men," or "the boat has a crew of picked men." It means that the whole event involving picked ones and boat's crew is in process.

As a hang-over from my education in chemical engineering, I relish an occasional chemical simile. Perhaps readers will catch what I mean when I say that the way the constituents are put together in these sentences of Shawnee and Nootka suggests a chemical compound, whereas their combination in English is more like a mechanical mixture. A mixture, like the mountaineer's potlicker, can be assembled out of almost anything and does not make any sweeping transformation of the overt appearance of the material. A chemical compound, on the other hand, can be put together only out of mutually suited ingredients, and the result may be not merely soup but a crop of crystals or a cloud of smoke. Likewise the typical Shawnee and Nootka combinations appear to work with a vocabulary of terms chosen with a view not so much to the utility of their immediate references as to the ability of the terms to combine suggestively with each other in manifold ways that elicit novel and useful images. This principle of terminology and way of analyzing events would seem to be unknown to the tongues with which we are familiar.

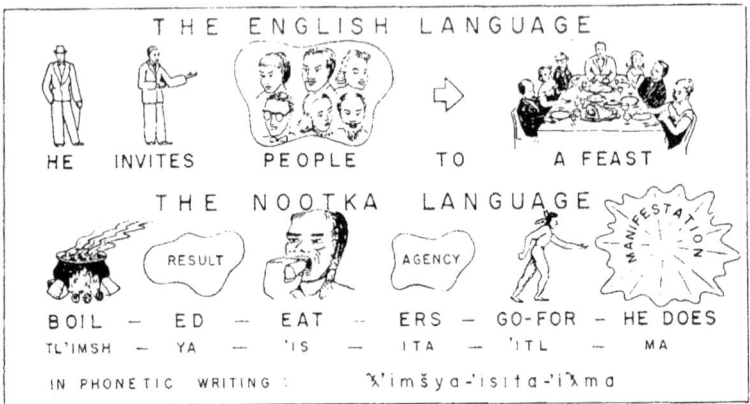

Fig. 2. Here are shown the different ways in which English and Nootka formulate the same event. The English sentence is divisible into subject and predicate; the Nootka sentence is not, yet it is complete and logical. Furthermore, the Nootka sentence is just one word, consisting of the root tl'imsh *with five suffixes.*

It is the analysis of nature down to a basic vocabulary capable of this sort of evocative recombinations which is most distinctive of poly-synthetic languages, like Nootka and Shawnee. Their characteristic quality is not, as some linguists have thought, a matter of the tightness or indissolubility of the combinations. The Shawnee term *l'θawa* could probably be said alone but would then mean "it (or something) is forked," a statement which gives little hint of the novel meanings that arise out of combinations—at least to our minds or our type of logic. Shawnee and Nootka do not use the chemical type of synthesis exclusively. They make large use of a more external kind of syntax, which, however, has no basic structural priority. Even our own Indo-

European tongues are not wholly devoid of the chemical method, but they seldom make sentences by it, afford little inkling of its possibilities, and give structural priority to another method. It was quite natural, then, that Aristotle should found our traditional logic wholly on this other method.

Let me make another analogy, not with chemistry but with art— art of the pictorial sort. We look at a good still-life painting and seem to see a lustrous porcelain bowl and a downy peach. Yet an analysis that screened out the totality of the picture—as if we were going over it carefully, looking through a hole cut in a card—would reveal only oddly shaped patches of paint and would not evoke the bowl and fruit. The synthesis presented by the painting is akin to the chemical type of syntax, and it may point to psychological fundamentals that enter into both art and language. Now the mechanical method in art and language might be typified by Fig 3, No. 3A. The first element, a field of spots, corresponds to the adjective "spotted," the second corresponds to the noun "cat." By putting them together, we get "spotted cat." Contrast the technique in Fig. 3, No. 3B. Here the figure corresponding to "cat" has only vague meaning by itself—"chevronlike," we might say—while the first element is even vaguer. But combined, these evoke a cylindrical object, like a shaft casing.

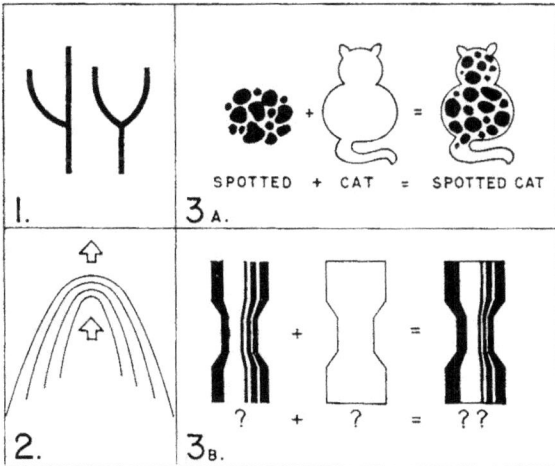

Fig. 3. Suggested above are certain linguistic concepts which, as explained in the text, are not easily definable.

The thing common to both techniques is a systematic synthetic use of pattern, and this is also common to all language techniques. I have put question marks below the elements in Fig. 3, No. 3B, to point out the difficulty of a parallel in English speech and the fact that the method probably has no standing in traditional logic. Yet examination of other languages and the possibility of new types of logic that has been advanced by modern logicians themselves, suggest that this matter may be significant for modern science. New types of logic may help us eventually to understand how it is that electrons, the velocity of light, and other components of the subject matter of physics appear to behave illogically, or that phenomena which flout the sturdy common sense of yesteryear can nevertheless be true. Modern thinkers have long since pointed out that the so-called mechanistic way of thinking has come to an impasse before the great frontier problems of science. To rid ourselves of this way of thinking is exceedingly difficult when we have no linguistic experience of any other and when even our most advanced logicians and mathematicians do not provide any other—and obviously they cannot without the linguistic experience. For the mechanistic way of thinking is perhaps just a type of syntax natural to Mr. Everyman's daily use of the western Indo-European languages, rigidified and intensified by Aristotle and the latter's medieval and modern followers.

As I said in an article, "Science and Linguistics," in The Review for April, 1940 [in this volume], the effortlessness of speech and the subconscious way we picked up that activity in early childhood lead us to regard talking and thinking as wholly straightforward and transparent. We naturally feel that they embody self-evident laws of thought, the same for all men. We know all the answers! But when scrutinized, they become dusty answers. We use speech for reaching agreements about subject matter: I say, "Please shut the door," and my hearer and I agree that "the door" refers to a certain part of our environment and that I want a certain result produced. Our explanations of how we reached this understanding, though quite satisfactory on the everyday social plane, are merely more agreements (statements) about the same subject matter (door, and so on), more and more amplified by statements about the social and personal needs that impel us to communicate. There are here no laws of thought. Yet the structural regularities of our sentences enable us to sense that laws are *somewhere* in the background. Clearly, explanations of understanding such as "And so I ups and says to him, says I; see here, why don't you . . . !" evade the true process by which "he" and "I" are in communication. Likewise psychological-social descriptions of the social and emotional needs that impel people to communicate with their fellows tend to be learned versions of the same method and, while interesting, still evade the question. In similar case [*sic*] is evasion of the question by skipping from the speech sentence, via physiology and "stimuli," to the social situation.

The *why* of understanding may remain for a long time mysterious; but the *how* or logic of understanding—its background of laws and regularities—is discoverable. It is the grammatical background of our mother tongue, which includes not only our way of constructing propositions but the way we dissect nature and break up the flux of experience into objects and entities to construct propositions about. This fact is important for science because it means that science *can* have a rational or logical basis even though it be a relativistic one and not Mr. Everyman's natural logic. Although it may vary with each tongue, and a planetary mapping of the dimensions of such variation may be necessitated, it is, nevertheless, a basis of logic with discoverable laws. Science is not compelled to see its thinking and reasoning procedures turned into processes merely subservient to social adjustments and emotional drives.

Moreover, the tremendous importance of language cannot, in my opinion, be taken to mean necessarily that nothing is back of it of the nature of what has traditionally been called "mind." My own studies suggest, to me, that language, for all of its kingly role, is in some sense a superficial embroidery upon deeper processes of consciousness which are necessary before any communication, signaling, or symbolism whatsoever can occur and which also can at a pinch effect communication (though not true *agreement*) without language's and without symbolism's aid. I mean "superficial" in the sense that all processes of chemistry, for example, can be said to be superficial upon the deeper layer of physical existence, which we know variously as intra-atomic, electronic, or subelectronic. No one would take this statement to mean that chemistry is *unimportant*—indeed the whole point is that the more superficial can mean the more important, in a definite operative sense. It may even be in the cards that there is no such thing as "Language" (with a capital L) at all! The statement that "thinking is a matter of *language*" is an incorrect generalization of the more nearly correct "thinking is a matter of *different tongues*." The different tongues are the real phenomena and may generalize down not to any such universal as "Language," but to something better—called "sublinguistic" or "superlinguistic"—and *not altogether* unlike, even if much unlike, what we now call "mental." This generalization would not diminish, but would rather increase, the importance of intertongue study for investigation of this realm of truth.

Botanists and zoologists, in order to understand the world of living species, found it necessary to describe the species in every part of the globe and to add a time perspective by including the fossils. Then they found it necessary to compare and contrast the species, to work out families and classes, evolutionary descent, morphology, and taxonomy. In linguistic science a similar attempt is under way. The far-off event toward which this attempt moves is a new technology of language and thought. Much progress has been made in classifying the languages of earth into genetic families, each having descent from a single precursor, and in tracing such developments through time. The result is called "comparative linguistics." This plots the outstanding differences between tongues–in grammar, logic, and general analysis of experience.

As I said in the April, 1940, Review, segmentation of nature is an aspect of grammar—one as yet little studied by grammarians. We cut up and organize the spread and flow of events as we do largely because, through our mother tongue, we are parties to an agreement to do so, not because nature itself is segmented in exactly that way for all to see. Languages differ not only in how they build their sentences but in how they break down nature to secure the elements to put in those sentences. This breakdown gives units of the lexicon. "Word" is not a very good "word" for them: "lexeme" has been suggested, and "term" will do for the present. By these more or less distinct terms we ascribe a semi-fictitious isolation to parts of experience. English terms, like "sky," "hill," "swamp," persuade us to regard some elusive aspect of nature's endless variety as a distinct *thing*, almost like a table or chair. Thus English and similar tongues lead us to think of the universe as a collection of rather distinct objects and events corresponding to words. Indeed, this is the implicit picture of classical physics and astronomy— that the universe is essentially a collection of detached objects of different sizes.

The examples used by older logicians in dealing with this point are usually unfortunately chosen. They tend to pick out tables and chairs and apples on tables as test objects to demonstrate the objectlike nature of reality and its one-to-one correspondence with logic. Man's artifacts and the agricultural products he severs from living plants have a unique degree of isolation; we may expect that languages will have fairly isolated terms for them. The real question is: What do different languages do, not with these artificially isolated objects but with the flowing face of nature in its motion, color, and changing form: with clouds, beaches, and yonder flight of birds? For as goes our segmentation of the face of nature, so goes our physics of the cosmos.

Here we find differences in segmentation and selection of basic terms. We might isolate something in nature by saying, "It is a dripping spring." Apache erects the statement on a verb *ga*: "be white (including clear, uncolored, and so on)." With a prefix *no-* the meaning of downward motion enters: "whiteness moves downward." Then *tó*, meaning both "water" and "spring," is prefixed. The result corresponds to our "dripping spring," but synthetically it is "as water, or springs, whiteness moves downward." How utterly unlike our way of thinking! The same verb *ga*, with a prefix that means "a place manifests the condition" becomes *gohlga*; "the place is white, clear; a clearing, a plain." These examples show that some languages have means of expression—chemical combination, as I called it—in which the separate terms are not separate as in English but flow together into plastic synthetic creations. Hence such languages, which do not paint the separate-object picture of the universe to the same degree as do English and its sister tongues, point toward possible new types of logic and possible new cosmical pictures.

The Indo-European languages and many others give great prominence to a type of sentence having two parts, each part built around a class of words—substantives and verbs—which those languages treat differently in grammar. As I showed in the April, 1940, Review, this distinction is not drawn from nature; it is just a result of the fact that every tongue must have some kind of structure, and these tongues have made a go of exploiting this kind. The Greeks, especially Aristotle, built up this contrast and made it a law of reason. Since then, the contrast has been stated in logic in many different ways: subject and predicate, actor and action, things and relations between things, objects and their attributes, quantities and operations. And, pursuant again to grammar, the notion became ingrained that one of these classes of entities can exist in its own right but that the verb class cannot exist without an entity of the other class, the "thing" class, as a peg to hang on. "Embodiment is necessary," the watchword of this ideology, is seldom *strongly* questioned. Yet the whole trend of modern physics, with its emphasis on "the field," is an implicit questioning of the ideology. This contrast crops out in our mathematics as two kinds of symbols—the kind like 1, 2, 3, x, y, z and the kind like $+, -, \div$, $\sqrt{}$, log—though in view of 0, $1/2$, $3/4$, π and others, perhaps no strict two-group classification holds. The two-group notion, however, is always present at the back of the thinking, although often not overtly expressed.

Our Indian languages show that with a suitable grammar we may have intelligent sentences that cannot be broken into subjects and predicates. Any attempted breakup is a breakup of some English translation or paraphrase of the sentence, not of the Indian sentence itself. We might as well try to decompose a certain synthetic resin into celluloid and whiting. The Algonquian language family, to which Shawnee belongs, does use a type of sentence like our subject and predicate but also gives prominence to the type shown by our examples in the text and in Fig. 1. To be sure, *ni-* is represented by a subject in the translation but means "my" as well as "I" and the sentence could be translated thus: "My hand is pulling the branch aside." Or *ni-* might be absent; if so, we should be apt to manufacture a subject, like "he," "it," "somebody," or we could pick out for our English subject an idea corresponding to any one of the Shawnee elements.

When we come to Nootka, the sentence without subject or predicate is the only type. The term "predication" is used, but it means "sentence." Nootka has no parts of speech; the simplest utterance is a sentence, treating of some event or event-complex. Long sentences are sentences of sentences (complex sentences), not just sentences of words. In Fig. 2 we have a simple, not a complex, Nootka sentence. The translation, "he invites people to a feast," splits into subject and predicate. Not so the native sentence. It begins with the event of boiling or cooking, *tl'imsh*; then comes *-ya* ("result") = cooked; then *-'is* ("eating") = eating cooked food; then *-ita* ("those who do") = eaters of cooked food; then *-'itl* ("going for"); then *-ma*, sign of third person indicative, giving *tl'imshya'isita'itlma*, which answers to the crude paraphrase, "he, or somebody, goes for (invites) eaters of cooked food."

The English technique of talking depends on the contrast of two artificial classes, substantives and verbs, and on the bipartitioned ideology of nature already discussed. Our normal sentence, unless imperative, must have some substantive before its verb, a requirement which corresponds to the philosophical and also naïve notion of an actor who produces an action. This last might not have been so if English had had thousands of verbs like "hold," denoting positions. But most of our verbs follow a type of segmentation that isolates from nature what we call "actions," that is, moving outlines.

Following majority rule, we therefore read action into every sentence, even into "I hold it." A moment's reflection will show that "hold" is no action but a state of relative positions. Yet we think of it and even see it as an action because language formulates it in the same way as it formulates more numerous expressions, like "I strike it," which deal with movements and changes.

We are constantly reading into nature fictional acting-entities, simply because our verbs must have substantives in front of them. We have to say "It flashed" or "A light flashed," setting up an actor , "*it*" or "light" to perform what we call an action, "to flash." Yet the flashing and the light are one and the same! The Hopi language reports the flash with a simple verb, *rehpi*: "flash (occurred)." There is no division into subject and predicate, not even a suffix like -*t* of Latin *tona-t* ("it thunders"). Hopi can and does have verbs without subjects, a fact which may give that tongue potentialities, probably never to be developed as a logical system for understanding some aspects of the universe. Undoubtedly modern science, strongly reflecting western Indo-European languages, often does as we all do, sees actions and forces [*sic*] where it sometimes might be better to see states. On the other hand, "state" is a noun, and as such it enjoys the superior prestige traditionally attaching to the subject or thing class; therefore science is exceedingly ready to speak of states if permitted to manipulate the concept like a noun. Perhaps in place of the "states" of an atom or a dividing cell, it would be better if we could manipulate as readily a more verblike concept but without the concealed premises of actor and action.

I can sympathize with those who say, "Put it into plain, simple English," especially when they protest against the empty formalism of loading discourse with pseudolearned words. But to restrict thinking to the patterns merely of English, and especially to those patterns which represent the acme of plainness in English, is to lose a power of thought which, once lost, can never be regained. It is the "plainest" English which contains the greatest number of unconscious assumptions about nature. This is the trouble with schemes like Basic English, in which an eviscerated British English, with its concealed premises working harder than ever, is to be fobbed off on an unsuspecting world as the substance of pure Reason itself. We handle even our plain English with much greater effect if we direct it from a vantage point of a multilingual awareness. For this reason I believe that those who envision a future world speaking only one tongue, whether English, German, Russian, or any other, hold a misguided ideal and would do the evolution of the human mind the greatest disservice. Western culture has made, through language, a provisional analysis of reality and, without correctives, holds resolutely to that analysis as final. The only correctives lie in all those other tongues which by aeons of independent evolution have arrived at different, but equally logical, provisional analyses.

In a valuable paper on "Modern Logic and the Task of the Natural Sciences," Harold N. Lee says: "Those sciences whose data are subject to quantitative measurement have been most successfully developed because we know so little about order systems other than those exemplified in mathematics. We can say with certainty, however, that there are other kinds, for the advance of logic in the last half century has clearly indicated it. We may look for advances in many lines in sciences at present well founded if the advance of logic furnishes adequate knowledge of other order types. We may also look for many subjects of inquiry whose methods are not strictly scientific at the present time to become so when new order systems are available."* To which may be added that an important field for the working out of new order systems, akin to, yet not identical with, present mathematics, lies in more penetrating investigation than has yet been made of languages remote in type from our own.

* *Sigma Xi Quarterly*, XXVIII (Autumn, 1940, 125).

Commentary on the essays of
Benjamin Lee Whorf

Grammatical Categories

In this paper Whorf discusses and in some instances establishes a variety of grammatical classifications: covert and overt categories, selective categories, moduli, lexemes, signatures, and more, all carefully set out with examples. Still, much of the paper seems like a sketch, waiting to be filled out with many more examples.[1]

Yet with such careful distinctions of classifications, Whorf never defines or gives an idea of what he understands by the terms "noun" and "verb" that he so often invokes.

Whorf mentions the distinction between full and empty words in Chinese (p. 181), but it is not clear that he understands those as Marcel Granet described them earlier.[2]

In the end, Whorf seems to be directing us to try to find universals across languages:

> Perhaps those of the second degree are the more important and ultimately the more valuable as linguistic concepts, as generalizations of the largest systemic formulations and outlines found in language when language is considered and described in terms of the whole human species. p. *187*

Science and Linguistics

Here is the statement of Whorf's relativity view:

> The categories and types that we isolate from the world of phenomena we do not find there because they stare every observer in the face; on the contrary, the world is presented in a kaleidoscope flux of impressions which has to be organized by our minds—and this means largely by the linguistic systems in our minds. We cut nature up, organize it into concepts, and ascribe significances as we do, largely because we are parties to an agreement to organize it in this way—an agreement that holds throughout our speech community and is codified in the patterns of our language. The agreement is, of course, an implicit and unstated one, *but its terms are absolutely obligatory*; we cannot talk at all except by subscribing to the organization and classification of data which the agreement decrees. p. 193

---

[1] Whorf sent this paper in 1937 to Franz Boas; it was not published in his lifetime.

[2] See p. 21 of "Language and the World" in this volume.

I believe that Whorf was right, is right. But his only evidence was
from comparing ordinary languages, and there was often debate about
whether the descriptions of their grammars were right, whether there
might be a misconception in the way the language was described.
A reaction pushing the classifications of grammar of Indo-European
languages commenced, as I trace in "Language and the World".

Yet Whorf made criticism of his work too easy:

> Whenever agreement or assent is arrived at in human affairs, and
> whether or not mathematics or other specialized symbolisms are
> made part of the procedure, *this agreement is reached by linguistic
> processes, or else it is not reached.* pp. 192–193

This is wrong. If it weren't wrong, no one could enter a very different
language-culture and learn a new language. Nor does it distinguish
between agreement and assent. Even speakers of English use gestures
to communicate, not necessarily conventional ones. But perhaps you
could say those are linguistic, too. The only way this pronouncement
could be interpreted as true is if by "agreement" Whorf meant something
much more substantial than my pointing at the fire and then towards the
woods and you getting some more firewood.

Much criticism has been directed at Whorf's analysis of time
in Hopi culture, as presented in this paper and in "The Relation of
Habitual Thought and Behavior to Language".[3] Some of it stems
from Whorf calling Hopi "timeless", as he shows that the Hopi do
not not conceive of time as a mass or flow or divided into bits. They
do not have, or at least do not talk as if they have a conception of
"Time as Such" as Chris Sinha et al. dub it, no idea of time separate
from experience.[4] But Whorf does show that the Hopi have a notion
of temporal ordering:

> Hopi grammar, by means of its forms called aspects and modes, also
> makes it easy to distinguish between momentary, continued, and
> repeated occurrences, and to indicate the actual sequence of reported
> events. p. 197

Nothing is suggested about time except the perpetual "getting later".[5]

---

[3] *Linguistic Relativities* by John Leavitt traces well that controversy.
[4] I dub it *Zeit an Sich* in analogy to the idea of a thing that is distinct from
all its"manifestations" that is dubbed *Ding an Sich.*
[5] Whorf's analysis is supported by studies of other languages. See, for
example, Vera da Silva Sinha, *Linguistic and Cultural Conceptualisations*

The Relation of Habitual Thought and Behavior to Language

If language shapes thought, we should be able to see cultural or behavioral consequences of speaking one language compared to another. Some psychologists have looked for that by concentrating on vocabulary, seeing how people react and classify according to the "ideas" of the words in their language. But Whorf stresses how the grammar as well as the vocabulary affect the conception of the world as expressed in the culture, reflecting the thought of the individual.

The comparisons he makes are between what he calls SAE languages and Hopi:

> Since with respect to the traits compared, there is little difference between English, French, German, or other European languages with the *possible* (but doubtful) exception of Balto-Slavic and non-Indo European, I have lumped these languages into one group called SAE, or "Standard Average European." p. 204

The exception of the Balto-Slavic languages seems apt because they are closer to mass-process languages, lacking articles comparable to "a" and "the" and so not forcing individualizing.

But Whorf makes claims that go far beyond what his research shows, for example:

> There is no such striking difference between Hopi and SAE about space as about time, and probably the apprehension of space is given in substantially the same form by experience irrespective of language. p. 223

> We see things with our eyes in the same space forms as the Hopi, but our idea of space has also the property of acting as a surrogate of non-spatial relationships like time, intensity, tendency, and as a void to be filled with imagined formless items, one of which may even be called "space." Space as sensed by the Hopi would not be connected mentally with such surrogates, but would be comparatively "pure," unmixed with extraneous notions. p. 224

Whorf has given no reason to believe that our perception of space is not as influenced by our language as our conceptions of time.

I suspect much of what Whorf says that is unhinged from research comes from his clinging to an idea with which he starts the paper:

---

of Time in Huni Kui, Awety´ and Kamaiurá, and Chris Sinha and Tania Kuteva, "Distributed Spatial Semantics".

In *Time and Space in Formal Logic* I develop a formal logic that takes account of time only with propositional connectives for before and after, assuming no notion of *Zeit an Sich*.

> And we shall always assume that the linguistic analysis made by our group reflects reality better than it does. p. 203

Where is the reality? What is the reality that our language does or does not reflect well? [6] In "Languages and Logic",Whorf seems to abandon reliance on a world that is the same for all.

It might seem that a certain vagueness was needed in these beginning studies. Concerning language and culture, Whorf says:

> That portion of the whole investigation here to be reported may be summed up in two questions: (1) Are our own concepts of "time," "space," and "matter" given in substantially the same form by experience to all men, or are they in part conditioned by the structure of particular languages? (2) Are there traceable affinities between (a) cultural and behavioral norms and (b) large-scale linguistic patterns? I should be the last to pretend there is anything so definite as "a correlation" between culture and language, and especially between ethnological rubrics such as "agricultural," "hunting," etc. and linguistic ones like "inflected," "synthetic," or "isolating." [1] When I began the study, the problem was by no means so clearly formulated, and I had little notion that the answers would turn out as they did.
>
> [1] We have plenty of evidence that this is not the case. Consider only the Hopi and the Ute, with languages that on the overt morphological and lexical level are as similar as, say, English and German. The idea of "correlation" between language and culture, in the generally accepted sense of correlation, is certainly a mistaken one.   p. 204

This depends on what you mean by "culture". It appears that Whorf was not aware of Dorothy Lee's paper "Conceptual Implications of an Indian Language" (reprinted in this volume) that had already dealt with the issue of time and cultural consequences.[7]

---

[6] Penny Lee in *The Whorf Theory Complex*, p. 110, notes that others have made a similar point:

> Hockett went on to argue . . . that although people like Whorf "have found themselves impelled to search for an absolute that they could use in their wanderings—an anchor to windward . . . no such point of reference is necessary". He said that: "It is not necessary to have a co-ordinate system in order to have a perfectly valid geometry" and suggested that perhaps "we can dispense with any cross-culturally valid co-ordinate system in making these measures of linguistic and cultural differences" [Hockett, 1954, p. 171].

[7] Dorothy Lee's name appears as one of the contributors to the fund that

In his discussion of mass versus thing and counting and how language connects to experience we see Whorf struggling to come up with a way to convey how experience could be so different depending on a language. In the long paragraph (pp. 214–215) about how thought connects directly with the rosebush, Whorf is trying to convey what I set out in my paper "Language and the World": If the world is flow, the flux of all, then there is no separation, we are not separate, distinct things; all is connected in the flow of all.

I started with the metaphysics and derived a language from that. Then I looked for consequences in behavior and thought that would follow from that view. Once we have seen that view in the abstracted way, we can ask if we can find the view of the world as flow, of mass-process descriptions dominating rather than thing-descriptions, in ordinary languages. We find some language—not a perfect match, but the overview highlights and makes clear the general conception. Then we look to see if some of the non-linguistic consequences described in "Language and the World" occur with speakers of that language. So we can read this long paragraph of Whorf with more insight, nodding that yes, this is what we had imagined would be, not exactly, not the details, but the broad view and conceptions as lived.

Languages and Logic

Whorf is explicit that the subject-predicate distinction need not appear in a language:

> Fig. 2. Here are shown the different ways in which English and Nootka formulate the same event. The English sentence is divisible into subject and predicate; the Nootka sentence is not, yet it is complete and logical. Furthermore, the Nootka sentence is just one word, consisting of the root tl'imsh with five suffixes. p. 228

> Our Indian languages show that with a suitable grammar we may have intelligent sentences that cannot be broken into subjects and predicates. Any attempted breakup is a breakup of some English translation or paraphrase of the sentence, not of the Indian sentence itself. p. 234

Whorf sets out more clearly than Nietzsche[8] the influence of language on logic:

---

paid for the publication of the volume in which this paper appeared. But I do not know if Whorf was aware of her work.

[8] " 'Reason' in Philosophy" reprinted in this volume.

Such symbolic methods lead to fruitful techniques of rational ordering, stimulate our thinking, and bring valuable insights. Yet we should realize that the similarities and contrasts in the original sentences, subsumed under the foregoing formula, are dependent on the choice of mother tongue and that the properties of the tongue are eventually reflected as peculiarities of structure in the fabric of logic or mathematics which we rear. p. 227

These examples show that some languages have means of expression — chemical combination, as I called it — in which the separate terms are not separate as in English but flow together into plastic synthetic creations. Hence such languages, which do not paint the separate-object picture of the universe to the same degree as do English and its sister tongues, point toward possible new types of logic and possible new cosmical pictures. p. 233

Perhaps in place of the "states" of an atom or a dividing cell, it would be better if we could manipulate as readily a more verblike concept but without the concealed premises of actor and action. p. 235

The *why* of understanding may remain for a long time mysterious; but the *how* or logic of understanding — its background of laws and regularities — is discoverable. It is the grammatical background of our mother tongue, which includes not only our way of constructing propositions but the way we dissect nature and break up the flux of experience into objects and entities to construct propositions about.
                                                                                    p. 231

Whorf knew the problem of the linguistic basis of logic in 1941.

I had to rediscover it. Without realizing it, I developed Whorf's program by creating a formal logic in *Reasoning and the World as the Flow of All*.

Whorf's view doesn't suppose any special human faculty for language but only the faculty we know that we and other animals have: pattern recognition and pattern making.[9] He says:

The thing common to both techniques is a systematic synthetic use of pattern, and this is also common to all language techniques. p. 229

We always look for patterns, or I would say similarities. This is like that. Such a capability is all that's needed for explaining how children learn language, though there must be some innate push that way, notable especially in that as we get older we have a much harder time to learn a language. Or perhaps it's just that our general patterning

_____

[9] See *The Animal Mind* by James L. Gould and Carol Grant Gould, especially pp. 25–27.

Commentary on the papers of Whorf 243

ability is so much stronger than that of chimpanzees, and that accounts
for language. And as we get older our imaginations atrophy as we are
"stuck" in our patterning.[10]

REFERENCES

EPSTEIN, Richard L.
  2021 *Time and Space in Formal Logic*
        To appear, AdvancedReasoningForum.
  2022 *Reasoning and the World as the Flow of All*
        To appear, AdvancedReasoningForum.org.
GOULD, James L. and Carol Grant GOULD
  1994 *The Animal Mind*
        Scientific American Library.
HOCKETT, Charles F.
  1954 Chinese versus English: An Exploration of the Whorfian thesis
        In Harry Hoijer, ed., *Language in Culture: Conference on the
        Interrelations of Language and Other Aspects of Culture*, University
        of Chicago Press, pp. 106–123.
LEAVITT, John
  2011 *Linguistic Relativities*
        John Benjamins Publishing Company.
LEE, Penny
  1996 *The Whorf Theory Complex: A Critical Reconstruction*
        John Benjamins Publishing Company.
SINHA, Chris and Tania KUTEVA
  1995 Distributed Spatial Semantics
        Nordic Journal of Linguistics, vol. 18, no. 2, pp. 167–199.
SINHA, Chris, Vera da Silva SINHA, Jörg ZINKEN, and Wany SAMPAIO
  2011 When Time is Not Space: The Social and Linguistic Construction
        of Time Intervals and Temporal Event Relations in an Amazonian
        Culture
        Language and Cognition, vol. 3, no. 1, pp. 137–169.

---

[10] In contrast, Noam Chomsky and others following him have postulated a
special biologically based mental faculty that allows humans to learn language.
From Whorf's view, we can explain mistakes by children as they learn a
language: they haven't enough information to make the necessary connections.
But how can Chomsky explain the mistakes? Not enough data to stimulate the
trigger? The trigger must be very prolonged, lasting many years. If it's there,
why isn't it triggered completely by very little data? If it takes a lot of data,
then the data isn't so impoverished. See Penny Lee, *The Whorf Theory
Complex*, pp. 186–188 for further on this.

SINHA, Vera da Silva

   2018   *Linguistic and Cultural Conceptualisations of Time in Huni Kui,*
           Awety´, and Kamaiurá Communities in Brazil
           Ph.D. thesis, University of East Anglia.

M. Dale Kinkade

Salish Evidence against the Universalityof 'Noun' and 'Verb' (1983)

M. Dale Kinkade (1933–2004) received his Ph.D. in linguistics from the University of Indiana in 1963. He taught at Central Washington University, the University of Kansas, and the University of British Columbia. From 1960 to 1976 he conducted fieldwork on Salishan languages. He was a member of the board of trustees of the Jacobs Research Fund, which supports fieldwork on Northwest American Indian languages and cultures.

Salish Evidence against the
Universality of 'Noun' and 'Verb'

It is usually claimed that languages contain at least two major word-classes, nouns and verbs. However, Salishan languages of North-western North America cannot be described in these terms. Instead, only predicates and particles can be distinguished. Nouns and verbs are variously defined for other languages. But whether looked at morphologically, syntactically, semantically, or logically, and whether at a surface or deep level, the notions of 'noun' and 'verb' (as well as other traditional parts of speech) are not relevant in Salish. A Salishan sentence contains at least a predicate, which may be inflected for pro-nomial subject and/or object (as well as aspect, control, transitivity, etc.). An overt subject or object may be expressed by adding another predicate in apposition to the pronomial elements affixed to the main predicate. Complex sentences may thus be built up by adding layers of embedded appositional and adjuncted predicates.

The claim has been made (Kuipers 1968; Kinkade 1976; Thompson and Thompson 1980; Thompson and Kinkade ms.) that Salishan languages do not distinguish word-classes that can be labelled 'noun', 'verb', 'adjective', or 'adverb', but rather have only two kinds of words, predicates and particles.[1] Neighboring Wakashan and Chemakuan

[1] Material on Upper Chehalis, Cowlitz, and Columbian used in this article was collected from 1960 onwards under the auspices of the American Philo-sophical Society Library, Indiana University, the National Science Foundation, the University of Kansas, and the University of British Columbia. I am par-ticularly grateful to my many informants for their patience and willingness to spend time with me: Silas Heck and Lillian Young for Upper Chehalis; Emma Mesplie and Lucy James for Cowlitz; Jerome Miller and Emily Peone for Columbian; and to Arnold Guerin for Halkomelem. I also wish to acknowledge with thanks the many helpful comments from the several people who read earlier drafts of this article, especially Laurence C. Thompson, M. Terry Thompson, James E. Hoard, Phillip W. Davis, Ross Saunders, William H. Jacobsen, Jr. and Thomas E. Hukari.

Abbreviations for languages cited in this article are Be Bella Coola, Ch Upper Chehalis, Cm Columbian, Cr Cœur d'Alène, Cz Cowlitz, Hl Halkomelem, IS Interior Salish, Ka Kalispel, Ld Lushootseed, Se Sechelt, Sh Shuswap, and Th Thompson. Other abbreviations used are compl. com-pletive aspect, cont. continuative aspect, fem. feminine, intr. intransitive, obj. object, sg. singular, subj. subject, trans. transitive. [continued next page]

languages have been described in the same way,[2] and this unusual
characteristic appears to be an important areal feature, since it has
not been proven that these three families are related. Except in Kuipers
(1968) this claim has been little more than an assertion on the part of
writers based on their experience with these languages; the point has
not been the major issue in the papers referred to, and hence has not
been explored and justified fully and unequivocably.[3] It is one of the
major points in Kuiper's article, which includes a formalization of the
relations involved, and attempts to demonstrate that there is no logical
necessity for such a distinction in language. I hope to show here that
not only is such an analysis just a possibility for Salishan languages,
but the only one that will account for a number of peculiar characteristics of these languages. Since some of these characteristics are syntactic, it will also be necessary to explain the relationship of various
elements that constitute sentences in these languages, and why the
notions of subject and object are not equatable to 'noun'. Furthermore,
this claim has some bearing on current syntactic theory, since some
theorists (e.g. Chomsky 1965; Chafe 1970) claim that a noun-verb
dichotomy must be present in every language, at least in underlying
structure. On the other hand, Bloomfield explicitly disclaims such a
universality: "some features such as, for instance, the distinction of

---

The notions 'adjective' and 'adverb' will not be discussed here, but all
arguments given apply to them as well as to 'noun' and 'verb'.

[2] For an opposing view see Jacobsen 1979.

[3] Thompson and Thompson (ms.), however, make a careful distinction
between nominals in Thompson and the notion of 'noun': "Nominals . . .
should not be confused with nouns in a language like English; like other
major words they are predicative. . . . They refer to actions, situations, states,
entities which are viewed as wholes or as facts, or as products, leftovers, or
results. They are opposed to non-nominals (without //s-//), which denote
actions and states in progress; active entities; or situations viewed as dynamic,
developmental in the past or generally." Examples follow, including the nominalization of both intransitives and transitives:

    (i) Th   zik-t '[A tree] fell over, has just fallen.' (fall-immediate)
    (ii)   s-zik 'It is a log [tree which has fallen].' (nominal-fall)
    (iii)   c'éw'-s-tn 'soap, way to wash face' (wash-face-way)
    (iv)   s-c'éw'-s-tn 'water someone has washed face with'
    (v)   wik-ne 'I see him' (see-[him]-I)
    (vi)   ʔe xéʔe séye-s e s-wik-ne 'that is the second time I saw him'
                       (there is that two-his direct nominal-see-[him]-I)

verb-like and noun-like words as separate parts of speech, are common to many languages but lacking in others" (1933: 20).

One criterion that is often used to distinguish word classes is the restriction placed on occurrence of affixes. I see no basis for claiming that there are limitations on such co-occurrences in Salish that are morphological or syntactic; certainly there are limitations having to do with semantic incompatibility, as in any language. Prefixes in Salishan languages typically indicate aspect, time, or position; suffixes indicate control, transitivity, redirection, and object (including reflexive and reciprocal). There are also lexical suffixes (with semantic, rather than grammatical, content), and reduplication for various purposes (usually some sort of plurality and diminutive; number in Upper Cehalis and Cowlitz is indicated by suffixes). All these things may occur on both the main predicate and on complements or adjuncts. Indeed, fully inflected transitive predicates are not at all uncommon as subject or object of a sentence. Imperative suffixes may not occur on complements, but that is probably a semantic restriction, since it would not be an appropriate notion there. There is a distinction in the use of subject markers, however. Normally, subject clitics or suffixes occur with the main predicate only; to indicate subject of a complement, one finds, at least in some Salishan languages, dependent subject markers. The two types of subject markers have different syntactic functions, but do not distinguish word classes. There are also a number of miscellaneous affixes with restricted distributions, but these do not occur frequently enough for delimiting functions to be claimed for them, and there is nothing about them to suggest that they need be restricted to any specific syntactic role.

It is readily demonstrable that any full word may constitute the main predicate of a Salishan sentence. This predicate may be accompanied by one or more particles (including subject clitics); particles are usually readily identifiable as such, and are uninflectable elements expressing temporal, aspectual, modal, or deictic notions, and the like. For convenience I will refer to all other words as 'full words'. There will be little question that such utterances as (1)–(4) are predicates, since they correspond to transitive and intransitive verbs in English:

    (1) Ch s-x̣ ə́p-w-n 'It's getting dry.' (continuative-dry-cont.
           intr.-cont. 3rd subj.)
    (2) Ch s-x̣ api-t-n 'He's drying it.' (x̣ api- 'dry',[4] -t- 'cont. 3rd obj.')

---

[4] Underlying ə in Ch surfaces stressed as ə́ and unstressed as *a* (or zero).

(3) Cm l-c-kic-x 'He came back home.' (back-cislocative..arrive-?)
(4) Be xɬsx-c-s 'He dislikes me.' (dislike-me-he)

But utterances that correspond to nouns or pronouns in English are also predicative, and often overtly so, with subject and/or object markers attached:

(5) Ch ʔit q'ʷalán' č 'You're all ears.' (compl. ear you sg. compl.)
(6) Sh (taʔa kə ʔ-séxʷ-m), me? xméy-nt-s-t '(Don't go swimming): you'll be flied (i.e. covered with flies).' (cf. xméye 'fly': not article your-swim/bathe-intr. expectation fly-trans.-you. obj-passive) (S. Bell, p.c.)
(7a) Cm s-q'á?-xn 'shoe' (cont.- wedge in-foot)
(7b) q'á?-xn 'I put a shoe on him.' (-xn 'foot' -nt- 'trans.', -n I; -xn-nt-n regularly collapses to -xn)
(7c) q'á?-x-s 'He put a shoe on him.' (-xn 'foot', -nt- 'trans.', -s 'he'; -xn-nt-s regularly collapses to -xs)
(7d) q'á?q'a?-x-s 'He put (his) shoes on him.'
(8a) Ka p'oxút 'father, parent' (Vogt 1940)
(8b) p'oxút-s 'He is his father.' (-s 'his')
(8c) an-p'oxút 'He is your father.' (an- 'your. sg')
(8d) kʷ in-p'oxoút 'You are my father.' (kʷ 'you sg.'. in-'my')
(9) Cm ʔincá kn staʔáwna 'I am Staʔáwna.' (ʔincá 'I', kn 'I' [subj. clitic])
(10) Cz ..., ʔus nəwi kn '... if I were you.'
(11) Se nəwil-stxʷ-la t'uc'ut *You* shoot it!' (you, sg.causative-imperative shoot) (R.C. Beaumont, p.c.)

Given the forms in (8b–8d), an alternative gloss presents itself for (8a), 'he is a father', and that is indeed an alternative (and more accurate) translation for *p'oxút*; similarly, Cm *s-q'á?xn* may be glossed 'it is a shoe', and Ch *q'ʷalán'* 'it is an ear.' If one reversed the procedure, and elicited these English sentences, *p'oxút, s-q'á?xn*, and *q'ʷalán'* are just the forms one would get. That is because they are predicates in the Salishan languages rather than either nouns or verbs. They are rather like gerunds in English, which are both noun and verb at the same time. Any such simple form may be translated into English either as a simple noun or an equational sentence with a dummy 'it' as subject, with the whole indicating a state rather than an entity. It is difficult for speakers of English to conceive of forms such as *p'oxút* as complete sentences because English requires a subject and predicate in every sentence, but there is no logical reason why one cannot perceive of 'father' (and other nouns) as a state such as 'being a father' (cf. Kuipers 1968). Words such as 'father', 'deer', 'shoe' may even be given imperative inflections in Salish, in which case they mean 'be a X!'[5]

Even names are predicative, although they usually occur as complements or adjuncts rather than as main predicates. But they *may* occur as main predicates:

(12) Sp   ppátiqs ɫu skʷ-és-t-s 'Ppátiqs was his name'
          (P. that name-stative-his) (B. Carlson, p.c.)
(13) Sp   nt'əláne? ɫu? skʷ-k'ʷúl'-mn 'It was Nt'əláne? who was
          the helper.' (N. that agentive-do-instrumental)
          (B. Carlson, p.c.)

A further example is seen in the way native speakers of Cm inflect the name of their language, even when used in an English context:

(14) Cm   the nxa?amxcin-m word (-m 'middle')

The phrase is considered incorrect without the *-m*, although *nxa?amxcin* is correct in other contexts.[6]

Further evidence of this unitary predicate class may be seen in the various aspectual usages in Ch. Here, the main predicate must be marked for one of three aspects: continuative (*s-*), stative (*?ac-*), or completive (*?it*, etc.) Continuative forms correspond almost exactly to English gerunds and to progressive *-ing* constructions. Thus *sqʷə́t'wn* may be translated either 'it is burning' or '(the) burning (i.e. fire)'. When used with a deictic particle (e.g. *tit sqʷə́t'wn*) it is normally translated as 'the fire', although 'the burning' would be more accurate. *sqʷə́t'wn* is the regular continuative form corresponding to completive *?it qʷə́ɫ* 'it burned'. By analogy, other forms with a prefixed *s-* should be considered as continuative forms, even when no completive form corresponds (presumably for semantic reasons), such as *sƛ'aláx̌* 'deer, it is a deer'. So many forms such as *sƛ'aláx̌* occur in all Salishan languages that this *s-* has often been called a nominalizer. But that it is not that at all—it is an aspectual marker, at least in Ch. Further evidence of this is the reinterpretation that occurs in borrowings such as Ch *skʷúl* 'school' vs. *kʷúlm* 'go to school', where the *s-* is deleted (as though it were a prefix) to produce a

---

5 This insight was provided by Philip W. Davis and Ross Saunders.

6 Jacobsen (1979) calls personal and place names in Makah 'particles'; although this is an interesting idea, I see no necessity of claiming they are anything but predicates in Salish.

completive form. Similarly, it, or other aspect prefixes, may be added
to a loan-word to produce an appropriate predicative form:

(15) Hl   pút 'boat' vs. ?u? spúpət 'He has (his own) boat. '
        (The *s-* in this example is the stative marker, which has
        merged phonologically with continuative *s-*.)

Stative aspect forms in Ch are commonly translated as English nouns,
because they indicate the state that results from a particular action.
Stative forms, marked by *?ac-*, are usually the main predicate, but
when they are used as subject or object are preceded by one of the
deictic particles:

(16) Ch   ?it lə́px^w- m'ł 'He made a hole (there).'
        (compl. be hole-detransitive)[7]

(17) Ch   ?it nə́m'- š -n tat ?ac-lə́px ^{w}- ł? ?ə́c-tm š 'He covered /
        filled in the hole (in the ground).' (compl. cover-indirective-he
        the stative-be hole-intr. in-ground)

(18) Ch   ?it mə́lk'^{w}-t-m'ł 'He wrapped something up.'

(19) Ch   s-mə́lk'^{w}-n 'He's wrapping it.'

(20) Ch   ?it wáł-t'aq-n tat ?ac-mə́lk'^{w}-ł 'He unwrapped the package.'
        (compl. loosen-tie he . . .)

(21) Ch   ?it k'^{w}ə́ł- ł tu ?ə́x-tm ča t lé? 'It reflected.'
        (compl. show-intr. from see-passive with a far)

(22) Ch   s-k'^{w}ə́łk'^{w}ł-w-n tat ?ac-k'^{w}ə́ł- ł 'The light is blinking.'

The stative and predicative nature of *?ac-*forms may be clearer from
the following (unattested) examples in which regular processes are
applied to the same basic material in order to provide a directly
contrasting set:

(23) Ch   ?ac-táw-ł tit ?ac-lə́px^w-ł   'The hole is big.'

(24) Ch   ?ac-lə́px^w-ł tit ?ac-táw-ł   'The big one is a hole.'

(25) Ch   ?ac-táw-ł tit ?ac-mə́lk'^{w}- ł 'The package is big.'

(26) Ch   ?ac-mə́lk'^{w}-ł tit ?ac-táw-ł 'The big one is wrapped.'

In each of (23)–(26), the first word is the predicate, the second full
word the subject. Sentence (24) is semantically odd, but exactly
parallel to sentence (26). In (25) and (26), English requires different
words to translate *?ac-mə́lk'^{w}-ł*, but they are obviously the same Ch
word; one might translate sentence (25) alternatively as 'the wrapped

---

[7] A detransitive suffix makes a normally transitive stem intransitive, with an
object only implied.

up one is big' to keep the translation of *mə́lkʷ-* the same. The difference, then, is in English syntax and semantics, not in Ch word classes.

But inflectional possibilities are only one of the means that has
been used to define word-classes. Lyons (1977) provides a good basis
for any discussion of the subject; he gives a careful review of how parts
of speech have been defined, and how they should be defined, distinguishing some of the rather different criteria that have been used (and
usually not carefully distinguished). He distinguishes nouns, noun-
forms, and nominals (or nominal expressions). "At least three different
strands must be unravelled in the rather tangled skein which makes up
the traditional theory of the parts-of-speech" (Lyons 1977: 425). These
three strands are morphological definitions (e.g. inflections for number,
tense, etc.), syntactic definitions (i.e. grouping expressions into
expression classes in terms of distribution, e.g. in nominal or verbal
expressions), and semantic definitions. It is clear that the notions of
'noun' and 'verb' as semantic concepts (which may be notions applied
to single lexical items) must be kept distinct from the syntactic relations
of 'subject', 'predicate', etc. Our thinking about these concepts has to
do with the way speakers of European languages structure the world
around them, and they are so ingrained that we ethnocentrically look
for analogous categories in other languages, which may well structure
these concepts in quite different ways.

I have already shown that there is no morphological evidence for a
noun-verb distinction in Salish, and Kuipers (1968) showed clearly that
there is no *logical* reason why there must be a noun-verb dichotomy;
his arguments were based on morphological and semantic criteria.
Lyons does not appear to be entirely convinced by semantic evidence
either, especially in regard to adjectives, which "traditionally" denote
states:

> "The fact that it is difficult sometimes to distinguish states from qualities,
> on the one hand, and from actions and processes, on the other, would
> suggest that states have a certain ontological ambivalence; and this is
> reflected in the various ways in which they are given lexical or
> grammatical recognition in languages" (Lyons, 1977: 441).

It would appear that everything in Salish may be considered to be a
state.

The noun-verb distinction is often justified on syntactic grounds,
often by claiming that certain kinds of relationships can be explained

only if there are these two categories. There are fundamental disagreements among theoreticians on the point, however. Chomsky generally
makes the distinction (e.g. Chomsky 1965), but McCawley (1971, e.g.
p. 221) and Bach (1968) claim that only one category is necessary.
Lyons does not quite commit himself:

> "*It is generally accepted by linguists* that although the traditional theory
> of the parts-of-speech . . . is inapplicable, in all its details, to languages
> whose grammatical structure differs significantly from that of the classical
> Indo-European languages, the distinction between nouns and verbs at least
> is universal. Furthermore, *it is generally accepted* that this distinction is
> intrinsically bound up with the difference between reference and predica-
> tion" (Lyons 1977: 429; my emphasis).

But, as I have shown, Salish uses only predications, and there is thus no
basis for claiming a distinction between nominal expressions and verbal
expressions (Lyons' syntactic categories) either. So far, I have based
my arguments on single predicates (which can constitute a simple sentence): I now turn to more complicated sentences, both to see what
evidence they provide, and because the role of elements within them
must be explained if there is no noun-verb, or nominal-verbal, distinction. Of particular importance are the notions of 'subject' and 'object'.

Sentences (1)–(4) were examples of single predicates used as
complete utterances (i.e. sentences). Such sentences, with or without
particles attached, are extremely common in Salishan languages, even
in texts. But longer sentences occur more commonly; these are made
up of a main predicate, complements which may be (translated as)
subject or object to that predicate, and optional prepositional phrases.[8]
Each of these basic elements may be accompanied by particles. Some
Salishan languages seem to allow both a nonpronomial subject and a
nonpronomial object to be expressed simultaneously as direct complements of a predicate; others allow only one complement (see Hukari
1976 for a particularly clear case of the latter; see also Hess 1973 and
Hukari 1977). Probably no Salishan language allowed two direct
complements aboriginally, but the restriction has been relaxed due

---

[8] The term 'preposition' may be misleading: some might insist that it implies
'noun'. I do not think that is a necessary implication, and I retain the term for
convenience. These particles are few in number in Salishan languages, and all
tend to have broad ranges of meaning. The function is to indicate an oblique
relationship of an adjunct to the main predicate of the sentence or to a complement.

to English influence; this does not affect my arguments, however.[9]
Thus the following are normal Salishan sentences.

(27) Ch (s-)wə́ š-c š-t-n t xiwó?s tat t'ə́č'-iq 'Wildcat was carrying
         a hind leg.' (cont.-carry-reflexive-it-he a wildcat the single-leg)

(28) Cm kn las-kɬ-hacáy'-n 'I will tease that Owl.'
         (I unrealized-under-tease-(her)-I that owl)

(29) Hl ni cən mə?émə-stəxʷ tə scéɬtən ?ə tə swə́y'qe?
         'I took the salmon to the man.' (non-proximal I take-causative
         the salmon to the man)

(30) Ld ɬu?kʷaxʷad čad tə stub š 'I will help the man.' (future-help
         I the man) (Hukari 1976)

(31) L   ?ukʷaxʷaɬəb ?ə tə stub š cə sɬadəy? 'The woman was
         helped by the man.' (?ukʷaxʷ(a)-t-b 'compl.-help-trans.-
         mediopassive) (Hukari 1976)

(32) Cr e-n-šcšc-úl'mxʷ xʷe gʷuɬ púl'ye 'Gophers make holes
         in the ground.' (customary-in-dig-ground the collective gopher)
         (Nicodemus 1975)

Sentences (28), (29), and (30) have pronominal objects; (32) has a
non-pronominal subject; and (27) has both. Sentence (31) is passive,
and has the agent (stubš) introduced by a preposition, while the patient
(sɬadəy?) is a direct complement (the subject). In each of these sentences, the main predicate would be an acceptable sentence by itself,
and subjects and objects would be considered fully indicated, even
though third person intransitive subjects and transitive objects are not
marked (in independent clauses; many Salishan languages mark third
person intransitive subject in dependent clauses), except in (27). Ch
does mark third person subjects in continuative aspect forms and third
person objects at all times.[10] But if the main predicate is complete in
itself, and the nonpronominal subjects and objects that are present are
also predicates, then their role can only be appositives[11] — they

---

[9] Some readers may wish to see surface nouns in words serving as complements or adjuncts. It is precisely this view that is disturbing when those
complements or adjuncts are clearly predicative, as in the case of transitive
forms. Such an analysis then begs the question whether all such complements
and adjuncts are not embedded predicates.

[10] Historically, these appear to be developed from transitive markers.

[11] I use 'apposition' in its traditional meaning, e.g. as defined by Bloomfield:
"The term *apposition* is used when paratactically joined forms are grammatically, but not in meaning, equivalent . . ." (1933:186). Definitions by other
authors are equally apposite, e.g. Curme: "A noun which explains or charac-

expand on a subject or object already present in the main predicate.
It is conceivable that they could alternatively be described as relative
clauses, although they are not necessarily dependent constructions.
Perhaps it is even possible to say that both appositives and relative
clauses occur in those languages (such as Thompson and Shuswap)
where some complements take dependent subject suffixes (and are
then relative clauses?); this argument is possible since relative clauses
are generally held to be subordinate/dependent, and appositives coordinate (e.g. Langendoen: "nonrestrictive relative clauses [i.e. apposi-
tives] are not felt to be subordinate to the nouns they occur with, but
rather coordinate" [1969: 93]). But whether relative or appositive,
complements and adjuncts in Salish are clearly secondary. Although
this is what several of us who have been studying Salishan languages
for several years have come to recognize, the best evidence I have seen
appeared in a recent book on Cr by Lawrence Nicodemus, a native
speaker who had some linguistic training from Gladys Reichard forty
years ago. In this book, Nicodemus often gives more literal (i.e. clause
by clause) translations for sentences which translate nonpronominal
subjects and objects with phrases beginning "the one who/which
is a . . ."; he translates sentence (32), for example, also as 'They dig
and dig in the ground those which are gophers.' Other Cr examples
(all Nicodemus 1975) are:

(33) Cr   x̣es-iɫc'e? xʷe c'i? 'Venison is delicious.' ('They are good
              to eat those which are deer.' (good-flesh the deer)

---

terizes another is placed alongside of it, and from its position is called an
appositive . . ." (1947: 129); or, in another camp, Langendoen: "Apposition. An
expression occurring after a noun phrase and having exactly the same reference
as that noun phrase. Traditionally, only a noun phrase may be in apposition to
another noun phrase . . ." (1969: 148). The last two definitions beg the question, of course, as to whether nouns are universally distinct from verbs.

A similar treatment of subjects and objects co-referenced to pronominal
affixes is suggested for Potawatomi (Algonquian): "In my view it is most useful
to say that the verb form with its affixes can stand as a complete sentence, and
that overt nominals of the kinds mentioned may be either 'included' or placed
in apposition" (Gathercole 1978: 29).

Thompson and Thompson (ms.) make a similar point, but do not call the
relationship between complement and predicate appositional: "The heads of
such complements are predicative words subordinated to their predicates by
position and their introductory particles." Adjuncts and complements in
Thompson are clearly dependent.

(34) Cr   jjón', ?ác'x̌nt xʷa? sx̌ax̌ł'il't 'Johnny, look at the puppy.'
          ('Johnny, look at it, that which is the little dog.')

(35) Cr   stim xʷe intgʷičn 'How do you see?' ('What is it, that
          which you see with?')

These translations can only have been made by a native speaker; the
idea of translating subjects and objects as separate clauses would hardly
occur to anyone not extremely familiar with one of these languages
(Nicodemus had no help from any such person in writing this book,
although he had discussed some of these notions earlier with one,
Clarence Sloat; Sloat assures me that Nicodemus came up with such
translations on his own, however). These sentences (27)–(35), and all
other sentences with more than one full word, are *complex* sentences,
rather than the simple sentences they have usually been treated as, with
additional predicates added to a simple sentence to amplify a subject or
object.

One difficulty in making no distinction between nouns and verbs
has been the presence of particles that precede nonpronominal subjects
and objects that have been translated as articles (*t* and *tat* in sentence
27, the demonstrative *?aci* in 28, *tə* in 29, 30, 31, *cə* in 31, *xʷe* and
xʷa? in 32–35). These are indeed deictic elements, and their use is
normally restricted to words that are not the main predicate; they may
themselves sometimes be predicative, but seem not usually to be so.
The translation as articles is somewhat misleading, although a role as
article is included in their use. They include notions of time as well
as space, however (and, in coastal Salishan languages, gender[12] or
indication of primary or secondary status). Their use in Ch and Cz is
particularly interesting. There is a set of eight of these deictics there:

(36) Cr

non-fem	fem	
t	c	indefinite
tit	tic, cic	definite, proximate
?it	?ic	definite, near
tat	tac, cac	definite, distal

Of these, *?it / ?ic* does not occur with subjects or objects, but it almost
always occurs with the main predicate when it is completive aspect,
as in sentences (5), (37), and (38):

---

[12] See Davis and Saunders (ms.) for arguments in favor of identifying nouns
partly on the basis of gender. But since gender is not the sole semantic feature,
or, in many Salishan languages, the major feature, of deictics, I do not find this
a compelling argument for saying Salishan languages distinguish nouns and verbs.

(37) Ch ʔit ʔax-ṣ́n 'He saw him.' (ʔṣ́x̣- 'see'.[13] -n 'compl. 3rd person obj.)

(38) Ch ʔit wáɬ-t'aq-n tat ʔac-mṣ́lk'ʷ-ɬ 'He unwrapped the package.' (=20)

But *t/c* and (less commonly) *tit/tic* also occur in these positions, and then indicate a spatial/temporal distinction from *ʔit/ʔic*. Thus it is clear that these deictic elements are not word-class markers, but give spatial/temporal information about the word with which they occur.

Another source of nouns in English translations of Salishan sentences is worth noting. This is the lexical suffixes, such as Cm *-xn* 'foot' in sentence (7), the Cr *-úl'mxʷ* 'ground' in sentence (32), and Cr *-iɬc'eʔ* 'flesh' in sentence (33). These suffixes are quite common, and often have very specific meanings, referring to body parts and various common objects. Sometimes words with these suffixes have the suffixes translated literally, and sometimes they are given a derived or metaphorical meaning as parts of a larger concept, as in (7a) Cm *sq'aʔxn* 'shoe'. They are the primary device in Salishan languages for creating new words. For the most part, these suffixes bear no phonological relationship to independent words for the same concept, e.g. Cm *kálx* and the suffix *-akst* both meaning 'hand, arm', or Cm *stxʷúl* and *-aɬxʷ* meaning 'house'. Words with these suffixes are used in the same way that simple predicative words are used — they may be transitive, intransitive, predicate, complement, or whatever. Several examples from Cm follow:

(39) Cm máʕ'ʷ-lqs 'He broke his nose.' (break-nose)

(40) Cm k-ʔalk'ʷ-ús-n 'I stirred the fire.' (on-fix-face/eye/door/road/fire-(it)-I)

(41) Cm n-k'ʷλ'-p-akst-átkʷ-n 'I (accidentally) dropped it into the water.' (in-release-inchoative-hand-water-(it)-I)

(42) Cm n-x̣ʷaʕ-qn-ús-xn 'He has a hole in the toe of his shoe.' (in-hole-head-face-foot)

(43) Cm ka-l'aʕ'ʷ-ikn'-xn 'button-hook' (on-put over-back-foot)

(44) Cm n-p'iy'-atkʷ-álqs-n 'washtub, washing-machine' (in-squeeze-water-dress-instrument)

The last two examples are recent formations. These suffixes are strictly bound forms, so there is no question of them being derived separately by a compounding rule or the like. In fact, their role should probably

---

[13] Cf. footnote 4.

be conceived as more adverbial than anything else. Alternate translations of (39) and (40) might then be 'he nose-broke' and 'I fire-stirred'; note further that (41) and (42) require translations with prepositional phrases in English for the lexical suffixes.[14]

Various problems with analysis of Salishan sentences are resolved if nonpronomial subjects and objects are treated as embedded appositive predicates. It resolves Hukari's (1976) indecision whether to derive Ld person markers from abstract pronouns or to generate them directly in the base; the latter is the only possibility (and the alternative preferred by Hukari) if the predicate can consist of only a single predicate. This simple predicate may have attached person markers, but they do not derive from some abstract pronoun (or other complement), since any such form that might appear overtly would, in my analysis, have to be in apposition to what is present in the predicate. This applies equally to the independent pronouns, which are predicative like all other full words (cf. 9, 10, 11). Lexical suffixes should likewise be considered as part of the base, rather than being copies of something elsewhere.

Another problem which is resolved in the treatment of different kinds of objects most clearly exemplified in IS languages (all from Thompson and Thompson 1980; morphological analysis is added):

(45) Th   n'-t-és e sinci?-s tə qʷú? 'He gave his younger brother
           some water.' (give-trans.-(him)-he direct complement younger
           brother-his oblique complement water)
(46) Th   n'cém-s tə qʷú? 'He gave me some water.'
           (give-(trans.)-me-he oblique water)
(47) Th   wik-t-xʷ e smútec 'You see the woman.'
           (see trans.-(her)-you sg. direct woman)
(48) Th   wik-x-t-xʷ e smútec 'You see what the woman has.'
           (see-indirective-trans.-her-you. sg. direct woman)

In these sentences, the particle e marks the direct complement (here

---

[14] Saunders and Davis (1975) claim some subcategorizations among lexical suffixes are evidence of noun-verb contrast in Bella Coola. Much of their argument depends on copying of information from a complement or adjunct onto the main predicate. Since, as indicated here, I do not see any need for the notion of copying in Salish, I cannot accept these arguments either. The notion of subcategorization of lexical suffixes has not been fully explored in more than two or three Salishan languages, and it is not clear that Bella Coola is typical in all respects in this.

equivalent to the direct object in English) and *t ə* marks the oblique
complement (here equivalent to the indirect object in English). But
note that sentence (48) uses the direct marker where the object has quite
a different relationship to the main predicate; the shift was indicated in
the main predicate by the suffix *-x* (underlying *//-xi//*). Thompson
and Thompson call this suffix 'indirective'. Other IS languages have
additional suffixes of this type, e.g. Cm *-xi-, -ł- -túł-* :

(49) Cm ?ac-yáy-x-t-n Mary sttám'tam' 'I made a bag for Mary.'
        (stative-weave-indirective-trans.-I Mary bag)
(50) Cm ?ac-yáy-ł-n sttám'tam ' k'l Mary 'I'm weaving a bag
        for Mary.'
(51) Cm q'iy'-xi-t-a? ani sm?ámm 'Write to that woman!'
        (mark-indirective-trans-imperative deictic woman)
(52) Cm q'iy'-ł-t-a? q'iy'-min-s Mary 'Write a letter for Mary!
        (mark-indirective-trans.-imperative mark-instrument-her Mary)
(53) Cm x̣áq'-n 'I paid him.' / x̣áq'-x-tn 'I paid for it, I paid his fare.' /
        x̣áq'-ł-n 'I paid (it) for him.'
(54) Cm wákʷ-n 'I hid it.' / wákʷ-ł-n 'I hid it for him.' /
        wákʷ-túł-n 'I hid it from him.'
(55) Cm tu-mi-st-m-n 'I sold it.' / tu-mi-st-m-túł-n ' I sold it to him.'

In each case, these suffixes shift the relationship of the object to the
predicate; the shift applies primarily to the suffixed pronomial object.
Any complement placed in appositive position to this object will be
direct if the pronomial object was the (re)focussed semantic object and
oblique otherwise. This accounts for the shifting of direct and oblique
markers among complements. The indirective and related suffixes are
then very much like case markers, but appear on the predicate itself,
and do not affect the form of subsequent pronominal object suffixes.

Languages such as these, where full words are predicates (whether
on the surface or in deep structure), are clearly vastly different from our
more familiar European languages. Syntactic theories have been largely formulated to account for phenomena in Indo-European languages,
and linguists have had varying amounts of difficulty in applying these
theories to languages in other parts of the world. Their applicability to
Salishan languages seems even more difficult than usual. I find none
of the currently popular theories adequate in all respects to describe
or explain these languages. Parts of several are useful, and allow the
description of parts of these languages in interesting ways. I hope that
theoreticians will examine the structure of Salishan (and Wakashan and

Chemakuan) languages more carefully since they seem to be so
radically different from European languages. Much of the problem
is the difficulty of being totally objective when looking at another
language; as educated people trained from childhood to look at
language in a particular way, we presuppose too much similarity
between languages, and almost inevitably describe them at least
partially in terms of what we are most familiar with. In any case,
unprejudiced attention to full treatments of these languages could
well lead to important new insights and advances in linguistic
method and theory.

References

Bach, Emmon, 1968. Nouns and noun phrases. In: Emmon Bach,
     Robert T. Harms (eds.). Universals in linguistic theory, 90 122.
     New York: Holt, Rinehart and Winston.
Bloomfield, Leonard, 1933. Language. New York: Henry Holt and
     Company.
Chafe, Wallace L., 1970. Meaning and the structure of language. Chicago:
     Univ. of Chicago Press.
Chomsky, Noam, 1965. Aspects of the theory of syntax. Cambridge, Mass.:
     MIT press.
Curme, George O., 1947. English grammar. New York: Barnes and Noble, Inc.
Davis, Phillip W., Ross Saunders, ms. Bella Coola *s-*.
Gathercole, Geoff. 1978. Instrumental phonetic studies and linguistic analysis:
     the case of Kansas Potawatomi. Kansas Working Papers in Linguistics 3,
     20–33.
Hess, Thom., 1973. Agent in a Coast Salish language. IJAL 39, 89–94.
Hukari, Thomas E., 1976. Person in a Coast Salish language. IJAL 42, 305–318.
Hukari, Thomas E., 1977. A comparison of attributive clause constructions
     in two Coast Salish languages. Glossa 11, 48–73.
Jacobsen, William H., Jr., 1979. Noun and verb in Nootkan. In Barbara S.
     Efrat (ed.), The Victoria conference on northwestern languages, Victoria,
     British Columbia, November 4/5, 1976, 83–155. British Columbia
     Provincial Museum Heritage Record No. 4. Victoria, B.C.: British
     Columbia Provincial Museum.
Kinkade, M. Dale, 1976. The copula and negatives in Inland Olympic Salish.
     IJAL 42, 17–23.
Kuipers, Aert H., 1968. The categories verb-noun and transitive-intransitive
     in English and Squamish. Lingua 21, 610–626.
Langendoen, D. Terence, 1969. The study of syntax. New York: Holt,
     Rinehart and Winston.

Lyons, John, 1977. Semantics, vol. 2. Cambridge Univ. Press.

McCawley, James D., 1971. Where do noun phrases come from? In: Danny D. Steinberg, Leon A. Jakobovits (eds.) Semantics: an interdisciplinary reader in philosophy, linguistics and psychology, 217–231. Cambridge: Cambridge Univ. Press.

Nicodemus, Lawrence, 1975. Snchitsu'umshtsn: The Cœur d'Alène language: a modern course. Plummer, Idaho: The Cœur d'Alène Tribe.

Saunders, Ross, Phillip W. Davis, 1975. Bella Coola referential suffixes. IJAL 41, 355–368.

Thompson, Lawrence C., M. Dale Kinkade, ms. Linguistic relations and distributions. To appear in: Handbook of North American Indians, volume VIII: The Northwest Coast.

Thompson, Laurence C., M. Terry Thompson, 1980. Thompson Salish //-xi //. IJAL 46, 27–32

Thompson, Laurence C., M. Terry Thompson, ms. Thompson. To appear in: Handbook of North American Indians, volume XV: Grammatical sketches.

Vogt, Hans, 1940. The Kalispel language. Oslo: Det Norske Videnskaps-Akademi.

Commentary on "Salish Evidence" by M. Dale Kinkade

Kinkade says,

> Salishan languages do not distinguish word-classes that can
> be labelled 'noun', 'verb', 'adjective', or 'adverb', but rather
> have only two kinds of words, predicates and particles. p. 246

This division is comparable to that of categorematic and syncategorematic words as I describe in "Language and the World". Kinkade suggests that such a division is "an important areal feature" of languages in the Northwest. But it is much wider spread than that. Chinese, for example, has just these two classes, as Marcel Granet noted in 1920 (p. 21 in this volume).

The huge problem Kinkade faced was how to describe and convey to English speakers this other way of encountering the world. He starts with the language and tries to talk about a word being like a gerund, both a noun and verb, which isn't wrong—it's how I describe it, too. But it misses why the words are treated this way. In that respect, this is a step backward from what Dorothy Lee did. He either can't or won't infer a metaphysics from the language. Yet if you start with the metaphysics, all that he says seems completely natural for a mass-process language. We need a new vocabulary of grammar, new classifications for mass-process languages, ones that arise from the languages not from the outside. I have no idea what he means by "subject" and "object" except as those show up in how he translates. And I can find no meaning for "predicate" as he uses it except as a part of speech meant for describing.

Friedrich Nietzsche

"Reason" in Philosophy   (1888)

Friedrich Nietzsche (1844–1900) was born in Germany and studied philology at Bonn University. Appointed professor of classical philology in 1869 at the University of Basel, Switzerland, he taught and wrote, though not on philology, while living mostly in Switzerland and Italy, until he became insane in 1888.

"Reason" in Philosophy

1

You ask me which of the philosopher's traits are really idiosyncrasies?
For example, their lack of historical sense, their hatred of the very idea
of becoming, their Egypticism. They think that they show their *respect*
for a subject when they de-historicize it *sub specie aeterni*—when they
turn it into a mummy. All that philosophers handled for thousands of
years turned into concept-mummies; nothing real escaped their grasp
alive. Whenever these honorable concept idolaters worship something,
they kill it and stuff it; they threaten the life of everything they worship.
Death, change, old age, as well as procreation and growth, are to their
mind objections—even refutations. Whatever has being does not
become; whatever becomes does not have being. Now they all believe,
desperately even, in what has being. But since they never grasp it,
they seek for reasons why it is kept from them. "There must be mere
appearance, there must be some deception which prevents us from
perceiving that which has being: where is the deceiver?"

"We have found him," they cry jubilantly; "it is the senses! These
senses, which are so immoral in other ways too, deceive us concerning
the true world. Moral: let us free ourselves from the deception of the
senses, from becoming, from history, from lies; history is nothing but
faith in the senses, faith in lies. Moral: let us say No to all who have
faith in the senses, to all the rest of mankind; they are all 'mob.' Let
us be philosophers! Let us be mummies! Let us represent monotono-
theism by adopting the manner of a gravedigger! And above all, away
with the body, this wretched *idée fixe* of the senses, disfigured by all
the fallacies of logic, refuted, even impossible, although it is impudent
enough to behave as if it were real!"

2

With the highest respect, I exclude the name of *Heraclitus*. When
the rest of the philosophic crowd rejected the testimony of the senses
because they showed multiplicity and change, he rejected their testimony because it represented things as if they had permanence and
unity. Heraclitus too did the senses an injustice. They lie neither in
the way the Eleatics believed, nor as he believed—they do not lie at
all. What we *make* of their testimony, that alone introduces lies;
for example, the lie of unity, the lie of thinghood, of substance, of

permanence. "Reason" is the cause of our falsification of the testimony of our senses. Insofar as the senses show becoming, passing away, and change, they do not lie. But Heraclitus will remain eternally right with his assertion that being is an empty fiction. The "apparent" world is the only one: the "true" world is merely added by lie.

3

And what magnificent instruments of observation we possess in our senses! This nose, for example, of which no philosopher has yet spoken with reverence and gratitude, is actually the most delicate instrument so far at our disposal: it is able to detect minimal differences of motion which even a spectroscope cannot detect. Today we possess science precisely to the extent to which we have decided to *accept* the testimony of the senses—to the extent to which we sharpen them further, arm them, and have learned to think them through. The rest is miscarriage and not-yet-science—in other words, metaphysics, theology, psychology, epistemology—or formal science, a doctrine of signs, such as logic and that applied logic which is called mathematics. In them reality is not encountered at all, not even as a problem—no more than the question of the value of such a sign-convention as logic.

4

The other idiosyncrasy of the philosophers is no less dangerous; it consists in confusing the last and the first. They place that which comes at the end—unfortunately! for it ought not to come at all! — namely, the "highest concepts," which means the most general, the emptiest concepts, the last smoke of evaporating reality, in the beginning, *as* the beginning. This again is nothing but their way of showing reverence: the higher *may* not grow out of the lower, may not have grown at all. Moral: whatever is of the first rank must be *causa sui*. Origin out of something else is considered an objection, a questioning of value. All the highest values are of the first rank; all the highest concepts, that which has being, the unconditional, the good, the true, the perfect—all these cannot have become and must therefore be *causa sui*. All these, moreover, cannot be unlike each other or in contradiction to each other. Thus, they arrive at their stupendous concept, "God." That which is last, thinnest, and emptiest is put first, as *the* cause, as the *ens realissimum*. Why did humanity have to take seriously the brain afflictions of sick web-spinners? We have paid dearly for it!

5

At long last, let us contrast the very different manner in which we conceive the problem of error and appearance. (I say "we" for politeness' sake.) Formerly, alteration, change, any becoming at all, were taken as proof of mere appearance, as an indication that there must be something which led us astray. Today, conversely, precisely insofar as the prejudice of reason forces us to posit unity, identity, permanence, substance, cause, thinghood, being, we see ourselves somehow caught in error, compelled into error. So certain are we, on the basis of rigorous examination, that this is where the error lies.

It is not different in this case than with the movement of the sun: there our eye is the constant advocate of error, here it is our language. In its origin language belongs in the age of the most rudimentary form of psychology. We enter a realm of crude fetishism when we summon before consciousness the basic presuppositions of the metaphysics of language, in plain talk, the presuppositions of reason. Everywhere it sees a doer and doing; it believes in the will as *the* cause; it believes in the ego, in the ego as being, in the ego as substance, and it projects this faith in the ego-substance upon all things—only thereby does it first *create* the concept of "thing." Everywhere "being" is projected by thought, pushed underneath, as the cause; the concept of being follows, and is a derivative of, the concept of the ego. In the beginning there is that great calamity of an error that the will is something which is effective, that will is a capacity. Today we know that it is only a word.

Very much later, in a world which was in a thousand ways more enlightened, philosophers, to their great surprise, became aware of the sureness, the subjective certainty, in our handling of the categories of reason: they concluded that these categories could not be derived from anything empirical—for everything empirical plainly contradicted them. When, then, were they derived? And in India, as in Greece, the same mistake was made: "We must once have been at home in a higher world (instead of a very much lower one, which would have been the truth); we must have been divine, *for* we have reason!" Indeed, nothing has yet possessed a more naïve power of persuasion than the error concerning being, as it has been formulated by the Eleatics, for example. After all, every word we say and every sentence speak in its favor. Even the opponents of the Eleatics still succumbed to the seduction of their concept of being: Democritus, among others, when he invented his atom. "Reason" in language—oh, what an old deceptive female she is! I am afraid we are not rid of God because we still have faith in grammar.

6

It will be appreciated if I condense so essential and so new an insight into four theses. In that way I facilitate comprehension; in that way I provoke contradiction.

First proposition. The reasons for which "this" world has been characterized as "apparent" are the very reasons which indicate its reality; any other kind of reality is absolutely indemonstrable.

Second proposition. The criteria which have been bestowed on the "true being" of things are the criteria of not-being, of *naught*; the "true world" has been constructed out of contradiction to the actual world: indeed an apparent world, insofar as it is merely a moral-optical illusion.

Third proposition. To invent fables about a world "other" than this one has no meaning at all, unless an instinct of slander, detraction, and suspicion against life has gained the upper hand in us: in that case, we avenge ourselves against life with a phantasmagoria of "another," a "better" life.

Fourth proposition. Any distinction between a "true" and an "apparent" world—whether in the Christian manner or in the manner of Kant (in the end, an underhanded Christian)—is only a suggestion of decadence, a symptom of the *decline of life*. That the artist esteems appearance higher than reality is no objection to this proposition. For "appearance" in this case means reality *once more*, only by way of selection, reinforcement, and correction. The tragic artist is no pessimist: he is precisely the one who says Yes to everything questionable, even to the terrible—he is *Dionysian*.

Benson Mates

Metaphysics and Linguistic Relativity

Extract from *The Philosophy of Leibniz*, 1986

Benson Mates (1919–2009) received his B.A. in Philosophy and
Mathematics at the University of Oregon in 1941. His graduate
study in philosophy at Cornell was interrupted by the Second
World War. He completed his Ph.D. studies at the University of
California, Berkeley in 1948, continuing there as a faculty
member until his retirement in 1989. Among the books he
published are *Stoic Logic*, *Elementary Logic*, *The Philosophy
of Leibniz*, and *The Skeptic Way: Sextus Empiricus's Outlines
of Pyrrhonism*.

Metaphysics and Linguistic Relativity

Extract from *The Philosophy of Leibniz*

Doubts about the cognitive content of metaphysics in general, or of Leibniz's metaphysics in particular, need not prevent us from indulging in some meta-metaphysical speculation about the origin of these kinds of doctrine. The first thing that meets the eye is the remarkable similarity of structure, no matter how one is going to account for it, between the sentences of our language, on the one hand, and the elements of the realms postulated by the metaphysicians, on the other. Philosophers have often noticed this close relationship and have sometimes exploited it. It led Carnap, for instance, to his distinction of the material and formal modes, and to such suggestions as that the cognitive content of "pseudo object" sentences (for example, "A rose is a thing and not an event") could be expressed less metaphysically by sentences about language ("The word 'rose' is a noun and not a verb").

The isomorphism is especially striking in Leibniz. For him, the elements of the real world are individual substances with accidents. The simplest thoughts or propositions, correspondingly, consist of a subject concept joined to a predicate concept, and the simplest sentences consist of a subject expression joined by the copula to a predicate expression. (Incidentally, the copula, since it does not correspond to any individual or concept, is often thought to be dispensable, that is, replaceable by mere juxtaposition.) In the Leibnizian scheme, therefore, it appears that our subject-predicate language is admirably well suited to providing pictures of our thoughts, which in turn are pictures of the constituents of the world.

For example, when I tell you truthfully that Socrates is wise, what happens is that I utter a sentence '*A* is *B*', where *A* and *B* are words or other linguistic expressions for concepts under which Socrates falls. In the real world there is the old man himself, with certain individual accidents that we may amalgamate under the heading "the wisdom of Socrates." The word "Socrates" expresses a complete individual concept under which our man Socrates and nobody else falls (or even could fall), and the word "wise" expresses a concept under which he also falls, this time by virtue of the aforementioned collection of individual accidents. So, in my assertoric utterance of the sentence

"Socrates is wise," I am expressing the thought or proposition that Socrates is wise, that is, the unique individual in the real world who comes under the concept expressed by "Socrates" comes also, by virtue of his accidents, under the concept expressed by "wise".

Of course, in all of this I do not succeed in conveying the full individuality of Socrates' wisdom; in effect I only inform you in that it lies within a certain range. But the range can be narrowed down, if desired, for our language offers a variety of further predicate expressions under which Socrates but not other wise people will fall by virtue of their particular brands of wisdom. We have seen that although the accidents of individuals are individual, things fall under various concepts by virtue of those accidents and hence, to the extent that they come under the same concepts, are thought of as similar. By the principle of the Identity of Indiscernibles we are assured that if individuals *A* and *B* are different, there is some concept under which one falls but not the other. In other words, it is in principle possible for a mind (by means of concepts, of course) to tell them apart; they cannot be completely similar.

At least two ways of accounting for this admirable isomorphism of language, thought, and the world present themselves. One is that somewhere back in the most remote history of the Indo-European languages our forebears, in their efforts to deal with the individual substances-with-accidents, were led by the structure of this world to develop ways of thought and speech reflecting that structure. For what could be more natural than to represent the existence of a fact or state of affairs by a picture, model, or some other moderate-sized, easily reproducible representation of the fact or state of affairs? On this hypothesis, the origin of the subject-predicate form of our simplest sentences, as well as that of the corresponding thoughts, is due to the fact that the world—"everything that is the case"—is made up of components that are structurally similar to the sentences of thoughts.

The other hypothesis is less flattering to metaphysics. It is that the causal connections are the other way around: what inclines us to say that the real world consists of substances-with-accidents is that our native language is one in which sentences have subjects and predicates. The metaphysician's insight into the most general features of Being qua Being is nothing more than a projection of the structure of language into the world. The speaker of a language in which the sentences do not have the subject-predicate form does not need to be pitied as having to work with a tool that is poorly adapted to its function; there is no reason whatever to suppose that the world fits our language in some way that it does not fit his.

This suggestion, that the basic outlines of traditional metaphysics, to which Leibniz adheres in the main, have no objective validity but are merely projections of certain grammatical features common to Indo-European languages, will, of course, remind the reader of the so-called Sapir-Whorf hypothesis of "linguistic relativity."[1] By considering the grammars of Semitic, Chinese, Tibetan, African, and American Indian languages, all of them fundamentally different from our own, Whorf and Sapir were led to "a new principle of relativity, which holds that all observers are not led by the same physical evidence to the same picture of the universe, unless their linguistic backgrounds are similar, or can in some way be calibrated."[2] The "unless" clause applies, of course, to our modern European languages. Here, Whorf explains, there is an apparent unanimity of major pattern; "but this unanimity exists only because these tongues are all Indo-European dialects cut to the same basic plan, being historically transmitted from what was long ago one speech community; because the modern dialects have long shared in building up a common culture; and because much of this culture, on the more intellectual side, is derived from the linguistic backgrounds of Latin and Greek." But speakers of languages with grammars radically different from ours cannot be expected to share our conceptualization of the world as consisting of objects that "have" properties and "stand in" relations to one another.

The whole matter is undeniably as puzzling and confusing as it is apparently important to philosophy.[3] We are admonished that even in our attempts to consider the relation of our language and our world picture, we are still looking at things through our own language, as it were; we are in the position of a person who cannot remove his glasses and yet is trying to find out, by peering intently at the environment, to what extent his visual perception is distorted by the glasses. When

---

[1] See, in particular, Whorf (1956) [*Language, Thought, and Reality*, ed. J. B. Carroll, The MIT Press.], especially the last four papers, and Sapir (1949) [*Selected Writings*, ed. D. Mandelbaum, University of California Press].

[2] Whorf (1956), 214 [in this volume, p. 194].

[3] Cf., e.g., the discussion of it by a group of noted linguists, anthropologists, social psychologists, and philosophers, in Hoijer (1954) [*Language and Culture*, University of Chicago Press].

Whorf tells us that a certain Nootka sentence, of which the English translation is "He invites people to a feast," has no subject or predicate,[4] we are strongly inclined to think that there *must* be a subject. If, as in Whorf's example, the element of the Nootka sentence that justifies the "he" in the translation is itself a Nootka sentence translatable as "He does" or "He acts," we try to save the subject-predicate structure by taking that element as subject anyway, arguing that there is no reason why one sentence should not be the subject of another. But are we doing anything more than insisting that if "He invites people to a feast" is true, there has got to be a state of affairs with a component that is denoted by "He" and that has an attribute expressed by "invites people to a feast"? So that if the Nootka sentence doesn't appear to have elements representing this component and its attribute, we should conclude only that we haven't analyzed it correctly? After all, we are told by the philosophers of language that the only way you can make a statement is to "identify" an object and then predicate something of it. Yet surely this point of view hints of provinciality and question begging.

It is indeed very difficult to know what moral should be drawn from the thought-provoking linguistic data put forward by Whorf and others. There is surely some philosophical significance, if only of an admonitory nature, in such facts as that the Nootka translations of "The boat is grounded on the beach" and "The boat is manned by picked men" not only fail to have the same grammatical structure but even do not—either of them—contain any unit corresponding to our word "boat,"[5] and in general that grammatically similar sentences of one language frequently have grammatically dissimilar translations in another. Whorf notes also that it is practically impossible to explain the use of basic metaphysical terms like "substance," "attribute," "event," "object," "relation," without what he calls "a circuitous return to the grammatical categories of the definer's language."[6] It must be granted that this is certainly true of Leibniz's metaphysics; in one of his explanations he even assigns grammatical cases to concepts.

Actually, we could cope fairly effectively with talk about substances and accidents, concepts, propositions, attributes, and the rest, if the projection of which I have been speaking were simple

---

[4] Whorf (1956), 242–243 [in this volume, p. 234].

[5] Op. cit, p. 235 [in this volume, p. 226].

[6] Op. cit., p. 215 [in this volume, p. 196].

enough. But unfortunately the correspondence is far from being one-to-one. Presumably to take account of the obvious fact that even in the same language different sentences or other expressions may be synonymous, the metaphysics has had to be refined. So it turns out that different sentences of the same language may express the same proposition and different propositions may be made true by the same fact, with the corresponding arrangements, mutatis mutandis, for predicates, attributes, and accidents. What is worse, the different expressions need not even have the same structure. This is important, because it appears that the only practical way to determine the structure of a proposition, attribute, or other concept is to read it off somehow from that of a corresponding linguistic expression.

Index

n = footnote
b = bibliography or references list
italics = quotation from that person

experience, 11–12
  about things?, 108
  abstracting from?, 41.
    See also abstracting.
  actualizes reality (Dorothy Lee),
    148, 155–156, 158
  basis of Weltanschauung, 46
  brain shapes?, 51
  beginnings and endings of, 82
  categories organize, 62, 64, 65–66
  child constructs things from?, 90–91
  describing, 80, 189–190, 191
  events and. *See* event(s).
  flow of, 4, 25
  fluid?, 90
  future and, 151–152
  generic, 147
  grammar crystallizes, 124
  language shapes, 79–80
  mass vs. thing reading?, 108, 113
  meaning and, 69–70, 72–74, 77–78.
    See also meaning.
  metaphysics shapes, 47, 49, 50.
    See also metaphysics.
  objective, 177–178. *See also*
    objectification; objective case;
    objective data; objective world;
    subjective.
  putting into words, 71
  reality is experienced, 158-159,
    163. *See also* reality.
  same, 189
  similar experiences, 63
    other creatures and, 74
  stories and, 81–82
  supernatural is part of, 138
  symbolizing and, 158, 164
  truth is beyond (Wintu), 124
  unconscious thoughts and.
    See unconsciousness thoughts.
  universals of?, 77
  Whorf and Trager on —, 35

experience (continued)
  See also background;
    categories; Wintu, evidence
    markers; platonic view;
    shape; thing(s); thing-
    in-itself.
external world, 103–104
  See also reality; world.

Firth, Raymond, 161, 168b
flow of all, 6–7, 10, 13, 23–25, 31,
    47, 92, 119, 233, 241
  cause and effect and, 90, 98–99
  not masses or processes, 115
  substance and, 102
  See also describing.
flux of experience, 193, 231, 242
form and substance, 207, 208,
    212, 215, 217, 218, 223, 224
form imposed by man. *See*
    Wintu, form imposed by man.
formal logic. *See* logic, formal.
free will/free agent. *See* Wintu,
    free will/free agent.
French, 114, 180, 183, 184, 204,
    206, 239
full word,
    Chinese, 21, 44n, 181, 237
    Salishan, 248, 251, 256, 258, 259
    See also categorematic part of
    speech.
function, 35, 146, 159, 164, 168,
    179, 182
functional basis of universals, 35
functional grammatical categories, 127,
    131, 134, 136, 138, 141, 174, 182,
future,
    Hopi and, 214
    Wintu. *See* Wintu, future.
    Whorf on —, 197, 209–210,
    214, 218
    See also tense.

$\int$ There is no end but only a continual beginning. $\int$